Dinner à Day

365 Delicious Meals You Can Make in Minutes

LYNETTE ROHRER SHIRK

A adamsmedia
avon, massachusetts

Published by
Adams Media, an F+W Publications Company
57 Littlefield Street, Avon, MA 02322. U.S.A.
www.adamsmedia.com

ISBN-10: 1-59869-615-7
ISBN-13: 978-1-59869-615-8

Printed in China.

J I H G F E D C B A

Library of Congress Cataloging-in-Publication Data
is available from the publisher.

This publication is designed to provide accurate and authoritative information
with regard to the subject matter covered. It is sold with the understanding that
the publisher is not engaged in rendering legal, accounting, or other professional advice. If legal advice or other expert assistance is required, the services
of a competent professional person should be sought.
   —From a *Declaration of Principles* jointly adopted by a Committee of the
American Bar Association and a Committee of Publishers and Associations

Many of the designations used by manufacturers and sellers to distinguish their
product are claimed as trademarks. Where those designations appear in this
book and Adams Media was aware of a trademark claim, the designations have
been printed with initial capital letters.

Contains material adopted and adapted from *The Everything® Quick and Easy
30-Minute, 5-Ingredient Cookbook* by Linda Larsen, Copyright © 2006 by F+W Publications, Inc.; *The Everything® Classic Recipes Book* by Lynette Rohrer Shirk, Copyright © 2006 by F+W Publications, Inc.; *The Everything® Italian Cookbook* by Dawn
Altomari, Copyright © 2005 by F+W Publications, Inc.; *The Everything® Healthy
Meals in Minutes Cookbook* by Patricia M. Butkus, Copyright © 2005 by F+W Publications, Inc.; *The Everything® Holiday Cookbook* by Margaret Kaeter, Copyright ©
2004 by F+W Publications, Inc.; and *The Everything® Low-Fat High-Flavor Cookbook*
by Lisa Shaw, Copyright © 1998 by F+W Publications, Inc.

*This book is available at quantity discounts for bulk purchases.
For information, please call 1-800-289-0963.*

Contents

Introduction

◯◡Dinnertime is a very important occasion for today's busy families. For most, family dinner is the only time when the whole gang can be together and share the events of the day. If family dinner is a staple in your household, then you've come to the right place.

Dinner a Day allows busy family cooks the opportunity to make a quick, easy, and delicious meal every night of the year. Gone are the days when women spend more than two hours preparing plain and monotonous meals. Today, with sports practices, rehearsals, appointments, and other commitments, you need a simple and satisfying solution to the dinnertime dilemma. So stop wasting time wandering the aisles of the supermarket and staring into your kitchen cabinets. With this book, you can easily flip through for something light, something hearty, or something in between—whatever the family wants that night, you can make it!

Finally, you only need one cookbook for a variety of tasty meals. With *Dinner a Day,* the days of "not that again!" are gone, and your family will be asking "what's new for tonight?"

Forget about takeout and throw away those frozen meals; now is the time to experiment with a different dinner every night—and to start enjoying your time with your family!

Soups

Tomato Bisque

A bisque is a rich soup that combines vegetables, stock, and milk or cream.
Serve for dinner with some chewy breadsticks and a mixed fruit salad.

SERVES 6

1 tablespoon olive oil

1 onion, finely chopped

1 (10-ounce) container refrigerated Alfredo sauce

1 cup chicken or vegetable broth

1½ cups whole milk

2 (14-ounce) cans diced tomatoes, undrained

½ teaspoon dried basil leaves

¼ teaspoon dried marjoram leaves

1. In heavy saucepan, heat olive oil over medium heat and add onion. Cook and stir until onion is tender, about 4 minutes. Add Alfredo sauce and chicken broth; cook and stir with wire whisk until mixture is smooth. Add milk and stir; cook over medium heat for 2 to 3 minutes.

2. Meanwhile, puree undrained tomatoes in food processor or blender until smooth. Add to saucepan along with seasonings and stir well. Heat soup over medium heat, stirring frequently, until mixture just comes to a simmer. Serve immediately.

Alfredo Sauce

Alfredo sauce is basically a white sauce, usually with some cheese added. You can find it in the refrigerated dairy section of your supermarket. It can also be found on the pasta aisle. In addition to Alfredo sauce, four-cheese sauce, cheddar pasta sauce, and roasted garlic parmesan pasta sauce are available.

tip

Cheesy Clam Chowder

This rich, thick, and super easy chowder can be made with any other seafood too. Think about using canned oysters, canned mussels, frozen cooked shrimp, or lump crabmeat.

SERVES 6–8

2 (10-ounce) cans condensed broccoli cheese soup

2 cups half and half

2 cups milk

3 cups refrigerated hash brown potatoes

½ teaspoon dried marjoram

2 (8-ounce) cans clams, undrained

⅛ teaspoon pepper

1. Combine soup, half and half and milk in large heavy saucepan. Bring to a boil, then add potatoes and marjoram.

2. Bring to a boil again, reduce heat, and simmer for 15 minutes. Add clams and pepper and simmer for 5–10 minutes longer until soup is hot and blended. Serve immediately.

Super Quick Beef Vegetable Stew

There are so many types of fully prepared meat entrées in your grocery store; browse the selection and stock up!

SERVES 6

3 tablespoons olive oil

1 onion, chopped

3 cloves garlic, minced

1 (16-ounce) package prepared roast beef in gravy

1 (16-ounce) package frozen mixed vegetables

1 (10-ounce) can cream of mushroom soup

2 cups water

½ teaspoon dried thyme leaves

1. In heavy large saucepan, heat olive oil over medium heat. Add onion and garlic; cook and stir until tender, 4–5 minutes. Meanwhile, cut the cooked roast beef into 1" chunks. Add to saucepan along with gravy, frozen mixed vegetables, soup, water, and thyme leaves.

2. Cook over medium high heat until soup comes to a boil, about 7–9 minutes. Reduce heat to low and simmer for 6–7 minutes longer until vegetables are hot and tender. Serve immediately.

Soup or Stew?

The difference between soup and stew is the thickness of the liquid. Soups are generally thin, sometimes made with just broth or stock. Stews have ingredients that thicken the liquid, including potatoes, flour, cornstarch, or pureed vegetables. You can make any soup into a stew by adding some cornstarch dissolved in water.

tip

Chicken Corn Chowder

Grate some cheese over this chowder, and you'll have a hearty, hot soup on the table in about 15 minutes. Serve with some crackers and fresh fruit.

SERVES 6–8

1 (26-ounce) jar double cheddar pasta sauce

2 (14-ounce) cans chicken broth

2 (15-ounce) cans corn

2 (9-ounce) packages frozen cooked Southwest chicken strips

½ teaspoon dried Italian seasoning

2 cups shredded sharp Cheddar cheese

1. In large saucepan, combine all ingredients except cheese and bring to a boil over medium high heat. Reduce heat to low, cover, and simmer for 6–8 minutes until chicken is hot.

2. Stir in Cheddar cheese, remove from heat, and let stand, covered, for 3–4 minutes. Stir thoroughly and serve.

Frozen Precooked Chicken

There are lots of varieties of frozen precooked chicken in your supermarket's meat aisle. You can find cooked grilled chicken, chicken strips, and chopped chicken in flavors that range from Southwest to plain grilled. Some varieties come with a sauce; be sure to read the label to make sure you're getting what you want.

tip

Tortellini Soup

*This rich soup is full of flavor. Serve it with some water crackers,
a chopped vegetable salad, and melon slices.*

SERVES 6

*1 pound sweet Italian bulk
sausage*

*1 (8-ounce) package sliced
mushrooms*

4 cloves garlic, minced

3 (14-ounce) cans beef broth

1½ cups water

*1 teaspoon dried Italian
seasoning*

⅛ teaspoon pepper

*1 (24-ounce) package frozen
cheese tortellini*

1. In large saucepan over medium heat,
brown sausage with mushrooms and garlic,
stirring to break up sausage. When sausage is
cooked, drain thoroughly. Add broth, water,
Italian seasoning, and pepper to saucepan
and bring to a boil over high heat. Reduce
heat to low and simmer for 8–10 minutes.

2. Stir in frozen tortellini and cook, stirring
frequently, over medium high heat for 6–8
minutes or until tortellini are hot and tender.
Serve immediately.

Frozen or Refrigerated Tortellini?

Refrigerated, or fresh, tortellini is found in the dairy aisle of
the regular grocery store. It is
generally more expensive than
the frozen and package sizes are
smaller. Frozen tortellini and tor-
telloni take a bit longer to cook.
Choose your favorite and
stock up.

tip

Cheesy Shrimp Chowder

This rich chowder is very simple to make and has a wonderful, rich flavor. Serve it with tiny oyster crackers, a baby spinach salad, and oatmeal cookies for dessert.

SERVES 6

2 tablespoons olive oil

1 onion, finely chopped

2 cups frozen hash brown potatoes

1½ cups water

2 (6-ounce) cans medium shrimp, drained

1 (16-ounce) jar four-cheese Alfredo sauce

1 (15-ounce) can evaporated milk

1. In large saucepan, heat olive oil over medium high heat. Add onion; cook and stir until tender, about 4–5 minutes. Add potatoes and water; bring to a boil, cover, lower heat, and simmer for 5 minutes until potatoes are hot and tender.

2. Add shrimp, Alfredo sauce, and evaporated milk to saucepan. Stir well and heat over medium heat until the soup comes to a simmer; do not boil. Serve immediately.

Savory Minestrone

Minestrone is a thick vegetable soup with beans and pasta. It's really a meal in one bowl; serve with some toasted garlic bread and tall glasses of milk.

SERVES 6

4 cups chicken broth

1 (16-ounce) package frozen mixed vegetables

1 (15-ounce) can cannellini beans, drained

½ teaspoon dried basil leaves

½ teaspoon dried oregano leaves

1 (14-ounce) can diced tomatoes with garlic, undrained

1 cup elbow macaroni

1. In large saucepan, combine chicken broth and vegetables; bring to a boil over medium high heat. When broth boils, add beans, basil, oregano, and tomatoes.

2. Bring to a simmer, lower heat, and cook for 5 minutes. Add macaroni; stir and simmer for 8–9 minutes until pasta is tender, then serve.

Canned Beans

Canned beans are a great convenience food to have on hand, but they do tend to be high in sodium. To reduce sodium, drain the beans, place them in a strainer or colander, and run cold water over them. Drain well again and use in the recipe.

tip

Mexican Beef Stew

*Serve this rich stew topped with a dollop of sour cream and
some chopped avocados or guacamole for a cooling contrast.*

SERVES 6

2 tablespoons olive oil

1 onion, chopped

1 (16-ounce) packaged cooked
ground beef in taco sauce

2 (15-ounce) cans chili beans,
undrained

2 cups frozen corn

1 (14-ounce) can Mexican
flavored chopped tomatoes,
undrained

1 tablespoon chili powder

½ teaspoon cumin

⅛ teaspoon cayenne pepper

1. In large saucepan heat olive oil over
medium heat. Add onion; cook and stir until
crisp tender, about 3–4 minutes.

2. Add remaining ingredients and stir well.
Bring to a simmer, reduce heat to medium
low and cook for 10–15 minutes until corn
is hot and soup has thickened slightly. Serve
immediately.

Spices

Spices have a shelf life of about
a year; after that time, they lose
flavor and intensity and should
be replaced. To keep track, write
the purchase date on the can
or bottle using a permanent
marker. Periodically, go through
your spice drawer or rack and
discard older spices; be
sure to write the ones you
need on your grocery list. *tip*

French Onion Soup

Because the onions need to sauté for a fairly long time to develop
carmelization, this recipe starts with frozen chopped onions.
You can chop your own, but the recipe will take longer than 30 minutes.

SERVES 6

2 tablespoons olive oil

2 tablespoons butter

2 (10-ounce) packages frozen chopped onions

2 tablespoons flour

2 (16-ounce) boxes beef stock

6 slices French bread

¼ cup butter, softened

1½ cups shredded Gruyere cheese

1. In large saucepan, combine olive oil and 2 tablespoons butter over medium heat until butter is foamy. Add onions; cook over medium heat for 10–12 minutes, stirring frequently, until onions brown around edges. Sprinkle flour over onions; cook and stir for 2–3 minutes.

2. Stir in stock, bring to a simmer, and cook for 10 minutes. Meanwhile, spread French bread slices with ¼ cup butter. In toaster oven, toast the bread until browned and crisp. Sprinkle with cheese and toast for 2–4 minutes until cheese melts. Divide soup among soup bowls and float the toasted cheese bread on top.

Boxed Stocks

If your grocery store carries boxed stocks, buy them. These stocks tend to be richer and less salty than canned stocks. If you don't use all of the stock, these boxes come with a flip top lid so you can close the box and store them in the refrigerator for a couple of weeks.

tip

Vegetable Meatball Soup

Frozen cooked meatballs are available in several flavors;
choose plain or Italian style for this super easy and delicious recipe.

SERVES 6

1 (16-ounce) package frozen meatballs

2 cups 8-vegetable juice

2 cups frozen mixed vegetables

1 (10-ounce) can beef broth

4 cups water

½ teaspoon dried Italian seasoning

⅛ teaspoon pepper

1½ cups mini penne pasta

1. In large saucepan or stockpot, combine all ingredients except for pasta and mix gently. Bring to a boil over high heat.

2. Stir in pasta, reduce heat to medium high, and cook for 9–11 minutes until meatballs are hot, vegetables are hot, and pasta is tender. Serve immediately.

Substituting Pasta

You can substitute one shape of pasta for another as long as they are about the same size and thickness. Whichever pasta you choose, be sure to cook it al dente; this means cooked through, but with a firm bite in the center.

tip

Pressure Cooker Beef Stew

*This stew tastes like it simmered for hours on your stove, but
the pressure cooker makes quick work of the recipe. Serve with
some crusty bread to soak up the wonderful sauce.*

SERVES 8

2 pounds bottom round steak

3 tablespoons flour

½ teaspoon garlic salt

⅛ teaspoon pepper

3 tablespoons olive oil

3 russet potatoes

1 (16-ounce) package baby
carrots

½ teaspoon dried thyme leaves

½ teaspoon dried oregano leaves

4 cups beef stock, heated

1 (14-ounce) can diced tomatoes
with garlic, undrained

1. Cut steak into 1" cubes. Sprinkle meat
with flour, garlic salt, and pepper and toss
to coat. Heat oil in the pressure cooker and
brown the coated beef, stirring frequently,
about 5–7 minutes. Add remaining ingredients and lock the lid.

2. Bring up to high pressure and cook for
20 minutes. Release pressure using quick
release method and stir stew. Serve
immediately.

Quick Posole

Posole is a Mexican stew made with hominy, green chiles, and cubes of tender pork. Serve it with some blue corn tortilla chips, guacamole, sour cream, and a green salad.

SERVES 4–6

1 (16-ounce) package pork roast au jus

1 (4-ounce) can chopped green chiles, undrained

2 (14-ounce) cans chicken broth

1 tablespoon chili powder

1 teaspoon ground cumin

½ teaspoon dried oregano leaves

1 (15-ounce) can hominy, drained

2 cups frozen corn

3 tablespoons flour

½ cup water

1. Remove pork from package and cut into 1" cubes. Combine in large saucepan along with juice from pork, chiles, broth, chili powder, cumin, oregano, hominy, and frozen corn. Bring to a boil over high heat, then reduce heat to low, cover, and simmer for 12–15 minutes until pork is hot and tender.

2. In small jar, combine flour and water and shake well to blend. Stir into stew and raise heat to medium. Cook and stir until stew thickens, about 5–8 minutes. Serve immediately.

Hominy

Hominy is made by removing the bran and germ from kernels of corn. It can be made by soaking the corn kernels in a weak solution of lye and water, or by physically crushing the corn. Yellow hominy is generally sweeter than the white. You can substitute barley for it in any recipe if you'd like.

tip

Cold Pea Soup

This elegant soup is perfect for a hot summer evening. Serve it with some crisp croutons, a fruit gelatin salad, and some buns fresh from the oven.

SERVES 4

1 (16-ounce) package frozen baby peas

1 avocado, peeled and chopped

1 tablespoon lemon juice

2 cups chicken broth

½ teaspoon salt

⅛ teaspoon white pepper

¼ cup chopped mint

Place frozen peas in a colander and run cold water over them for 2–3 minutes to thaw, tossing occasionally. Place in blender container or food processor along with avocado and sprinkle with lemon juice. Add chicken broth, salt, and pepper and process until smooth. Pour into serving bowl and sprinkle with chopped mint.

Baby Peas

Try to find baby peas in the frozen aisle of your supermarket. They are much more tender than regular peas and have a sweet fresh flavor. Do not cook them before adding to recipes; when adding to a pasta recipe, drain the pasta over the peas in a colander, or add them to a soup at the very end of cooking time.

tip

Tex-Mex Cheese Soup

As with all Tex-Mex foods, serve this hearty soup with salsa, sour cream, chopped avocado or guacamole, and crumbled crisp tortilla chips.

SERVES 4

2 tablespoons olive oil

1 onion, chopped

1 (1.25-ounce) envelope taco seasoning mix

1 (15-ounce) can creamed corn

1 (10-ounce) can condensed chicken broth

1½ cups water

2 cups shredded Pepper Jack cheese

2 tablespoons flour

1. In heavy saucepan, heat olive oil over medium heat. Add onion; saute until crisp tender, about 3–4 minutes. Sprinkle taco seasoning mix over the onions and stir, then add corn, chicken broth, and water. Bring to a simmer and cook for 10 minutes, stirring occasionally.

2. Meanwhile, in medium bowl toss cheese with flour. Add to soup and lower heat; cook and stir for 2–3 minutes until cheese is melted and soup is thickened. Serve immediately.

Black Bean Soup

Serve this delicious soup with sour cream, chopped avocado
for toppings, a spinach salad, and crisp breadsticks.

SERVES 6

2 *tablespoons olive oil*

1 *onion, chopped*

3 *cloves garlic, minced*

2 *(15-ounce) cans black beans, drained and rinsed*

1 *(14-ounce) can diced tomatoes with green chiles*

2 *(14-ounce) cans chicken broth*

½ *teaspoon cumin*

⅛ *teaspoon white pepper*

1. In heavy saucepan, heat olive oil over medium heat. Add onion and garlic; cook and stir for 3–4 minutes until crisp tender.

2. Meanwhile, place black beans in a colander, rinse, and drain thoroughly. Using a potato masher, lightly mash some of the beans. Add all beans to saucepan along with remaining ingredients. Bring to a simmer; cook for 10–12 minutes until blended.

Dried Beans

You can substitute dried beans for canned to reduce sodium. Rinse the beans and sort to remove any dirt or pebbles. Cover with cold water, bring to a boil, and boil for 1 minute. Cover and let stand for 1 hour. Drain the beans and cover with cold water. Simmer for about 2 hours until beans are tender.

tip

Potato Soup

*This creamy and rich soup uses two kinds
of potatoes for a nice depth of flavor.*

SERVES 6

4 slices bacon

1 onion, chopped

*1 (5-ounce) package cheese
scalloped potato mix*

3 cups water

*1 (15-ounce) can evaporated
milk*

*2 cups frozen hash brown
potatoes*

½ teaspoon dried dill weed

⅛ teaspoon white pepper

1. In heavy saucepan, cook bacon until crisp. Remove bacon, drain on paper towels, crumble and set aside. Cook onion in bacon drippings until tender, about 5 minutes.

2. Add potato mix and seasoning packet from potato mix along with remaining ingredients. Bring to a boil and simmer for 17–20 minutes until potatoes are tender. If desired, puree using an immersion blender. Sprinkle with bacon and serve.

Precooked Bacon?

When recipes call for crumbled bacon, you can use the pre-cooked version. But, if the recipe calls for cooking the bacon and using the bacon fat to saute other ingredients, you must used uncooked bacon. Or you can use the precooked bacon and use butter or olive oil as a substitute for the bacon fat.

tip

Two-Bean Chili

This vegetarian chili can be varied in so many ways. Add more beans, salsa, cooked ground beef or pork sausage, jalapeño peppers, or tomato sauce.

SERVES 4

2 tablespoons olive oil

1 onion, chopped

1 (1.25-ounce) package taco seasoning mix

1 (15-ounce) can kidney beans, drained

1 (15-ounce) can black beans, drained

2 (14-ounce) cans diced tomatoes with green chiles

1 cup water

1. In heavy saucepan over medium heat, add olive oil and saute onion until tender, about 4–5 minutes.

2. Sprinkle taco seasoning mix over onions; cook and stir for 1 minute. Add drained but not rinsed beans, tomatoes, and water.

3. Bring to a simmer; cook for 10–12 minutes until thickened and blended.

Taco Seasoning Mix

You can make your own taco seasoning mix by combining 2 tablespoons chili powder, 2 teaspoons onion powder, 2 tablespoons cornstarch, 1 teaspoon dried oregano, 1 teaspoon dried red pepper flakes, 2 teaspoons salt, and ½ teaspoon cumin. Blend well and store in a cool dry place: 2 tablespoons equals one envelope mix.

tip

Bean and Bacon Soup

This simple soup can be great for kids' lunch boxes the next day.
Pack into an insulated Thermos along with some crackers, baby
carrots, and shredded cheddar cheese for topping the soup.

SERVES 4–6

1 (8-ounce) package bacon

1 onion, chopped

1 (14-ounce) can diced tomatoes, undrained

2 (15-ounce) cans pinto beans, drained

2 cups chicken broth

1. In large saucepan, cook bacon until crisp. Drain bacon on paper towels, crumble, and set aside. Drain off all but 2 tablespoons bacon drippings.

2. Cook onion in drippings over medium heat for 3–4 minutes. Add remaining ingredients and bring to a simmer.

3. Simmer for 10–12 minutes, then use a potato masher to mash some of the beans. Add reserved bacon, stir, and simmer for 5 minutes longer. Serve immediately.

Egg Drop Soup

Because this soup is so simple it demands the best chicken stock. Try to find the boxed chicken stock at your grocery store, or order it online. You can also make your own stock.

SERVES 4

5 cups chicken broth

1 cup shredded carrots

½ cup grated onion

2 eggs

1 egg yolk

1. In heavy saucepan, combine chicken broth, carrots, and onion. Bring to a simmer; cook for 3–5 minutes until vegetables are tender. Meanwhile, in small bowl place eggs and egg yolk; carefully remove the chalazea (the white ropy strand that connects the egg white and the yolk). Beat eggs and egg yolk with a fork until smooth; do not overbeat.

2. Remove the saucepan from the heat. Using a fork, drizzle the egg mixture into the soup. When all the egg is added, stir the soup for 30 seconds, then serve immediately.

Make Your Own Chicken Stock

This recipe takes some time, but you can freeze it and it will add lots of flavor to your recipes. Cover one stewing chicken, some chopped onion, carrots, 1 bay leaf, some parsley, and celery with water and simmer for 3–4 hours. Strain broth, cool, pour into ice cube trays, and freeze, then package in freezer bags.

tip

Sweet and Sour Pork Stew

Serve this delicious stew with a mixed lettuce salad,
some crisp breadsticks, and a bakery layer cake for dessert.

SERVES 4–6

2 tablespoons olive oil

1 onion, chopped

1 red bell pepper

1 (8-ounce) can pineapple tidbits

1 (16-ounce) package cooked
sweet and sour pork

2½ cups water

½ cup long grain rice

2 tablespoons cornstarch

⅓ cup water

1. In large saucepan, heat olive oil over medium heat. Add onion; cook and stir for 3 minutes until crisp tender. Add red bell pepper; cook and stir for 2–3 minutes longer. Add undrained pineapple, pork with sauce, and 2½ cups water. Bring to a simmer, stir in rice, and cook for 10 minutes.

2. Meanwhile, in small bowl combine cornstarch and ⅓ cup water and mix well. Stir into stew; cook and stir over medium heat for 5–8 minutes until rice is tender and stew is thickened. Serve immediately.

Asian Pork Stew

As a general rule, you can store soups and stews in the refrigerator, covered,
for three to four days. Freeze soup in individual containers for six to eight weeks.

SERVES 4

2 tablespoons all-purpose flour

2 teaspoons Chinese five-spice
powder

1½ pounds pork tenderloin,
trimmed of excess fat and cut
into ¾-inch cubes

2 tablespoons olive oil

1 cup sliced celery

¾ cup sliced red onion

½ cup diced green peppers

1 tablespoon minced garlic

1 cup chicken stock

2 tablespoons hoisin sauce

2 tablespoons tamari

½ teaspoon ground ginger

8 ounces zucchini, cut into
¼-inch-thick rounds and halved

3 tablespoons toasted sesame
seeds

Fresh cilantro leaves

1. Combine the flour and five-spice powder in a shallow bowl. Dredge the pork pieces in the flour and shake off the excess, reserving the excess flour.

2. Heat 1 tablespoon of the oil in a large nonstick skillet over medium-high heat. Add the pork and brown, stirring occasionally, about 6 minutes. Transfer the meat to a plate and tent with tinfoil.

3. Add the remaining tablespoon of oil and the celery, onions, peppers, and garlic. Cook until soft, about 4 minutes, stirring occasionally. Return the pork to the pan and add the stock, hoisin, tamari, ginger, and zucchini. Bring to a simmer and cook until the vegetables are crisp and the meat is tender and cooked through, about 18 minutes.

4. Add 3 to 4 tablespoons of the pan juices to the reserved flour and whisk until there are no lumps. Add the flour mixture to the stew and whisk to combine. Cook and stir until thick. To serve, ladle the stew into warm shallow soup bowls and garnish with the sesame seeds and cilantro leaves.

Asparagus Soup with Truffle Oil

If truffle oil isn't available, swirl a small dollop of
crème fraîche in the center before serving.

SERVES 4

2½ pounds asparagus, medium-sized stalks

1 tablespoon butter

1 teaspoon salt

½ cup half-and-half

2 teaspoons white truffle oil

Freshly cracked pepper, to taste

1. Snap off and discard the woody bases from each asparagus stalk. Use a vegetable peeler to peel the stalks, leaving the tips intact. Cut off the tops about 1½ inches down. Cut the stalks into 1-inch pieces. Bring a pot of salted water to a boil and cook the asparagus tips until bright green, about 2 minutes. Remove with a slotted spoon and set aside to cool.

2. Melt the butter in a medium-sized nonstick skillet over medium heat. Add the stalk pieces and salt to taste, and cook until crisp-tender, about 4 to 5 minutes. Slowly add the half-and-half and bring to a simmer; cook until the asparagus is tender, about 1 minute. Do not overcook. Use a slotted spoon to transfer the asparagus to a blender or food processor fitted with a metal blade. Allow to cool, then process until smooth. Add a few tablespoons of the hot half-and-half if needed.

3. Transfer the purée back to the pan with the half-and-half. Stir to combine, and adjust seasoning to taste. Heat through without boiling, 1 or 2 minutes. Ladle into bowls and top with several of the asparagus tips. Drizzle the truffle oil over each bowl and top with black pepper.

Basil and Zucchini Soup

You can add a shot of hot pepper sauce if desired,
or substitute tarragon for a different twist.

SERVES 6

6 cups sliced zucchini

*½ cup fresh basil leaves
(about 20)*

3 cups chicken stock

1 teaspoon salt

2 tablespoons lemon juice

½ cup plain yogurt

Julienned fresh basil

1. Place the zucchini and basil leaves in a medium-sized saucepan with the stock and salt. Bring to a boil, reduce heat, and simmer for 10 minutes.

2. Remove the saucepan from the heat, add the lemon juice, and allow the vegetables to cool slightly. Use a slotted spoon to transfer the vegetables to a food processor fitted with a metal blade, or a blender; process to a smooth purée, adding a few tablespoons of the broth if needed. Transfer to a bowl and chill. (The soup may be made ahead up to this point.)

3. Serve in chilled soup bowls with a dollop of plain yogurt. Garnish with basil and serve chilled.

Onion and Mushroom Soup

This is a great dish to serve in the spring when mushrooms come into season. Use morels, chanterelles, and other domestic exotics for a flavorful presentation.

SERVES 4

3 tablespoons butter

6 ounces assorted mushroom caps, thinly sliced

½ cup thinly sliced yellow onion

4 cups beef broth

¼ cup dry sherry

¼ teaspoon salt

Freshly cracked black pepper

2 tablespoons freshly grated Parmesan

Chopped fresh thyme

1. Melt the butter in a medium-sized non-stick skillet over medium heat. Add the mushrooms and onions; cook, stirring frequently, until translucent, about 8 minutes.

2. Add the beef broth, sherry, salt, and pepper; simmer for about 5 to 7 minutes. Taste and adjust seasoning as needed. To serve, ladle the hot soup into 4 soup bowls and garnish with a sprinkling of Parmesan and fresh thyme leaves.

Beef Stroganoff Soup

Make sure the pan is really hot when you sear the meat to ensure the
meat stays tender and the flavorful juices stay inside the meat.

SERVES 6

2 pounds top sirloin steak,
trimmed of visible fat and cut
into ½-inch cubes

½ teaspoon salt

Freshly ground black pepper

4 tablespoons all-purpose flour

4 tablespoons butter

1 tablespoon olive oil

½ cup sliced yellow onions

3 cups sliced mushrooms

2 tablespoons minced garlic

¼ cup dry white wine

2 cups beef stock

2 tablespoons chopped parsley,
plus extra for garnish

2 teaspoons Worcestershire sauce

½ cup sour cream

1. Pat the meat dry with paper towels and season with salt and pepper. Place the flour in a shallow bowl. Dredge the meat in the flour, shaking off excess. Reserve remaining flour.

2. Melt the butter in a large nonstick skillet over high heat until bubbling. Add the meat and brown on all sides, stirring occasionally to cook evenly, about 6 minutes. Use a slotted spoon to transfer the meat to a plate and tent with tinfoil to keep warm.

3. Heat the oil over medium-high heat and add the onions, mushrooms, and garlic. Cook until soft, about 6 minutes, stirring occasionally.

4. Sprinkle the reserved flour over the vegetables. Cook and stir until thick. Add the white wine and cook until thick and reduced, about 4 minutes. Add the stock, parsley, and Worcestershire; bring to a simmer and cook until somewhat reduced, about 6 minutes.

5. Add the meat and any accumulated juices and simmer, uncovered, for 10 minutes. To serve, stir in the sour cream and heat through. Serve hot in warm shallow bowls.

Cheddar Cheese Soup

Use a quality aged Cheddar for a rich, creamy taste.
Using a sharp Cheddar will increase the intensity of this dish.

SERVES 4

2 tablespoons butter

¼ cup chopped yellow onion

½ cup chopped celery

2 tablespoons all-purpose flour

½ teaspoon ground cayenne pepper

¼ teaspoon dry mustard

½ tablespoon Worcestershire sauce

1 cup whole milk

1½ cups chicken stock

2 cups shredded Cheddar cheese

Seasoned salt, to taste

Freshly cracked black pepper

Paprika, for garnish

1. Melt the butter in a medium-sized saucepan and sauté the onion and celery until tender, about 4 minutes. Add the flour, cayenne pepper, mustard, and Worcestershire, and mix to combine.

2. Add the milk and chicken stock and bring to a boil. Cook for 1 minute, stirring constantly. Reduce heat to low, add the cheese, and stir occasionally just until the cheese is melted.

3. Add seasoned salt and pepper to taste. To serve, ladle hot soup into small decorative cups and sprinkle with paprika.

Healthy Chicken Soup

This recipe is easy to oversalt, as the stock and chicken are already well seasoned.
Taste frequently and be stingy with the salt until the very end.

SERVES 2

2 tablespoons olive oil

½ cup sliced yellow onions

1 cup chopped broccoli

½ cup carrots, peeled and cut into ¼-inch rounds

½ cup chopped bell pepper

Salt

Freshly ground black pepper

2 cups low-sodium chicken stock

1 cup diced cooked chicken, skinless

2 tablespoons chopped parsley

1. Heat the oil in a medium-sized stockpot over medium-high heat. Add the onions and cook until soft, about 4 minutes, stirring occasionally. Add the broccoli, carrots, and peppers; cook until the broccoli starts to turn bright green, about 4 minutes. Add the salt, pepper, and stock, and bring to a simmer. Cook until the vegetables are crisp-tender, about 8 minutes.

2. Add the chicken and parsley, and return to a simmer. Serve hot.

Chilled Cucumber Soup with Salmon

You can add a shot of cayenne pepper or hot pepper sauce if desired.
Plan your schedule to allow some time for the soup to chill.

SERVES 6

1 cup sliced yellow onion

3 cups fish stock (or clam stock)

3 cups peeled, seeded, and diced cucumber (about ½-inch dice)

2 tablespoons chopped dill

2½ cups plain yogurt

Salt, to taste

Freshly cracked black pepper, to taste

1½ pounds salmon fillet

Snipped fresh dill, for garnish

Lemon wedges, for garnish

1. Combine the onions, fish stock, and cucumbers in a medium-sized saucepan and bring to a simmer over low heat. Cook for about 5 minutes, until the cucumbers are tender but not mushy. Transfer the mixture to a food processor fitted with a metal blade and process until smooth. Add the dill and yogurt, and pulse until just combined. Season with salt and pepper and transfer to a bowl. Refrigerate until chilled. (The soup can be made ahead up to this point.)

2. To cook salmon: Preheat oven to 375°. Place salmon fillet on a tinfoil-lined pan, skin-side down. Lightly season with salt and pepper. Bake, uncovered, until cooked through, about 12 to 15 minutes.

3. When ready to serve, flake the salmon and gently stir it into the soup. To serve, ladle the soup into chilled soup cups and garnish with dill. Serve the lemon wedges on the side.

Chilled Zucchini Squash Soup with Basil

*This soup is best served when very chilled. You can prepare the
soup in advance up to the point where you purée the vegetables.*

SERVES 6

3 tablespoons olive oil

½ cup finely chopped leeks
(white and light green parts only)

4 cups thinly sliced zucchini squash

4 cups chicken stock

1 tablespoon lemon juice

½ cup half-and-half

½ cup sour cream

2 tablespoons finely chopped
fresh chives

6 tablespoons chopped basil

Salt and freshly ground black
pepper, to taste

Cleanup Tip

To clean the bowl of a blender
or food processor after puréeing,
put about ½ cup of warm soapy
water in the bowl and process
for about 30 seconds.

tip

1. Heat the oil in a large saucepan over
medium heat and sauté the leeks until softened, about 5 to 7 minutes. Add the squash
and sauté for another 5 minutes.

2. Add the stock, cover, and cook for about
15 minutes. Use a slotted spoon to transfer
the zucchini to a food processor fitted with
a metal blade or to a blender; process to a
smooth purée, adding a few tablespoons of
the hot stock if necessary. Transfer the soup
to a bowl and refrigerate.

3. After the soup has been chilled, add the
lemon juice, half-and-half, sour cream, chives,
and 3 tablespoons of the basil. Season with
salt and pepper. Taste and adjust seasoning
as desired.

4. Serve in chilled bowls, garnished with the
remaining 3 tablespoons basil.

Creamy Avocado Soup with Chives

Make sure you read the dietary label on the vegetable stock, if you're concerned about your diet. Some stocks can be high in sodium.

SERVES 4

2 large avocados, ripe

1½ cups vegetable stock (Hains is a good choice)

1 tablespoon Worcestershire sauce

¾ cup plain yogurt

¼ cup sour cream

¼ teaspoon kosher salt

Dash hot pepper sauce

⅛ teaspoon red pepper flakes

2 tablespoons snipped fresh chives

1. Cut the avocados in half and remove the pits. Use a spoon to remove the flesh from the skin and process in a food processor fitted with a metal blade until smooth.

2. Add the remaining ingredients and process until smooth, about 1 minute. Taste and adjust seasoning as desired. Refrigerate, covered, until ready to serve.

CHAPTER

2

Salads

Roasted Corn Salad

*Roasting corn helps concentrate the sweetness of
this vegetable, and makes the kernels slightly chewy.
It's delicious mixed with crisp peppers and ripe tomatoes.*

SERVES 6

1 (10-ounce) package frozen corn

2 tablespoons oil

1 green bell pepper, chopped

1 red bell pepper, chopped

2 tomatoes, chopped

¾ cup creamy garlic salad dressing

½ teaspoon dried Italian seasoning

½ teaspoon salt

⅛ teaspoon pepper

1. Preheat oven to 400°F. Brush baking sheet with oil and set aside. Thaw corn under running water and drain well; dry with paper towels and spread onto prepared baking sheet. Roast at 400°F for 10–15 minutes, stirring once during cooking, until corn browns slightly around edges. Remove to serving bowl.

2. Add bell peppers and tomatoes and toss to mix. In small bowl, combine salad dressing, Italian seasoning, salt, and pepper and mix well. Drizzle over corn mixture and toss to coat. Serve immediately or cover and chill up to 8 hours.

Broccoli Swiss Cheese Salad

This salad is similar to a popular deli salad;
to make it identical, add some golden raisins.

SERVES 4–6

1 pound fresh broccoli

1 cup sliced fresh mushrooms

3 strips bacon, cooked and crumbled

½ cup honey mustard salad dressing

½ cup cubed Swiss cheese

1. Cut florets from broccoli, and cut stems into 2" pieces. Place in heavy saucepan, cover with water, and bring to a boil. Simmer for 6–8 minutes until broccoli is crisp tender. Drain well and place in serving bowl.

2. Add mushrooms and bacon; toss gently. Drizzle with salad dressing and toss again. Sprinkle with cheese and serve.

Salad Substitutions

Salad recipes are made for substituting! Just about any vegetable can be substituted for another. Crumble cauliflower florets into a salad in place of mushrooms, slice crisp jicama as a substitute for bell peppers, and use blanched asparagus in place of green or wax beans (and vice versa!).

tip

Greek Lentil Salad

This vegetarian salad offers complete protein with the combination of cracked wheat and lentils. Top it with some crumbled feta cheese for even more flavor.

SERVES 6

¾ cup cracked wheat

1½ cups boiling water

¾ cup lentils

2 cups water

½ cup red wine vinaigrette salad dressing

¼ teaspoon dried oregano leaves

2 tomatoes

1 cucumber

1. Place cracked wheat in medium bowl and cover with boiling water. Set aside. In heavy skillet, combine lentils and 2 cups water and bring to a boil; cover and simmer for 20 minutes until tender; drain if necessary. Drain cracked wheat, if necessary. In small bowl combine salad dressing and oregano.

2. Meanwhile, cut tomatoes in half, gently squeeze out the seeds, and chop. Peel cucumber, cut in half, remove seeds, and slice.

3. In serving bowl, combine cracked wheat, lentils, vegetables, and salad dressing; toss gently to coat and serve immediately.

Apple and Greens Salad

*You can make the dressing ahead of time, but be sure
to prepare the apples just before serving, or they will turn dark.*

SERVES 4

⅓ cup oil

3 tablespoons apple cider vinegar

¼ cup sugar

½ teaspoon celery seed

¼ teaspoon salt

⅛ teaspoon pepper

2 apples, cored and sliced

4 cups butter lettuce

1 cup curly endive

1. In small bowl, combine oil, vinegar, sugar, celery seed, salt, and pepper and mix well with wire whisk to blend.

2. Place apples, lettuce, and endive in serving bowl and pour dressing over salad; toss gently to coat. Serve immediately.

Apple Varieties

Choose apple varieties depending on if you want a sweet or tart taste. Granny Smith apples are generally tart, while Golden Delicious and Red Delicious apples are sweeter. Gala apples have a sweet and honey-like taste, while Jonathans, McIntosh apples, and Cortlands are more tart.

Bacon and Spinach Salad

Baby spinach is wonderfully tender, with a rich and mild taste.
It's perfect in this salad, accented with crisp bacon and creamy Havarti cheese.

SERVES 6–8

4 strips bacon

1 pound baby spinach leaves

1 cup cubed Havarti cheese

½ cup mayonnaise

½ cup buttermilk

½ teaspoon seasoned salt

⅛ teaspoon white pepper

1. In medium saucepan, cook bacon until crisp. Drain on paper towels until cool enough to handle, then crumble. Combine cooked bacon, spinach, and cheese in serving bowl.

2. In small bowl combine mayonnaise, buttermilk, salt, and pepper and mix well with wire whisk to blend. Drizzle half of dressing over spinach mixture and toss to coat. Serve with remaining dressing.

Paella Rice Salad

Paella is a Spanish dish that combines rice with shrimp, sausages, chicken, peas, and saffron. This salad is a simplified version of the classic recipe.

SERVES 4

1 cup uncooked long grain rice

2 cups water

¼ teaspoon saffron

1 cup frozen baby peas

1 cup sliced celery

½ pound cooked, shelled shrimp

⅔ cup creamy Italian salad dressing

1. In medium saucepan over high heat, combine rice, water, and saffron. Cover and bring to a boil; lower heat and cook for 15–20 minutes until rice is tender. Stir in baby peas during final 3 minutes of cooking time.

2. Place rice mixture in serving bowl and add celery and shrimp; toss gently. Drizzle with salad dressing and toss again, then serve, or cover and refrigerate up to 8 hours.

Refrigerated Salad Dressings

Browse through your grocery store's produce aisle and you'll find many flavors of refrigerated salad dressings. These dressings are usually richer than typical bottled dressings, and made with fresh ingredients. They must be stored in the refrigerator; keep a supply of your favorites on hand.

tip

Chicken Salad with Nectarines

Use any combination of fresh fruit in this simple and elegant salad.
You can also try different flavors of chutney to vary the taste.

SERVES 4–6

2 cups cooked cubed chicken breast

1½ cups blueberries

3 nectarines, sliced

¾ cup mayonnaise

¼ cup mango chutney

½ teaspoon curry powder

1. In serving bowl, combine chicken, blueberries, and nectarines and toss gently.

2. In small bowl, combine mayonnaise, chutney, and curry powder and mix well. Spoon over chicken mixture and toss gently to coat. Serve immediately.

Chutney

Chutney is a cooked sauce made of fruit juices, dried fruits, and spices. You can usually find pineapple chutney, mango chutney, or cranberry chutney in the condiment aisle of your grocery store. There are also many recipes for making your own chutney; blueberry is a homemade favorite.

tip

Wilted Lettuce Salad

This warm salad can be a meal in itself.
Serve it with some bread and fresh fruit for a light supper.

SERVES 4–6

1 head romaine lettuce

1 head butter lettuce

1 cup sliced crimini mushrooms

5 slices bacon

2 tablespoons apple cider vinegar

½ teaspoon dry mustard

¼ teaspoon salt

⅛ teaspoon pepper

1. Wash lettuces and tear into bite size pieces; place in serving bowl along with mushrooms. Cook bacon in heavy skillet over medium heat, turning frequently, until crisp. Remove bacon to paper towels to drain; crumble when cool enough to handle.

2. Drain all but ¼ cup bacon drippings from pan. Place over medium heat and add remaining ingredients; bring to a boil. Immediately pour over lettuces and mushrooms in salad bowl; toss to wilt lettuce. Sprinkle with bacon and serve immediately.

Crimini Mushrooms

Crimini mushrooms can be found in most supermarkets in the produce section. They are actually small Portobello mushrooms, those large dark mushrooms that are so perfect for grilling or stuffing. They have more flavor than button mushrooms; wipe them with damp paper towels, cut off the end of the stem, and slice.

tip

Lemon Cucumber Salad

The cucumbers are sprinkled with salt and sugar before dressing to draw out any sour taste and to reduce their high water content, so the salad dressing isn't diluted.

SERVES 6

3 cucumbers

1 teaspoon salt

2 tablespoons sugar

1 (6-ounce) container lemon-flavored yogurt

⅓ cup sour cream

2 tablespoons lemon juice

1 teaspoon sugar

½ teaspoon dried thyme leaves

⅛ teaspoon white pepper

1. Peel cucumbers and thinly slice. Place in colander and sprinkle with salt and sugar. Let stand for 15 minutes, then toss cucumbers and press to drain out excess liquid. Rinse cucumbers, drain again, and press between paper towels to dry.

2. In large bowl, combine yogurt, sour cream, lemon juice, sugar, thyme, and pepper and mix well to blend. Gently stir in drained cucumbers, then serve.

Summer Squashes

Summer squashes, like zucchini and yellow squash, are thin skinned and excellent eaten raw. They can be substituted for cucumbers and mushrooms in most salads. Unless the skins are waxed, they don't need to be peeled, just cut into sticks, julienned, cubed, or sliced.

tip

Fruit and Cheese Salad

The fruits of summer, strawberries, raspberries, melons, peaches,
and blackberries can all be used in this refreshing and beautiful salad.

SERVES 6

2 nectarines

2 cups sliced strawberries

2 cups blueberries

1 cup cubed Havarti cheese

½ cup poppy seed salad dressing

1. Slice nectarines and discard pit. Combine with remaining ingredients in a serving bowl and toss gently to coat. Serve immediately or cover and refrigerate up to 2 hours before serving.

Turkey Waldorf Salad

Waldorf Salad is traditionally made from chopped apples and walnuts in a creamy dressing. Adding turkey to this salad elevates it to a main dish delight.

SERVES 6

3 Granny Smith apples

1 cup golden raisins

1 cup coarsely chopped toasted walnuts

2 cups chopped cooked turkey breast

1½ cups mayonnaise or yogurt

⅛ teaspoon allspice

⅛ teaspoon white pepper

1. Core apples and coarsely chop. Combine in medium bowl with raisins, walnuts, and turkey.

2. In small bowl combine mayonnaise, allspice, and pepper and blend well. Spoon over turkey mixture and toss to coat.

3. Cover and refrigerate for 10–15 minutes to blend flavors. Store leftovers in refrigerator.

Toasting Walnuts

Toasting walnuts concentrates and brings out the flavor. To toast them, spread on a shallow baking sheet and bake in a 350°F oven for 10–15 minutes, stirring twice during baking time. Or microwave the nuts: place in a single layer on microwave safe plate and heat at 100% power for 2–4 minutes until fragrant.

tip

Greens with Basil Dressing

This dressing can be served with any green or vegetable salad.
It will keep, well covered, in the refrigerator for about 3–4 days.

SERVES 6

6 cups salad greens

½ cup yogurt

½ cup mayonnaise or yogurt

¼ cup buttermilk

⅓ cup chopped fresh basil leaves

½ teaspoon dried basil leaves

½ teaspoon salt

⅛ teaspoon white pepper

1. Place salad greens in a serving bowl.

2. In a food processor or blender container, combine remaining ingredients. Process or blend until the basil leaves are very finely chopped.

3. Drizzle dressing over the salad, toss, and serve.

Fresh and Dried Herbs

Using fresh and dried herbs in the same recipe is an easy way to increase the depth of flavor. Many dried herbs taste different than their fresh counterparts. Dried basil, for instance, has a smokier flavor than fresh. And dried thyme has a more intense mint flavor, while the fresh tends to be more lemony.

tip

Pasta and Cheese Salad

Of course, you can add any number of fresh vegetables to this simple salad. Sliced mushrooms, yellow summer squash, cucumbers, and spring onions would all be nice additions.

SERVES 6

1 (10-ounce) container basil pesto

½ cup mayonnaise

1 cup cubed smoked Gouda cheese

2 red bell peppers, chopped

1 (18-ounce) package frozen cheese tortellini

1. Bring large pot of salted water to a boil.

2. Meanwhile, in large bowl, combine pesto and mayonnaise and blend well. Stir in cheese and chopped peppers.

3. Add tortellini to pot of water and cook according to package directions until done. Drain well and stir into cheese mixture. Serve immediately or cover and chill for 2–3 hours.

Simple Spinach Salad

This beautiful salad can be served with some corn bread or hot biscuits
for a simple dinner, or as a side dish for a casserole, soup, or stew.

SERVES 4

4 cups baby spinach leaves

½ cup toasted pine nuts

1 cup frozen baby peas

1 cup grape tomatoes

½ cup basil vinaigrette salad dressing

1. Toss together spinach and pine nuts in serving bowl. Place peas in a colander and run hot water over them for 1–2 minutes to thaw. Drain well and add to spinach mixture along with grape tomatoes.

2. Drizzle with half of the salad dressing and toss gently. Serve immediately with remaining dressing on the side.

Tiny Tomatoes

There are some new small tomatoes on the market. Grape tomatoes are about the size of grapes; they are sweet, tender, and juicy. Cherry tomatoes are less popular since grape tomatoes burst onto the scene but they are still available; they come in red and yellow varieties. And sweet currant tomatoes are about half the size of cherry tomatoes.

tip

Three-Bean Salad

*Three-Bean Salad is typically marinated in a sweet-and-sour salad dressing.
You can use any combination of beans you'd like, selecting from green beans,
wax beans, kidney beans, chick peas, black beans, red beans, and soybeans.*

YIELDS 6 CUPS

2 cups frozen soybeans

*1 (15-ounce) can green beans,
drained*

*1 (15-ounce) can wax beans,
drained*

*¾ cup red wine vinaigrette salad
dressing*

2 tablespoons red wine vinegar

⅓ cup sugar

*¼ teaspoon dried tarragon
leaves*

Dash black pepper

1. Bring large pot of water to a boil and cook
frozen soybeans for 2–3 minutes until tender.
Drain and rinse with cold water. Combine
in serving bowl with green beans and wax
beans.

2. In small saucepan combine salad dressing,
vinegar, sugar, tarragon, and pepper; whisk
over low heat until sugar is dissolved. Pour
over bean mixture and stir gently. Let stand
for 10 minutes, then serve. Store leftovers in
refrigerator.

Smoked Turkey Fruit Salad

*This delicious dressing, made by pureeing ripe strawberries with yogurt
and minty fresh thyme leaves, makes this salad simply spectacular.*

SERVES 6–8

1 quart strawberries

½ cup vanilla yogurt

¼ teaspoon salt

¼ teaspoon dried thyme leaves

1 ripe cantaloupe

2 cups chopped smoked turkey

1 pint raspberries

1. Wash and hull the strawberries and cut in half. In food processor or blender, combine yogurt, salt, thyme, and ½ cup of the sliced strawberries. Process or blend until smooth.

2. Cut cantaloupe in half and remove seeds. Cut into wedges.

3. In serving bowl, combine strawberries, cantaloupe, and turkey. Drizzle dressing over and toss gently to coat. Top with raspberries and serve.

Raspberries

Raspberries are a very delicate fruit. They must be used within a day or two of purchase. Do not rinse raspberries before you are ready to use them because they mold very easily. Never toss them with a salad; use them as a garnish on top.

tip

Layered Ham Salad

Layered salads were big in the 1970s and 1980s. They are a great choice for a buffet.
Be sure to use a clear glass serving dish so all the beautiful layers are exposed.

SERVES 6

2 tablespoons olive oil

2 cups chopped ham

2 cups frozen bell pepper and onion stir fry

1 head romaine lettuce

1 cup mayonnaise

1 tablespoon brown sugar

2 tablespoons grated Parmesan cheese

1. In heavy skillet, heat olive oil over medium heat. Add ¼ cup of the chopped ham; cook and stir until ham pieces are crisp around the edges. Remove ham to paper towel to drain. Add bell pepper and onion mixture; cook and stir for 3–5 minutes until vegetables are hot and tender.

2. Clean and chop romaine lettuce. In large bowl, layer half of the lettuce followed by half the bell pepper mixture and half the remaining 1¾ cups ham. Repeat layers.

3. In small bowl combine mayonnaise with sugar and cheese. Spread over top of salad and sprinkle with the fried ham bits. Serve immediately or cover and refrigerate for 2–3 hours before serving.

Sugared Almond Green Salad

Sugared almonds add wonderful crunch and flavor to this simple salad made with tender salad greens and sweet mandarin oranges.

SERVES 4–6

2 tablespoons butter

½ cup sliced almonds

3 tablespoons sugar

6 cups mixed salad greens

1 (15-ounce) can mandarin oranges, drained, reserving juice

2 tablespoons reserved juice from oranges

½ cup honey mustard salad dressing

1. In small heavy saucepan, melt butter over medium heat until foaming. Stir in almonds; cook and stir for 2–4 minutes until almonds begin to show color. Sprinkle sugar over almonds; cook and stir for another minute. Remove to paper towel to drain and cool.

2. In serving bowl, combine salad greens and drained oranges and toss gently. In small bowl, combine 2 tablespoons reserved orange juice and the salad dressing and whisk to blend. Drizzle over salad and top with sugared almonds.

Sugared Almonds

Sugared almonds are easy to make, but you must make sure to watch them carefully as they cook and never leave the stove. They burn easily! Make a large batch and store them in an airtight container in a cool place. You can sprinkle them over many salads. They'll keep up to 3 weeks.

tip

Ambrosia

Ambrosia is an old-fashioned salad that is sweet and delicious. It always includes oranges and coconut along with a sweet whipped dressing; the rest is up to you!

SERVES 6

1 (8-ounce) container frozen whipped topping, thawed

⅓ cup reserved mandarin orange juice

1 cup cottage cheese

2 (14-ounce) cans mandarin oranges, drained, reserving juice

1 (15-ounce) can crushed pineapple, drained

1 cup shredded coconut

In serving bowl, combine whipped topping, orange juice, and cottage cheese; stir with wire whisk until blended. Fold in remaining ingredients. Cover and chill for 15 minutes before serving. Store leftovers in refrigerator.

Whipped Cream or Frozen Topping?

You can use heavy cream, whipped until stiff with a few spoonfuls of powdered sugar, for the frozen whipped topping in this simple salad. If you are watching fat and calories, look for low fat nondairy frozen whipped toppings in your grocery store's frozen food aisle. Any frozen topping must thaw in the refrigerator for 6–8 hours.

tip

Pesto Pasta Salad

*This is an antipasto salad with salami and provolone cheese.
You may use other shapes of pasta, such as corkscrew or
tortellini, and vary the vegetables to suit your taste.*

SERVES 4

1 cup pesto

4 cups cooked penne pasta

¼ cup diced red onion

¼ cup sliced black olives

½ cup cherry tomatoes

¼ cup diced roasted red bell
peppers

¼ cup chopped artichoke hearts

4 ounces cubed salami

4 ounces cubed provolone cheese

1 clove minced garlic

Combine everything and chill. You can keep
this in the fridge and use it for both dinner
and lunch, either to stay in or to pack and go.

Macaroni Salad

Serve this classic with hot dogs and hamburgers from the backyard grill, pack it in a basket for a picnic in the park or take it in a cooler to the beach and serve it in a clean plastic sand pail.

SERVES 6

4 cups cooked macaroni

4 sliced hardboiled eggs

½ cup thinly sliced celery

1 tablespoon minced pimento

1 cup mayonnaise

¼ cup sliced green olives

2 tablespoons chopped fresh parsley

Salt and pepper to taste

Paprika

1. Mix all ingredients except eggs in a bowl, and chill for 1 hour.

2. Cover the surface with sliced eggs, sprinkle with paprika and serve.

Retro Salad

Mix 1 can of drained tuna into 1 recipe of macaroni salad and top it with tomato wedges for a popular lunch salad from the past.

tip

Potato Salad

*This potato salad has potatoes with the skin on and the robust
flavors of mustard seeds and pickles. Adjust the consistency
with more mayonnaise if it gets dry after being chilled.*

SERVES 6

*30 boiled baby red skinned
potatoes*

¼ cup diced red onion

3 baby dill pickles

2 tablespoons coarse mustard

2 tablespoons Dijon mustard

¾ cup mayonnaise

1 hardboiled egg

¼ teaspoon paprika

½ teaspoon salt

¼ teaspoon pepper

1 tablespoon pickle juice

2 tablespoons chopped chives

1. Quarter the potatoes and put in a bowl.

2. Cut the pickles into fine dice and add to the potatoes.

3. Chop the hardboiled egg and add it to the potatoes.

4. Add the rest of the ingredients to the bowl and stir until well mixed.

5. Chill and adjust seasoning before serving.

Sour Cream Potato Salad

This is a creamy potato salad with no potato skins. Since it requires overnight chilling in the refrigerator, it can be prepared the day before it is needed and free up the kitchen to make other things.

SERVES 8

8 medium potatoes—peeled, cubed, and boiled

1½ cups mayonnaise

1 cup sour cream

1½ teaspoons horseradish

1 teaspoon celery seed

½ teaspoon salt

½ cup parsley flakes

2 medium onions minced

Combine and chill 8–24 hours. Like other potato salads, you can add this to any protein-based meal or bring it as a side to a party.

Warm Potato Salad

This is sometimes called German Potato Salad.
Unlike most potato salads, this one is served warm.

SERVES 6

6 cooked, peeled medium potatoes, warm

3 sliced green onions

4 slices fried bacon, crumbled

2 tablespoons lemon juice

2 tablespoons white wine vinegar

1 tablespoon olive oil

Salt and pepper to taste

1. Cube the potatoes.

2. Toss everything else in a bowl with the potatoes.

3. Serve warm.

Sweet Potato Salad

Mix together 1 cup Oven-Roasted Sweet Potatoes, ½ cup Oven-Roasted Red Potatoes, cubed, ½ cup diced apples, 2 tablespoons malt vinegar, and 1 tablespoon olive oil. Season with 1 teaspoon minced fresh rosemary, and salt and pepper to taste. Serve warm.

tip

Pea Salad

*For extra crunch, add 1 cup salted peanuts and ¼ cup chopped celery
to this salad and sprinkle it with crisp bacon bits before serving.*

SERVES 4

2 cups fresh or thawed frozen peas

½ cup diced red onions

1 cup shredded cheddar cheese

1 chopped hardboiled egg

1 tablespoon diced red bell pepper

1 tablespoon diced green bell
pepper

2 tablespoons chopped fresh dill

¼ cup sour cream

½ cup mayonnaise

1 teaspoon lemon juice

Salt and pepper to taste

Mix everything in a bowl; season with salt
and pepper to taste. Enjoy this as a light dinner or side to a summer meal.

Interesting Additions

Some people add raisins and
mayonnaise to shredded carrots
to make carrot slaw, but you
could instead add sliced whole
green onions and honey mustard for a more savory version of
carrot slaw.

tip

Caesar Salad

This is the authentic version with dressing make in the bowl, not ahead of time. A wooden salad bowl is necessary to make this classic of tableside restaurant service.

SERVES 2

1 smashed clove of garlic

1 coddled egg

1 teaspoon Dijon mustard

4 anchovies

¼ cup olive oil

1 tablespoon white wine vinegar

3 dashes Worcestershire sauce

Dash cayenne pepper sauce

Salt and pepper to taste

1 lemon

Parmesan cheese

Croutons

3 hearts of romaine lettuce

1. In a wooden salad bowl rub the garlic around with a fork. Remove garlic clove.

2. Add egg, mustard, salt and pepper and stir with fork to make an emulsion.

3. Add 2 anchovies, mashing them into the emulsion, then add vinegar, oil, Worcestershire sauce and cayenne pepper sauce and stir with fork or whisk to combine. Adjust seasoning with salt and pepper.

4. To the dressing in the bowl add hearts of romaine leaves. Squeeze the juice of ½ lemon onto the lettuce, then add croutons.

5. Toss lettuce and croutons with dressing and top with grated parmesan cheese, anchovies and black pepper.

Greek Salad

Use kalamata olives and Greek olive oil for the authentic taste of Greece.

SERVES 4

1 head lettuce, chopped

1 large tomato, chopped

¼ red onion, sliced

¼ cup black olives

½ cucumber, sliced

4 ounces feta cheese, crumbled

1 teaspoon dried oregano

½ cup olive oil

3 tablespoons red wine vinegar

Salt and pepper

1. Make dressing by mixing together oregano, oil and vinegar. Season with salt and pepper.

2. Toss lettuce with dressing and put in a serving bowl.

3. Scatter vegetables and cheese over the dressed lettuce.

Cobb Salad

*A California-born classic. This is a staple on menus
across America—why not make it at home?*

SERVES 6

1 head iceberg lettuce, chopped

2 diced tomatoes

½ cup diced cooked chicken

1 diced avocado

½ cup crumbled blue cheese

¼ cup bacon bits

3 chopped hardboiled eggs

½ cup chopped green onions

½ cup salad dressing

1. Toss lettuce leaves with dressing. Mound dressed lettuce on an oval platter.

2. Top dressed lettuce with all the other ingredients arranged in separate stripes.

Brown Derby

The Cobb Salad was invented at the Brown Derby restaurant in Los Angeles, a famous hangout of stars and gossip columnists since its opening in 1926.

tip

Seafood Pasta Salad

*A great way to change up a pasta salad is to include surprise
ingredients—in this recipe, experiment with seafood. Shrimp will
bring a whole new element to your plain old pasta salad.*

SERVES 4

½ pound dry tricolored spiral
pasta, cooked and chilled

1 cup cooked and peeled shrimp

1 green bell pepper, diced

¼ cup sliced carrots

½ cup sliced zucchini

⅓ cup Worcestershire sauce

⅓ cup low-fat mayonnaise

Salt and pepper to taste

1. In a bowl, combine the pasta, shrimp, bell
pepper, carrots, and zucchini, mixing gently.
Add the Worcestershire sauce, mayonnaise,
salt, and pepper and toss lightly to combine.

2. Cover and refrigerate for at least 30 minutes before serving.

Apricot-Coriander Salad

This refreshing salad would go great with a piece of meat or some barbecued chicken in the summer, or as a light meal on its own.

SERVES 6

2 cups bean sprouts

Boiling water as needed

1 can (17 ounces) apricot halves in syrup

3 tablespoons white wine vinegar

1 teaspoon peanut oil

2 tablespoons soy sauce

1½ teaspoons ground ginger

4 cups shredded lettuce

¼ cup minced fresh coriander

2 scallions, sliced on the diagonal

1 can (8 ounces) water chestnuts, drained and sliced

1. Place the bean sprouts in a colander or large sieve. Pour boiling water over them; drain and cool. Drain the apricots, reserving 2 tablespoons syrup. Cut the apricots into strips and set aside.

2. In a jar with screw-top lid, combine the syrup, vinegar, oil, soy sauce, and ginger. Cover and shake well. Place the lettuce into a bowl or onto a platter. Top with the coriander, scallions, bean sprouts, and water chestnuts. Place the apricot strips over the salad. Shake the dressing again and pour over the salad. Toss well and serve.

CHAPTER

3

From the Deli

Ham and Three-Bean Salad

*Make sure that you taste the three-bean salad from your deli
before using it in this recipe. Most delis will offer you a taste if you ask.*

SERVES 4

3 cups deli three-bean salad

1 cup cubed cooked ham

1 cup grape tomatoes

1 yellow bell pepper, seeded and
chopped

1 cup mushrooms, sliced

1. Drain salad and reserve ½ cup of the
dressing.

2. Combine all ingredients in medium bowl
and toss with enough reserved dressing
to moisten. Serve immediately; refrigerate
leftovers.

Southwest Potato Salad

If you like your food extra spicy, use more chili powder or add
more jalapeño peppers. If you're really brave, try habanero peppers!

SERVES 8

1 quart deli potato salad

1 tablespoon chili powder

2 red bell peppers, chopped

1 pint cherry tomatoes

1 jalapeño pepper, minced

2 cups canned corn, drained

1. Place potato salad in serving bowl and sprinkle evenly with chili powder.

2. Add remaining ingredients and gently stir to mix thoroughly. Serve immediately or cover and chill for 1–2 hours to blend flavors.

Dress Up Potato Salad

It's easy to dress up plain potato salad; to make a curried potato salad, mix curry powder with chutney and stir into potato salad along with sliced green onions and sliced celery. For an All-American potato salad, add grape tomatoes, some chopped dill pickles, and some yellow mustard.

Spicy Veggie Pizza

Boboli pizza crusts are available in any deli and you can usually find plain pizza crusts there too. This easy pizza is delicious served with some deli fruit salad and cold milk.

SERVES 4

2 cups marinated deli vegetables

1 Boboli pizza crust

1 (10-ounce) container garlic and herb cream cheese

1 cup shredded Provolone cheese

½ cup grated Parmesan cheese

1. Preheat oven to 400°F. Chop the marinated vegetables into smaller pieces and place in saucepan with the marinade. Bring to a simmer over medium heat; simmer for 3–4 minutes until vegetables are tender. Drain thoroughly.

2. Place pizza crust on a cookie sheet and spread with the cream cheese. Arrange drained vegetables on top and sprinkle with Provolone and Parmesan cheeses. Bake at 400°F for 15–18 minutes until crust is hot and crisp and cheese is melted and begins to brown.

Make Your Own Crust

Make your own crust by combining 2 cups flour, 1 cup cornmeal, 3 tablespoons oil, 1 package yeast, and 1⅓ cups water in a bowl. Knead thoroughly, let rise, punch down, divide in half, and roll out. Prebake the crust at 400°F for 8–10 minutes, then cool, wrap well, and freeze until ready to use.

tip

Snickers Salad

In many delis, there is a fabulous sweet whipped cream salad made with chopped candy bars. It stretches the definition of "salad," but it makes a delicious treat.

SERVES 12

1 sheet puff pastry, thawed

3 cups deli candy bar salad

1 cup milk chocolate chips

½ cup chopped walnuts

1. Preheat oven to 425°F. On lightly floured surface, roll out puff pastry to a 12 × 18" sheet. Cut in half horizontally to make two 6 × 18" pieces. Cut each into six 6 × 3" pieces and place on baking sheet. Bake at 425°F for 8–10 minutes until puffed and golden brown. Remove to wire rack and let cool for 10–15 minutes.

2. Split each rectangle of pastry in half horizontally and put the halves together with some of the salad. Meanwhile, melt chocolate chips in microwave oven for 2 minutes on 50% power; stir until smooth. Drizzle chocolate over filled rectangles and sprinkle with walnuts. Cover and refrigerate, or serve immediately.

Recreating Deli Salads

If you can't find certain deli salads, recreate them! Most salads use a combination of fruits with whipped cream or nondairy whipped topping. The Snicker Bar Salad is made with vanilla pudding, chopped candy bars, chopped walnuts, nondairy whipped topping, and chopped apples.

tip

Simple Fruit Parfaits

Make these pretty parfaits ahead of time and keep them in the refrigerator until you're ready to serve them. After a big or late lunch, this light and sweet dinner is a great choice!

SERVES 8

2 cups frozen nondairy topping, thawed

1 cup deli vanilla pudding

½ teaspoon cinnamon

2 cups deli fruit salad

1 cup granola

1. In medium bowl, combine topping, pudding, and cinnamon and fold together gently.

2. Make parfaits by layering the fruit salad, topping mixture, and granola into tall parfait glasses, ending with granola. Serve immediately or cover and refrigerate for up to 4 hours.

Deli Fruit Salads

There are usually several kinds of deli fruit salads. You'll find plain mixed fruit with no dressing or a simple clear dressing, gelatin fruit salads, and fruit salads made with whipped cream or whipping topping. For this recipe, look for the plain mixed fruit salad.

tip

Barbecued Roast Beef Sandwiches

This recipe is great for using up leftover roast beef.
The sauce can also be used to make Sloppy Joe sandwiches;
use 1½ pounds of cooked and drained ground beef for the roast beef.

SERVES 12

2 tablespoons olive oil

1 onion, chopped

½ cup steak sauce

1 (8-ounce) can tomato sauce

1½ pounds thin sliced cooked deli roast beef

12 sandwich buns, split and toasted

1. In heavy skillet, heat olive oil over medium heat. Add onion and cook, stirring frequently, for 5–6 minutes until onions are tender. Add steak sauce and tomato sauce and bring to a simmer. Stir in roast beef; simmer for 5–6 minutes, stirring frequently, until sauce thickens slightly and roast beef is heated through.

2. Make sandwiches using roast beef mixture and split and toasted sandwich buns. Serve immediately.

Hot Submarine Sandwiches

Use any combination of meats and cheeses for this easy and hearty sandwich recipe.
Serve it with a deli fruit salad and a bakery pie for dessert.

SERVES 4–6

1 loaf Italian bread, unsliced

½ cup honey mustard/mayo combo

½ pound sliced deli ham

½ pound sliced deli turkey

½ pound sliced Muenster cheese

1. Preheat oven to 400ºF. Slice bread in half crosswise and place, cut sides up, on work surface.

2. Spread cut surfaces with the honey mustard/mayo combo. Arrange ham, turkey, and Muenster cheese on one half of the bread, then top with second half. Wrap entire sandwich in foil.

3. Bake at 400ºF for 20–23 minutes or until sandwich is hot, cheese is melted, and bread is toasted, opening foil for last 5 minutes of baking time to crisp bread. Slice into four to six portions and serve.

Mustard Combinations

There are many types and varieties of mustard combinations in the grocery store these days. From honey mustard to grainy mustard to mustard and mayonnaise blends, there's a large selection to choose from. Keep a supply on hand for making sandwiches from just about any leftover meat.

tip

Corned Beef Sandwiches

These hearty sandwiches are perfect for a St. Patrick's Day celebration.

SERVES 4

8 slices deli pumpernickle rye swirl bread

¼ cup mustard mayonnaise combo

½ pound sliced deli corned beef

2 cups deli coleslaw

4 slices deli Swiss cheese

1. Spread mustard mayonnaise combo on the bread slices and make sandwiches with the corned beef, coleslaw, and Swiss cheese.

2. Cut in half and serve with some deli dill pickles.

Salads in Sandwiches

When you're using any kind of prepared salads in sandwich recipes, you may need to drain the salad by placing it in a colander and letting it stand for a few minutes, or by using a slotted spoon to scoop the salad out of the container. If you're making sandwiches ahead of time, leave the salad out and add it just before serving.

tip

Chicken Tortellini Salad

Most delis have a selection of prepared salads. Serve this
gorgeous salad on some baby spinach leaves along with iced tea.

SERVES 4–6

1 quart deli tortellini salad

2 cups chopped deli chicken

1 red bell pepper, chopped

1 cup chopped Havarti cheese

½ cup mayonnaise

In large bowl, combine all ingredients and toss gently to coat. Serve immediately or cover and refrigerate up to 24 hours.

Salad Inspirations

Take some time to browse through your supermarket to find ideas for salads. In the produce section you'll find salad kits and lots of refrigerated dressings to inspire you. Many companies make salad kits that are placed in the meat aisle and some are in the grocery aisle near the bottled salad dressings.

tip

Monte Cristo Sandwiches

Find fish batter mix near the fish in the supermarket's meat aisle.
It makes a wonderful crispy coating on these delicious sandwiches.

SERVES 4

¼ pound thinly sliced deli ham

¼ pound thinly sliced deli turkey

¼ pound thinly sliced deli Colby cheese

8 slices whole grain bread

1 cup fish batter mix

⅓ cup oil

1. Heat heavy saucepan over medium high heat. Make sandwiches using ham, turkey, cheese, and bread. In shallow bowl, prepare batter mix as directed on package.

2. Pour oil into heated saucepan. Dip sandwiches into batter mixture and place in oil in saucepan. Cook over medium heat, turning once, until bread is golden brown and cheese is melted, about 3–4 minutes per side. Cut sandwiches in half and serve immediately.

Monte Cristo Sandwich Dips

Serve these dips with Monte Cristo Sandwiches or any grilled sandwich. For a sweet dip, combine ½ cup sour cream with ¼ cup raspberry jam and mix well. For a spicy dip, combine ½ cup mayonnaise with 2 tablespoons honey dijon mustard and a teaspoon of chili sauce and blend well.

tip

Crispy Chicken Stir-Fry

Hot cooked rice is a must for this simple stir-fry recipe.
Serve with chopsticks and some green tea for a quick Asian meal.

SERVES 4

2 *fried chicken breasts*

2 *tablespoons olive oil*

1 *onion, chopped*

2 *cups mixed salad vegetables from deli salad bar*

⅔ *cup sweet and sour simmer sauce*

1. Cut chicken meat off the bone; be sure to include some crisp skin on each piece. Set aside. If necessary, cut salad vegetables into uniform pieces.

2. In large saucepan or wok, heat olive oil over medium high heat. Add onion and salad vegetables and stir-fry for 4–7 minutes until crisp tender.

3. Add chicken pieces; stir-fry for 2–3 minutes until hot. Add simmer sauce and stir fry for 3–5 minutes until hot. Serve immediately.

Roasted Chicken Penne

A tender baby spinach salad with a raspberry vinaigrette with some raspberries and toasted slivered almonds is all you need to make this easy recipe a complete meal.

SERVES 4

2 cups penne pasta

2 roasted deli chicken breasts

1 (10-ounce) jar garlic Alfredo sauce

½ cup chicken gravy (from deli or 10-ounce jar)

2 cups frozen mixed vegetables

1. Bring a large pot of water to a boil and cook penne pasta according to package directions. Meanwhile, remove meat from chicken and shred. Combine with Alfredo sauce, chicken gravy, and vegetables in a large saucepan over medium heat. Cook, stirring occasionally, until sauce bubbles and chicken and vegetables are hot.

2. When pasta is cooked al dente, drain thoroughly and add to chicken mixture, stirring and tossing gently. Cook for another 1–2 minutes to heat through and serve.

Roast Beef Calzones

Calzones are a baked Italian sandwich, usually made with pizza crusts.
This version, made with pie crusts, is more delicate and flaky.

SERVES 6

1 package refrigerated pie crusts

1 (7-ounce) can artichoke hearts, drained

2 cups chopped deli roast beef

1½ cups diced swiss cheese

⅓ cup sour cream

1. Preheat oven to 400°F. Let pie crusts stand at room temperature while preparing filling. Drain artichoke hearts, place on paper towels to drain further, and cut into smaller pieces. In medium bowl, combine artichoke hearts, beef cubes, cheese, and sour cream, and mix gently.

2. Place pie crusts on cookie sheet, placing the edges in the center of the cookie sheet, about 1" apart, and letting excess hang beyond the cookie sheet. Divide filling between pie crusts, placing on one half of each crust, leaving a one inch border. Fold the unfilled half of the pie crust (the part hanging beyond the cookie sheet) over the filling to form a half moon shape. Press edges with a fork to firmly seal. Cut decorative shapes in the top of each crust. Bake at 400°F for 18–24 minutes until crust is golden brown and crisp and filling is hot. Let stand for 5 minutes, then cut into wedges to serve.

Pesto Potato Salad

This excellent salad is perfect for a picnic or cookout. Be sure to pack it in an insulated cooler with some ice packs and discard leftovers after the picnic.

SERVES 6–8

1 (10-ounce) container
refrigerated pesto

½ cup mayonnaise

6 cups deli potato salad

½ cup grated Parmesan cheese

2 cups cubed Havarti cheese

In large bowl, combine pesto and mayonnaise; stir in potato salad until coated. Stir in cheeses and mix well. Serve immediately or cover and chill for up to 8 hours before serving.

Menu Ideas

Serve this potato salad with steak, lots of tortilla chips and potato chips, and maybe some asparagus. For dessert, make s'mores by toasting marshmallows over the coals and making sandwiches with the marshmallows, graham crackers, and chocolate bars.

tip

Spinach and Fruit Ham Salad

For this recipe, purchase the deli fruit salad with a clear dressing, not the salad with the whipped cream dressing.

SERVES 6

1 (10-ounce) bag baby spinach

2 cups (8 ounces) cubed deli ham

2 cups deli fruit salad

½ cup peach pie filling

1 cup pecan halves

In large serving bowl, arrange spinach. In medium bowl, combine ham with deli fruit salad and fold in pie filling. Add pecan halves and spoon salad over baby spinach; serve immediately.

Menu Suggestions

On hot summer days, serve cold main dish salads on your back porch under a ceiling fan with some chewy bakery breadsticks on the side, some iced tea or lemonade. A real summer treat!

tip

Smoked Salmon Pizza

If your deli makes a marinated vegetable salad that you like, cook it for a few minutes over medium heat until tender, then drain thoroughly and substitute it for the artichoke hearts in this simple recipe.

SERVES 4

1 10-inch focaccia bread

¾ cup garlic Alfredo sauce (from 10-ounce jar)

8 ounces cold smoked salmon

1 (8 ounce) jar plain artichoke hearts, drained

1½ cups shredded Gouda cheese

1. Preheat oven to 400°F. Place focaccia on baking sheet. Spread with Alfredo sauce. Arrange salmon and artichoke hearts on pizza, then sprinkle with Gouda cheese.

2. Bake at 400°F for 18–22 minutes until pizza is thoroughly heated and cheese is melted and beginning to brown. Serve immediately.

Smoked Salmon

Salmon is available hot smoked or cold smoked. Hot smoked salmon, also called kippered salmon, is generally hard and slightly chewy and is a deep red color. Cold smoked salmon, or lox, is pink and tender and is sliced very thinly. Either type of salmon will work in this easy pizza.

tip

Seafood Enchiladas

*Serve these easy enchiladas with one of the refreshing
salads from this book for a cool summer meal.*

SERVES 6

½ pound deli Muenster cheese

3 cups deli seafood salad

1 cup salsa

1 (10-ounce) jar enchilada sauce

12 corn tortillas

1. Preheat oven to 400ºF. Shred cheese into large bowl or ask the deli to shred it.

2. In another large bowl combine seafood salad and salsa; stir in 1½ cups shredded cheese. Divide among corn tortillas and roll up.

3. Place ½ cup enchilada sauce in bottom of 2 quart baking dish and lay filled tortillas on top. Drizzle with rest of enchilada sauce and sprinkle with remaining cheese.

4. Bake at 400ºF for 20–23 minutes until casserole is hot and bubbly. Serve immediately.

Asian Beef Rolls

This cold entrée wraps tender roast beef around
crunchy coleslaw mix seasoned with Asian ingredients.

SERVES 6

3 tablespoons hoisin sauce

¼ cup plum sauce

1½ cups coleslaw mix

¼ cup chopped green onion

6 slices cooked deli roast beef

1. In medium bowl, combine hoisin sauce and plum sauce and mix well. Stir in coleslaw mix and green onion and mix gently.

2. Place roast beef slices on work surface and divide coleslaw mixture among them. Roll up beef slices, enclosing filling. Serve immediately or cover and refrigerate up to 8 hours before serving.

Menu Suggestions

These spicy and crunchy rolls are delicious paired with a cold soup and sweet bread for dinner on the porch on a hot summer day.

tip

Grilled Meatloaf Sandwiches

These great sandwiches are also the perfect way to use up leftover meatloaf. Serve with large dill pickles from the deli and some deli coleslaw, along with root beer and ice cream for dessert.

SERVES 4

4 slices deli meatloaf

½ cup tomato sauce

4 slices deli Cheddar cheese

8 slices deli pumpernickel bread

¼ cup butter, softened

1. Preheat dual contact indoor grill or large skillet over medium high heat.

2. Spread tomato sauce onto meatloaf slices. Make sandwiches with coated meatloaf, cheese, and pumpernickel bread.

3. Spread outside of sandwiches with softened butter and cook on grill or skillet, turning once, until bread is hot and crisp and cheese begins to melt, about 4–6 minutes. Serve immediately.

Dual Contact Grills

These grills are an easy way to grill just about any food. Just cut the cooking time in half, because the food cooks on both sides at the same time. Be sure to press the grill closed gently but firmly, to make good contact with the food.

tip

Curried Egg Salad

*Crunchy cashews and a dash of curry powder turn ordinary
egg salad into a flavorful entrée. Serve this egg salad on bread
with honey mustard, chopped cashews, and green lettuce.*

SERVES 2

3 hardboiled eggs

2 tablespoons diced celery

*1 tablespoon chopped green
onions*

¼ cup mayonnaise

1 tablespoon plain yogurt

2 tablespoons Dijon mustard

2 teaspoons honey

¼ teaspoon curry powder

¼ cup chopped toasted cashews

Salt to taste

Pepper to taste

1. Peel and chop the hardboiled eggs and put in a bowl with celery and green onions. Toss to mix briefly.

2. Add mayonnaise, yogurt, mustard, honey and curry powder to the bowl and mix well.

3. Season with salt and pepper to taste.

4. Sprinkle the cashews over the egg salad and fold them into the mixture.

Hero

A submarine sandwich made with various sliced meats, cold cuts, and cheeses is sometimes called a hero. When served hot, a hero can have steak, meatballs, or even hamburger patties lined up on the bun.

tip

Tuna Salad

Use soft white bread and lettuce when making this lunchbox classic, or dress it up on a croissant with alfalfa sprouts, lemon mayonnaise and tomato slices.

SERVES 4

1 (6-ounce) can tuna packed in water, drained

¼ cup red onion, diced

2 tablespoons celery, diced

1 tablespoon sweet relish

¼ cup mayonnaise

Salt to taste

Pepper to taste

1 tablespoon chopped parsley

1 tablespoon lemon juice

1. Combine all ingredients in a bowl with a spatula.

2. Adjust seasoning with salt and pepper.

Club Sandwich

This double-decker sandwich combines a BLT with a turkey sandwich and is best eaten with potato chips, carrot sticks, and pickle slices, lunch-counter style.

SERVES 1

3 *pieces white bread, toasted*

2 *pieces bacon, cut in half*

2 *slices tomato*

2 *leaves lettuce*

2 *tablespoons mayonnaise*

2 *ounces roast turkey, sliced thin*

1 *slice American cheese (optional)*

4 *toothpicks*

2 *black olives*

2 *green olives*

1. Put mayonnaise on all three pieces of toast.

2. Put lettuce, tomato, and bacon on one piece of toast, turkey and cheese on another piece of toast and stack them with the turkey on the bottom and the third piece of toast on the top.

3. Slice sandwich into 4 triangles and insert toothpicks in each quadrant. Top each toothpick with an olive.

Smoked Salmon Bagel

A fresh, chewy bagel is a must for this deli favorite. Smoked salmon or lox may be used and additions of avocado, tomato, and/or sprouts build up the classic bagel and schmear combination.

SERVES 1

1 plain bagel, sliced

2 ounces whipped cream cheese

3 slices smoked salmon

1 slice red onion

1 teaspoon capers (optional)

1. Smear the cream cheese on the cut sides of the un-toasted bagel.

2. Top cream cheese on the bottom half with smoked salmon, onion, and capers.

3. Top with the other half of the bagel and cut sandwich in half.

Grinder

A submarine sandwich made with sliced meat and cheese is sometimes called a grinder. Other names are gondola, torpedo, bomber, zeppelin, and hoagie.

tip

Gourmet BLT

Bacon, Lettuce, and Tomato make this sandwich classic;
basil mayonnaise and focaccia bread make it gourmet.

SERVES 1

One 4-inch square piece of focaccia

2 pieces cooked bacon

3 slices tomato

2 butter lettuce leaves

1 tablespoon mayonnaise

1 chopped basil leaf

1. Slice the focaccia horizontally. Cut the bacon pieces in half.

2. Mix basil and mayonnaise together and spread on underside of the top half of the focaccia.

3. Layer the lettuce, tomato and bacon on the bottom piece of focaccia. Top with the focaccia with the basil mayonnaise and slice the sandwich on the diagonal into 2 triangles.

Cheesesteak

There is controversy over which cheese to use in this hot hero sandwich,
so feel free to drizzle processed melted cheese sauce on it instead of shredded
provolone. Red cherry peppers and sautéed mushrooms are a tasty addition.

SERVES 2

1 pound strip steak, sliced thin

1 tablespoon butter

1 tablespoon olive oil

½ cup sliced onions

¼ cup sliced green peppers

1 cup shredded provolone cheese

1 foot-long sub bun

1. Sauté onions and peppers in olive oil, set aside.

2. Sauté steak in butter until cooked through.

3. Toss onions and peppers in with the meat.

4. Top the meat with the provolone.

5. Scoop meat with everything on it onto bun. Cut sandwich in half.

Italian Submarine Sandwich

This sandwich can be served cold or heated open-face in the
oven and then dressed with the salad after it's taken out of the oven.
Cut sub into smaller pieces for appetizers for more people.

SERVES 2

1 (12-inch-long) sub bun

6 slices ham lunchmeat

6 slices salami

6 slices provolone cheese

¼ cup sliced hot banana peppers

1 cup shredded lettuce

2 tablespoons bottled Italian dressing

5 slices tomato

1. Slice the sub bun lengthwise, but not all the way through. Open it up flat like a book.

2. Lay the slices of ham to cover the bread. Lay the salami on top of the ham. Line up the cheese on top of the salami. Layer the lettuce, tomato and banana peppers on the meats and cheese.

3. Drizzle dressing on the lettuce and fold the sandwich closed.

4. Cut sandwich in half with a serrated knife.

Muffaletta

A famous New Orleans sandwich is the muffaletta, which is made with olive salad on a round loaf of bread with sliced lunchmeat and cheese.

tip

Meatball Sandwich

You can make your own meatballs and sauce for this or go with prepared meatballs and tomato sauce for a quicker meal. I like green peppers, onions, black olives, and parmesan cheese on my meatball sandwich.

SERVES 2

2 six-inch sub buns

6 two-inch meatballs

1 cup marinara sauce

4 slices provolone cheese

½ cup shredded mozzarella cheese

1. Heat the meatballs in the sauce.

2. Open the buns flat and line them with provolone cheese.

3. Put 3 meatballs with sauce on each sandwich.

4. Sprinkle mozzarella cheese on top of meatballs.

5. Heat sandwiches in the oven until cheese melts.

Po'Boy

A po'boy is a sandwich on a submarine bun, sometimes filled with fried oysters, shrimp, or catfish. Originally a French-fried potato sandwich, it was invented in New Orleans in the 1920s to keep striking workers ("poor boys") fed.

tip

Reuben

Perhaps invented in Omaha, but made famous in the delicatessens of the Lower East Side of Manhattan, this combination of corned beef, sauerkraut, and Russian dressing perfectly balances salty and tangy flavors. Serve with a garlic pickle spear.

SERVES 2

4 slices rye bread

8 ounces thinly sliced corned beef brisket

½ cup drained sauerkraut

¼ cup Russian or Thousand Island dressing

2 slices Swiss cheese

2 tablespoons butter

1. Butter one side of each slice of bread.

2. For each sandwich, layer one slice of bread, butter side out, with cheese, corned beef, sauerkraut, dressing, and another slice of bread, butter side out.

3. Grill sandwich in a skillet or on a griddle until toasted.

4. Cut in half and serve warm.

Grilled Chicken Sandwich

*The chicken in this recipe can also be sliced and
served cold or warm on top of any salad.*

SERVES 2

2 kaiser rolls or hamburger buns

2 boneless, skinless chicken
breasts

1 clove garlic, minced

2 tablespoons olive oil

1 teaspoon fresh rosemary,
minced

¼ teaspoon salt

⅛ teaspoon pepper

4 lettuce leaves

2 tablespoons an aioli sauce

1. Marinate chicken in garlic, oil, rosemary,
salt and pepper for at least one hour.

2. Grill marinated chicken on preheated
grill or grill pan on both sides until cooked
through.

3. Put aioli on top of bun and grilled chicken
and lettuce on the bottom half.

Gyro

A gyro is a Greek sandwich
made with pita bread, lamb,
tomatoes, onions, and yogurt-
garlic-cucumber sauce (tziziki).
The meat for the sandwich is
usually cooked on a revolving
spit, from which the person preparing the gyro slices the meat
to put it on the warm pita. The
gyro (which means "to turn" in
Greek) is named after this
spit.

tip

Grilled Vegetable Sandwich

Any combination of grilled or roasted vegetables can be used to create your sandwich. The following is a list of suggestions to be layered on the focaccia with cheese and condiments.

SERVES 1

Focaccia

Grilled eggplant

Grilled zucchini

Grilled yellow squash

Sun-dried tomatoes

Roasted red bell pepper

Caramelized onions

Aioli

Pesto

Tapenade

1. Spread one condiment on the top half and another on the bottom half of the focaccia.

2. Lay slice of cheese on the bottom half of focaccia and build on top of that with vegetables of your choice.

3. Lettuce is optional.

Gourmet PBJ

Sliced strawberries and chopped peanuts elevate this perennial favorite.

SERVES 1

2 thick slices white bread
(AKA Texas Toast bread)

2 ounces peanut butter

2 tablespoons strawberry jam

¼ cup sliced fresh strawberries

2 tablespoons chopped peanuts

1. Spread peanut butter on one slice of bread and jam on the other.

2. Arrange strawberry slices on the jam and peanuts on the peanut butter.

3. Put bread together with the filling in the middle and serve whole.

Good for You Steak Subs

Enjoy these steak subs without the guilt!

SERVES 6

1 pound boneless beef sirloin steak, all fat trimmed

Shredded lettuce

1 loaf French bread, 1 pound, split lengthwise

1 jar (7 ounces) roasted red peppers, drained

Salt and pepper to taste

½ cup shredded fat-free mozzarella cheese

1. Prepare a fire in a charcoal grill. Grill the steak until done to your liking.

2. In the meantime, spread the lettuce over the bottom half of the split bread loaf. Spread the peppers over the lettuce.

3. Carve the steak into thin slices, and season with salt and pepper. Spread the steak slices over the peppers; top with the cheese. Put the top on the loaf, and cut into 6 portions. Serve at once.

Steak-Vegetable Pockets

These hearty "pockets" will satisfy your hunger without plumping you up!

SERVES 4

¾ pound top round

3 tablespoons soy sauce

¼ cup water

1½ teaspoons cornstarch

1½ cups broccoli florets

1 small carrot, diced

1 small onion, chopped

½ green bell pepper, chopped

8 snow peas, halved crosswise

6 mushrooms, sliced

1 small tomato, chopped

1 tablespoon olive oil

4 pita bread rounds, halved

1. Thinly slice the beef into bite-sized strips. Set aside.

2. In a small bowl, stir together the soy sauce, water, and cornstarch until the cornstarch dissolves; set aside.

3. Spray a wok or large skillet with nonstick cooking spray and place over high heat. Add broccoli, carrot, onion, green pepper and stir-fry until carrot is tender, about 7 minutes. Add the snow peas, mushrooms, and tomato and stir-fry for 2 minutes.

4. Remove the vegetables from the pan and set aside. Add the oil and heat over high heat. Add the beef and stir-fry until beef is tender, about 3 minutes. Quickly stir the cornstarch mixture and add to the pan. Cook and stir until bubbly and the pan juices thicken. Return the vegetables to the pan and heat through.

5. To serve, cut the pita breads in half, forming 8 pockets. Spoon the vegetable-beef mixture into the pockets and serve.

Roast Beef Pita Bread Sandwich with Tomato

*These quick sandwiches are perfect for a night when
the family gets home late or the cook is tired.*

SERVES 6

½ cup chopped fresh basil

⅛ cup prepared horseradish

½ cup plain low-fat yogurt

¾ pound delicatessen-style sliced roast beef

1 head butter lettuce, separated into leaves

3 pita breads

1 large tomato, cored and cut into 12 slices

1. In a large bowl, stir together the basil, horseradish, and yogurt. Spread the horse-radish-yogurt mixture on the beef slices and wrap each slice in a lettuce leaf.

2. Cut the pita breads in half, forming 6 pockets. Put the lettuce-wrapped beef and 2 slices of tomato into each half. Serve immediately.

Corn Dogs

A classic summer festival treat comes to your own kitchen!

SERVES 8

1 cup all-purpose flour

2 tablespoons sugar

1½ teaspoons baking powder

1 teaspoon salt

⅔ cup cornmeal

2 tablespoons shortening

1 egg

¾ cup milk

1 pound Healthy Choice Frankfurters

Ketchup

Mustard

1. Preheat oven to 350°F. In a bowl, sift together the flour, sugar, baking powder, and salt. Stir in the cornmeal. Using a pastry blender or 2 knives, cut in the shortening until the mixture resembles coarse meal. In a separate bowl, whisk together the egg and milk until blended and stir into the cornmeal mixture, again mixing until blended.

2. Insert a wooden skewer into the end of each hot dog. Working in batches, coat the hot dogs evenly with the batter and arrange on a cookie sheet sprayed with nonstick spray.

3. Bake for 15 minutes or until batter is lightly browned. Serve immediately with ketchup and mustard.

Burgers, Wraps, & Sandwiches

The Basic Burger

*Experiment with your basic burger by trying out
the three different cooking methods.*

SERVES 4

1¼ pounds ground round beef

½ teaspoon seasoned salt

*Freshly cracked black pepper,
to taste*

Getting the Basics Down

There are many versions of the basic burger; some contain egg yolk, bread crumbs, and any other number of additions. This is the simplest basic burger; therefore, the quality of the ground meat is key. Be sure not to overhandle meat when forming hamburger patties. Use a very light touch and make sure you don't compact the meat too much. Don't use a spatula to press down on the patty while cooking, either, because you'll press out the natural juices and you'll lose the juiciness and flavor to boot.

1. Lightly mix the ground round with salt and pepper and form into 4 evenly sized patties. Cook by your choice of the following methods.

2. *To grill:* Clean grill rack and lightly oil to prevent sticking. Preheat grill to medium-high. Cook for about 5 minutes per side for medium, turning once. Transfer burgers to a plate and tent with foil to keep warm. Let rest for 1 to 2 minutes to allow the juices to reabsorb. Serve hot. If using an indoor grill, follow manufacturer's directions.

3. *To broil:* Clean broiler rack and lightly oil to prevent sticking. Set broiler rack 4 inches from heat source. Preheat broiler to medium-high. Cook 5 minutes per side for medium, turning once. Transfer burgers to a plate and tent with foil to keep warm. Let rest for 1 to 2 minutes to allow juices to reabsorb. Serve hot.

4. *On stovetop:* Heat 2 tablespoons oil in a nonstick skillet over medium-high heat. Cook for about 5 minutes per side for medium, turning once. Transfer burgers to a plate and tent with foil to keep warm. Let rest for 1 to 2 minutes to allow the juices to reabsorb. Serve hot.

tip

Seasoned Bistro Burgers

You can add a different blend of herbs or use a flavored
or seasoned Dijon mustard for a unique twist.

SERVES 4

1¼ pounds ground round beef

¾ teaspoon seasoned salt

⅛ teaspoon lemon pepper

1 tablespoon chopped fresh parsley

3 tablespoons butter

1 tablespoon Dijon mustard

1 tablespoon fresh lemon juice

2 teaspoons quality steak sauce

1. Lightly mix the ground round with the seasoned salt, lemon pepper, and chopped parsley, and form into 4 evenly sized patties. Melt the butter in a medium-sized nonstick skillet over medium-high heat. Add the mustard and quickly blend to combine. Add the burgers to the skillet and cook for about 4 minutes per side, turning once. (Burgers will be returned to the pan for additional cooking.) Transfer the burgers to a plate and tent with foil to keep warm.

2. Add the lemon juice and steak sauce to the pan and blend to combine. Return the burgers and any accumulated juices to the pan and let simmer for 2 to 3 minutes while basting. Remove the pan from heat and allow the burgers to rest for 2 to 3 minutes. Serve with sauce ladled over the top; serve hot.

How to Handle a Burger

Use tongs or a spatula to turn burgers during cooking. The idea is to make sure you don't pierce the meat, because doing so will allow the flavorful juices to escape. Always make sure the pan or grill is hot before putting burgers on to cook. The goal is to quickly sear the outside so the flavorful juices are trapped inside during the cooking process.

tip

Bacon Burgers

These have a winning combination of flavors—bacon and sharp Cheddar.
This is definitely a hearty grill-time recipe.

SERVES 4

1¼ pounds ground round beef

¾ teaspoon seasoned salt

⅛ teaspoon fresh cracked pepper

¼ cup crispy bacon crumbles

8 (1-ounce) slices sharp Cheddar cheese

1. Lightly mix the ground round with the seasoned salt, pepper, and bacon crumbles, and form into 4 evenly sized patties. Clean and oil grill rack and preheat grill to medium-high.

2. Cook the burgers for about 5 minutes on each side for medium. Add 2 slices of cheese per burger during the last 2 minutes of cooking.

3. Transfer the burgers to a plate and tent with foil to keep warm. Let rest for 1 to 2 minutes to allow the juices to reabsorb. Serve hot.

Nothing Beats a Good Burger on the Grill!

Lean burgers are a staple in the diet plan of many people who are controlling carbs, so we've created a few special recipes that you can show off to your friends. A bunless burger is really no different from the classic Salisbury steak preparation that was popular in the 1970s. It was named after a nineteenth-century physician who recommended that his patients reduce their starch intake and eat plenty of beef.

tip

Wisconsin Burgers

Right from the heart of Milwaukee—sprinkle the kraut with a few caraway seeds, if desired. This recipe is great on the grill or stovetop.

SERVES 4

1¼ pounds ground round beef

½ teaspoon seasoned salt

⅛ teaspoon fresh cracked pepper

¼ cup sauerkraut, rinsed and drained

8 slices Muenster cheese

1. Lightly mix the ground round with the seasoned salt and pepper, and form into 4 evenly sized patties. Clean and oil grill rack and preheat grill to medium-high.

2. Cook the burgers for about 5 minutes on each side for medium. During the last 2 minutes of cooking, top each burger with 1 tablespoon of the kraut and 2 slices of cheese per burger.

3. Transfer the burgers to a plate and tent with foil to keep warm. Let rest for 1 to 2 minutes to allow the juices to reabsorb. Serve hot.

Before You Eat

It's best to let burgers "rest" on a warm plate for 1 or 2 minutes before serving. This allows the juices to release and reabsorb into the burger, which adds to the juiciness and tenderness.

tip

Blues Burgers

Let the burgers sit for a minute or two after
mixing to make sure the meat binds with the cheese.

SERVES 4

1¼ pounds ground round beef

½ teaspoon seasoned salt

⅛ teaspoon red pepper flakes

½ cup blue cheese crumbles

¼ cup thinly sliced scallions

2 tablespoons vegetable oil

1. Lightly mix the ground round with the seasoned salt, pepper flakes, blue cheese crumbles, and scallions, and form into 4 evenly sized patties. Heat the oil in a medium-sized nonstick skillet over medium-high heat.

2. Cook for about 5 minutes per side for medium, turning once.

3. Transfer the burgers to a plate and tent with foil to keep warm. Let rest for 1 to 2 minutes to allow the juices to reabsorb. Serve hot.

Be Sanitary!

Use disposable plastic or latex gloves when working with burgers. It's more sanitary and prevents the burger from sticking to your hands. Dip your gloved hand into cold water to prevent the meat from sticking to your gloves. Whenever dealing with meat that may be served at any temperature other than well done, it's worth the extra sanitation effort.

tip

Feta Burgers

It's best to cook these delicacies on the grill. The melting feta cheese tends to stick to the skillet, making them hard to handle.

SERVES 4

1¼ pounds ground round beef

½ teaspoon garlic salt

¼ teaspoon cayenne pepper

½ cup feta cheese crumbles

1. Lightly mix the ground round with the garlic salt, cayenne pepper, and feta cheese crumbles, and form into 4 evenly sized patties. Clean and oil grill rack and preheat grill to medium-high.

2. Cook the burgers for about 5 minutes on each side for medium.

3. Transfer the burgers to a plate and tent with foil to keep warm. Let rest for 1 to 2 minutes to allow the juices to reabsorb. Serve hot.

Pizza Burgers

*Get the kids—this is a family favorite. It's an easy recipe that
you can cook on the grill, in the broiler, or on the stovetop.*

SERVES 4

1¼ pounds ground round beef

½ teaspoon garlic salt

¼ teaspoon red pepper flakes

½ teaspoon dried Italian
seasoning

6 ounces pizza sauce

8 (1-ounce) slices mozzarella
cheese

1. Lightly mix the ground round with the garlic salt, pepper flakes, and Italian seasoning, and form into 4 evenly sized patties. Clean and oil grill rack and preheat grill to medium-high.

2. Cook the burgers about 5 minutes on each side for medium. During the last 2 minutes of cooking, top each burger with a generous tablespoon of the pizza sauce and 2 slices of cheese per burger.

3. Transfer the burgers to a plate and tent with foil to keep warm. Let rest for 1 to 2 minutes to allow the juices to reabsorb. Serve hot.

South of the Border Burgers

Spicy salsa equals spicy burgers; mild salsa equals mild burgers!
This recipe works well on the grill, in the broiler, or on the stovetop.

SERVES 4

1¼ pounds ground round beef

½ teaspoon garlic salt

¼ teaspoon red pepper flakes

4 (1-ounce) slices pepper jack cheese

1 cup quality salsa, such as Frontera Grill brand

¼ cup canned jalapeño slices

¼ cup chopped fresh cilantro

1. Lightly mix the ground round with the garlic salt and pepper flakes, and form into 4 evenly sized patties. Clean and oil grill rack and preheat grill to medium-high.

2. Cook the burgers for about 5 minutes on each side for medium. During the last 2 minutes of cooking, top each burger with a slice of cheese.

3. Transfer the burgers to a plate and tent with foil to keep warm. Let rest for 1 to 2 minutes to allow the juices to reabsorb. Serve hot, topped with the salsa, jalapeños, and cilantro leaves.

Indoor or Outdoor?

The little indoor grills that are popular these days, such as the George Foreman Grill, are a convenient and easy alternative to using the larger charcoal or gas grills.

tip

Basic Chicken Wraps

Cream cheese is the "glue" that holds a wrap together.
It's very simple to flavor the cream cheese for a nice twist.

SERVES 4

3 ounces cream cheese, at room temperature

1 tablespoon mayonnaise

1 tablespoon fresh lemon juice

¼ teaspoon seasoned salt

Freshly cracked pepper

2 (8-inch) low-carb tortillas, at room temperature

2 cups sliced or cubed cooked chicken

½ cup thinly sliced red onion

1 cup baby spinach leaves

1. Mix together the cream cheese, mayonnaise, lemon juice, salt, and pepper in a small bowl (or use a food processor to blend until smooth).

2. Place the tortillas on a clean work surface. Spread half of the cream cheese mixture on the upper third of each tortilla, about ½ inch from the edge. Place half of the chicken on the lower third of each tortilla. Top each with onions and spinach.

3. Roll up each wrap: Starting from the bottom, fold the tortilla over the filling and roll upward, compressing slightly to form a firm roll. Press at the top to "seal" the wrap closed with the cream cheese mixture. Cut the sandwich in half and wrap in plastic film. Refrigerate until ready to serve.

Beef and Blue Wraps

Use a good-quality deli roast beef for this delicious and flavorful wrap.
You can also add 1 tablespoon of bacon crumbles for an extra treat.

SERVES 4

3 ounces cream cheese, at room temperature

1 tablespoon mayonnaise

2 ounces blue cheese crumbles

¼ teaspoon seasoned salt

Freshly cracked pepper, to taste

2 (8-inch) low-carb tortillas, at room temperature

⅓ pound lean deli roast beef, trimmed of visible fat, sliced, and cut into ½-inch strips

¼ cup diced roasted red pepper

1 cup chopped romaine hearts

The Truth about Tortillas!

They're so thin, how bad can they be? If you're watching carbs or watching fat, it's important to read the label. A plain flour tortilla has 21g of carbs, 3g of protein, 4g of fat, and 2g of fiber. A tomato basil wrap has 36g of carbs, 8g of protein, 3g of fat, and 5g of fiber. A whole-wheat low-carb tortilla has 11g of carbs, 5g of protein, 2g of fat, and 8g of fiber.

tip

1. Mix together the cream cheese, mayonnaise, blue cheese, salt, and pepper in a small bowl (or use a food processor to blend until smooth).

2. Place the tortillas on a clean work surface. Spread half of the cream cheese mixture on the upper third of each tortilla, about ½ inch from the edge. Place half of the roast beef on the lower third of each tortilla. Top each with peppers and lettuce.

3. Roll up each wrap: Starting from the bottom, fold the tortilla over the filling, compressing slightly to form a firm roll. Press at the top to "seal" the wrap closed with the cream cheese mixture. Cut the sandwich in half and wrap in plastic film. Refrigerate until ready to serve.

Turkey Time

Use a good-quality deli turkey for this delicious wrap.
You can add a few bacon crumbles to this wrap for added flavor.

SERVES 4

3 ounces cream cheese, at room temperature

1 tablespoon mayonnaise

2 tablespoons cranberry sauce

¼ teaspoon seasoned salt

Freshly cracked pepper

2 (8-inch) low-carb tortillas, at room temperature

⅓ pound honey-roasted turkey breast, sliced and cut into ½-inch strips

¼ pound Cheddar cheese, shredded

1 cup chopped mesclun greens

Substitution Suggestions

Consider using smoked meats in place of regular meats. There are excellent smoked chickens, smoked pork tenderloins and chops, and smoked ducks available at specialty stores. Substituting with a smoked meat can add a whole new flavor to the old standby recipes.

tip

1. Mix together the cream cheese, mayonnaise, cranberry sauce, salt, and pepper in a small bowl (or use a food processor to blend until smooth).

2. Place the tortillas on a clean work surface. Spread half of the cream cheese mixture on the upper third of each tortilla, about ½ inch from the edge. Place half of the turkey on the lower third of each tortilla. Top each with Cheddar cheese and greens.

3. Roll up each wrap: Starting from the bottom, fold the tortilla over the filling, compressing slightly to form a firm roll. Press at the top to "seal" the wrap closed with the cream cheese mixture. Cut the sandwich in half and wrap in plastic film. Refrigerate until ready to serve.

Tuna Melts

Tartar sauce is made of mayonnaise, pickles, and seasonings. It is delicious paired with mild canned tuna and Swiss cheese in these quick and easy sandwiches.

SERVES 4

4 pita breads, unsplit

4 slices Swiss cheese

1 avocado

1 6-ounce can tuna, drained

½ cup tartar sauce

¾ cup shredded Swiss cheese, divided

½ teaspoon dried dill weed

1. Preheat oven to 400°F. Toast pita breads in oven until crisp, about 5 minutes. Remove from oven and top each one with a slice of Swiss cheese.

2. Peel avocado and mash slightly, leaving some chunks. Spread this on top of the Swiss cheese. In small bowl, combine tuna and tartar sauce with ¼ cup shredded Swiss cheese. Spread on top of avocado.

3. Sprinkle sandwiches with remaining shredded Swiss cheese and the dill weed. Bake for 7 to 11 minutes, until cheese melts.

Sandwich Melts

Melts are open-faced sandwiches, or sandwiches without a "lid," that are usually grilled, baked, or broiled to heat the filling and melt the cheese. Serve them with a knife and fork, and with a simple fruit salad or green salad for a hearty, quick dinner.

tip

Salmon Avocado Sandwiches

Look for salmon packed in pouches in your supermarket. The new varieties are boneless and skinless, eliminating the step of discarding them from canned salmon.

SERVES 4

1 7-ounce pouch pink salmon, drained

1 avocado, peeled and diced

½ cup mayonnaise

½ teaspoon dried basil leaves

½ cup chopped tomato

4 hamburger or hoagie buns, split, toasted if desired

In small bowl, combine all ingredients except hamburger or hoagie buns and mix gently but thoroughly. Divide mixture evenly between the hamburger or hoagie buns and serve.

Shrimp Sandwiches

You can add some butter lettuce or watercress leaves to the bottom half of the focaccia bread before adding the shrimp filling. This is a good salad for a picnic because it's easy to carry.

SERVES 8

2 3-ounce packages cream cheese, softened

¼ cup sour cream

½ teaspoon dried dill weed

3 6-ounce cans small shrimp, drained

1½ cups chopped celery hearts

1 10-inch focaccia bread

1. In medium bowl, beat cream cheese with sour cream and dill weed until smooth and fluffy. Stir in shrimp and chopped celery hearts.

2. Using serrated knife, cut focaccia bread in half horizontally. Spread bottom layer with cream cheese mixture and top with top layer. Cut into 8 wedges and serve.

Canned Seafood

Canned seafood can have a salty taste. You can rinse it before use, but be sure to drain it very well, and don't soak it. Canned salmon, crabmeat, and tuna, as well as surimi, or frozen faux crab, can all be substituted for canned shrimp in just about any recipe.

tip

Stuffed Panini

You can stuff a hollowed-out loaf of bread with just about any combination of meats, cheeses, and salad dressings. Experiment, and have a taste-test party!

SERVES 4

1 1-pound loaf round unsliced Italian bread

¼ cup creamy Italian salad dressing

¼ pound thinly sliced smoked turkey

¼ pound thinly sliced salami

½ pound sliced provolone cheese

1. Preheat oven to 400°F. Slice the top off the bread round and remove the center of the loaf, leaving a 1-inch border on the edges and the bottom.

2. Spread half of the salad dressing in bottom and up sides of bread. Layer turkey, salami, and provolone cheese in the bread and drizzle with remaining salad dressing. Cover with top of bread round and place on baking sheet. Place an ovenproof skillet on top of sandwich to press it down as it bakes.

3. Bake sandwich for 15 to 20 minutes, until bread is toasted, filling is hot, and cheese is melted. Cut into wedges and serve.

Curried Chicken Sandwiches

Keep this delicious sandwich spread in your refrigerator and let hungry teenagers make their own sandwiches! You could substitute pitted, halved cherries for the red grapes if you'd like.

SERVES 4–6

2 cups cubed, cooked chicken

½ cup plain yogurt

⅓ cup chutney

1 teaspoon curry powder

1 cup red grapes, cut in half

3 pita breads, cut in half

1. In medium bowl, combine all ingredients except pita breads and stir well to combine.

2. Fill pita breads with chicken mixture and serve.

Cooking Chicken

To cook chicken breasts for use in any recipe, place boneless, skinless breasts in a pot and cover with half water and half canned chicken broth. Bring to a simmer, then reduce heat and poach chicken for 8 to 12 minutes, until chicken is thoroughly cooked. Let chicken cool in refrigerator, then chop. Reserve the broth for use in other recipes.

tip

Bacon Crisp Sandwiches

This unusual way of cooking bacon makes these sandwiches simply superb. Be sure the tomatoes are ripe and juicy for best results. You could also add some fresh lettuce leaves or baby spinach.

SERVES 4

8 slices bacon

¾ cup grated Parmesan cheese, divided

½ teaspoon dried thyme leaves

¼ cup mayonnaise

4 hoagie buns, sliced

2 tomatoes, thickly sliced

1. Dip bacon slices in ½ cup Parmesan cheese and press to coat. Place 4 slices of the coated bacon on microwave-safe paper towels in a 12×8" microwave-safe baking dish. Cover with another sheet of microwave-safe paper towels. Microwave on high for 3 to 4 minutes or until bacon is light golden brown. Repeat with remaining bacon slices.

2. Meanwhile, in small bowl, combine thyme, mayonnaise, and remaining ¼ cup Parmesan cheese and spread on cut sides of hoagie buns. Toast in toaster oven or under broiler until cheese mixture bubbles. Make sandwiches with the cooked bacon, tomatoes, and toasted buns and serve immediately.

Bacon-Salmon Spread Sandwich

This fabulous spread is perfect to keep in the fridge for lunch on the run. Have English muffins, pita breads, and whole wheat sandwich buns on hand and let your family make their own.

YIELDS 3 CUPS

8 slices bacon

1 8-ounce container cream cheese with herbs, softened

⅓ cup mayonnaise

1 7-ounce pouch pink salmon, drained

½ cup chopped green onions

1. Cook bacon until crisp; drain on paper towels until cool enough to handle. Crumble bacon into small pieces.

2. In medium bowl, beat cream cheese until fluffy. Stir in mayonnaise and beat until smooth. Add reserved bacon, salmon, and green onions, and gently fold together. Cover and store in refrigerator up to 3 days. Make sandwiches using the spread.

Italian Favorites

Substitute your favorite salami or Italian cheeses.
You can also add a few roasted vegetables.

SERVES 4

3 ounces cream cheese, at room temperature

1 tablespoon mayonnaise

1 tablespoon chopped oil-packed sun-dried tomatoes, with a little of the oil

2 teaspoons dried Italian seasoning

¼ teaspoon seasoned salt

Freshly cracked pepper

2 (8-inch) low-carb tortillas, at room temperature

⅛ pound each: Genoa salami, mortadella, and provolone cheese, sliced and cut into ½-inch strips

¼ cup chopped pepperoncini, rinsed and drained

1 cup chopped arugula leaves

1. Mix together the cream cheese, mayonnaise, sun-dried tomatoes, Italian herbs, salt, and pepper in a small bowl (or use a food processor to blend until smooth).

2. Place the tortillas on work surface. Spread half of the cream cheese mixture on the upper third of each tortilla, about ½ inch from the edge. Equally divide the salamis and cheese between the tortillas, placing the ingredients on the lower third of the tortillas. Top each with the pepperoncini and arugula.

3. Roll up the wraps: Starting from the bottom, fold the tortilla over the filling and roll upward, compressing slightly to form a firm roll. Press at the top to "seal" the wrap closed with the cream cheese mixture. Cut the sandwich in half and wrap in plastic film. Refrigerate until ready to serve.

South of the Border Favorites

Try salsa-roasted turkey or sliced flank steak instead of chicken, too.
Drain the salsa slightly to prevent dripping while you eat.

SERVES 4

3 ounces cream cheese, at room temperature

1 tablespoon mayonnaise

¼ teaspoon seasoned salt

Freshly cracked pepper

2 (8-inch) low-carb tortillas

⅓ pound roasted chicken breast, sliced and cut into ½-inch strips

¼ pound pepper jack cheese, sliced and cut into ½-inch strips

¼ cup chopped cilantro

¼ cup spicy salsa, drained

1 cup chopped romaine hearts

Mexican Cheeses

Authentic Mexican cheeses enhance your south-of-the-border entrées. Good melting cheeses are Chihuahua and quesadilla. Queso Cotija is a flavorful cheese used for grating or crumbling as a garnish for dishes. Cream-style Mexican cheeses include crema Mexicana, a flavorful addition where spicy chilies are used.

1. Mix together the cream cheese, mayonnaise, salt, and pepper in a small bowl (or use a food processor to blend until smooth).

2. Place the tortillas on work surface. Spread half of the cream cheese mixture on the upper third of each tortilla, about ½ inch from the edge. Place half of the chicken on the lower third of each tortilla. Top each with the cheese, cilantro, salsa, and lettuce.

3. Roll up each wrap: Starting from the bottom, fold the tortilla over the filling and roll upward, compressing slightly to form a firm roll. Press at the top to "seal" the wrap closed with the cream cheese mixture. Cut the sandwich in half and wrap in plastic film. Refrigerate until ready to serve.

tip

California-Style BLT Wraps

*Eliminate the avocado if you're going to make this
in advance—it will oxidize and look unappealing.*

SERVES 4

3 ounces cream cheese, at room
temperature

2 tablespoons mayonnaise

¼ teaspoon seasoned salt

Freshly cracked pepper

2 (8-inch) low-carb tortillas, at
room temperature

6 slices smoked bacon, cooked

¼ cup diced avocado

¼ cup seeded and diced ripe
tomato

1 cup chopped romaine hearts

1. Mix together the cream cheese, mayonnaise, salt, and pepper in a small bowl (or use
a food processor to blend until smooth).

2. Place the tortillas on work surface. Spread
half of the cream cheese mixture on the
upper third of each tortilla, about ½ inch
from the edge. Place half of the bacon on the
lower third of each tortilla. Top each with the
avocado, tomato, and lettuce.

3. Roll up each wrap: Starting from the bottom, fold the tortilla over the filling and roll
upward, compressing slightly to form a firm
roll. Press at the top to "seal" the wrap closed
with the cream cheese mixture. Cut the sandwich in half and wrap in plastic film. Refrigerate until ready to serve.

Wrap It Up

There are a variety of options for
wraps other than bread or tortillas. Some ideas: lettuce leaves,
radicchio cups, large spinach
leaves, grape leaves, dried corn-
husks, and banana leaves. A little
creativity produces a beautiful
and unique presentation.

tip

Thai-Inspired Spicy Beef Lettuce Wraps

Kids especially enjoy using Boston lettuce leaves to roll their sandwiches. Adjust the spiciness of the beef according to the likes of your family.

SERVES 4

2 tablespoons peanut oil or vegetable oil

1½ pounds lean ground sirloin

¼ cup diced red pepper

¼ cup sliced scallions

¼ cup chopped cilantro, plus extra for garnish

½ cup peanut sauce

Asian chili sauce, to taste

Salt, to taste

12 Boston lettuce leaves

½ cup chopped unsalted peanuts

1. Heat the oil in a large nonstick skillet over medium-high heat. Add the sirloin, stirring to break up the meat into small pieces. Cook, stirring frequently, until the meat starts to brown, about 5 minutes. Use a small ladle to remove and discard excess fat.

2. Add the red pepper and stir to incorporate; cook for about 3 minutes. Add the scallions, cilantro, peanut sauce, chili sauce, and salt; stir to blend. Cook until heated through, about 3 to 4 minutes. Taste and adjust seasoning as desired.

3. To serve, arrange the lettuce leaves on a serving platter. Spoon the beef mixture into the center of each leaf and garnish with the peanuts and cilantro.

Grading Beef

Prime cuts are usually the most expensive and flavorful meat with the highest amount of marbling. Choice cuts are slightly below prime in cost and marbling. Select cuts are the leanest meats and therefore the least tender and usually require slower cooking methods to make them tender.

tip

Wraps with Spicy Beef and Cucumber Raita

You can adjust the spiciness by adjusting the quantity of Asian chili sauce—
start mild and you can always add more to top your lettuce wrap.

SERVES 4

8 ounces plain yogurt

1 tablespoon chopped fresh mint

¼ teaspoon honey

¼ cup peeled and diced cucumber

Salt, to taste

Freshly cracked black pepper

2 tablespoons olive oil

1½ pounds ground sirloin

¼ teaspoon garlic salt

Lemon pepper, to taste

⅛–¼ cup (to taste) Asian chili sauce

¼ teaspoon garam masala

12 Boston lettuce leaves

1. Prepare the raita by mixing together the yogurt, mint, honey, cucumber, salt, and pepper in a small bowl. Cover and refrigerate until ready to use.

2. Heat the oil in a large nonstick skillet over medium-high heat. Add the sirloin, stirring to break up the meat into small pieces. Add the garlic salt and lemon pepper. Cook, stirring frequently, until the meat starts to brown, about 5 minutes. Use a small ladle to remove and discard excess fat. Add the chili sauce and stir to incorporate; cook for about 3 minutes. Add the garam masala and stir to blend. Cook until heated through, about 3 minutes. Taste and adjust seasoning as desired.

3. To serve, arrange the lettuce leaves on a serving platter. Spoon the beef mixture into the center of each leaf and garnish with additional chili sauce, if desired.

Grilled Chicken Breast Sandwiches

*This simple sandwich tastes so good, especially
cooked on a real charcoal grill—there's nothing like it!*

SERVES 4

1 tablespoon butter

4 large onions, sliced

½ cup oil-packed sun-dried
tomatoes, drained and chopped

2 cloves garlic, minced

1 tablespoon water

2 boneless, skinless whole chicken
breasts, split

4 hamburger buns

1. Prepare a fire in a charcoal grill.

2. In a large skillet, melt the butter over
medium heat. Add the onions and cook,
stirring occasionally, for 10 minutes, or
until translucent. Add the tomatoes, garlic,
and water and cook for 5 minutes, stirring
occasionally.

3. Meanwhile, place the chicken over
medium-hot coals and grill, turning once,
until done, about 10 minutes. Spread some
of the onion mixture over the bottom half
of each bun. Top with a piece of the chicken,
the remaining onion mixture, and then the
tops of the buns. Serve hot.

Grilled Vegetable Sandwich

One of the most important parts of a sandwich is the dressing!
Here, learn to make something fresh, delicious, and healthy!

SERVES 6

Dressing:

1 cup plain nonfat yogurt

3 tablespoons Dijon mustard

Pepper to taste

2 tablespoons nonfat cottage cheese

⅓ teaspoon Tabasco sauce

2 tablespoons minced shallot

1 clove garlic, minced

1 teaspoon lemon juice

1. To make the dressing, combine all the ingredients and blend until smooth. Transfer to a bowl, cover, and refrigerate.

(To make sandwich, keep reading.)

Grilled Vegetable Sandwich

(continued)

Sandwiches:

1 small eggplant, cut into ¼-inch-thick rounds

1 medium-sized yellow squash, cut into ¼-inch-thick rounds

1 medium-sized zucchini, cut into ¼-inch-thick rounds

1 medium onion

1 tablespoon Italian seasoning

¼ teaspoon cayenne pepper

2 baguettes

1 large tomato, sliced

Pepper to taste

2 tablespoons chopped jalapeño pepper

8 fresh basil leaves

8 arugula leaves

2 red bell peppers, roasted and quartered

2. Preheat broiler. Spray a baking sheet with nonstick cooking spray. Arrange the eggplant, yellow squash, zucchini and onion in a single layer on the baking sheet. Sprinkle the Italian dressing and cayenne pepper over all of the rounds. Broil, turning once, for about 5 minutes on each side, or until browned. Remove the baking sheet, but leave the broiler on.

3. Cut each of the baguettes in half lengthwise and scoop out the soft inner dough. Place in the broiler and toast for 2 minutes on each side.

4. Put a few slices of tomato into the well in each baguette half. Dust with black pepper and sprinkle with the jalapeño pepper.

5. Place 4 basil leaves, 4 arugula leaves, and 4 pieces of roasted pepper onto the bottom half of each baguette. Layer slices of eggplant, yellow squash, zucchini, and onion on top. Coat the inside of the remaining half of each baguette with the dressing and place it on top of the vegetables. Cut each baguette crosswise into 3 equal pieces and serve.

California-Style Turkey Burger

Turkey burgers are a great alternative to beef burgers and to turkey sandwiches!
Spice things up with this recipe; the burgers are something different and delicious.

SERVES 6

1 pound ground turkey breast

1 cup old-fashioned or quick-
cooking rolled oats

¼ cup ketchup

1 egg, beaten

¼ cup minced onion

1½ teaspoons garlic salt

½ teaspoon pepper

1 teaspoon Worcestershire sauce

¼ teaspoon Tabasco sauce

6 hamburger buns

1. Prepare a fire in a charcoal grill.

2. Combine all the ingredients except the buns in a large bowl. Mix well and shape into 6 patties. Place the patties on the grill rack and grill for about 6 minutes on each side, or until done; the timing with depend on the thickness. Serve plain or on buns.

Chicken Pocket Sandwich

With this healthy sandwich recipe, you'll fill up but you won't fill out.

SERVES 5

1⅔ cups diced cooked chicken

1 cup plain low-fat yogurt

½ cup chopped almonds

¼ cup chopped nectarine

⅓ cup chopped scallions

1 tablespoon lemon juice

⅛ teaspoon pepper

⅛ teaspoon dried dill, crumbled

5 large pita breads

10 lettuce leaves

1. In a bowl, combine all the ingredients except the pita bread and lettuce. Toss gently to mix well.

2. Using a sharp knife, cut each pita bread in half, forming 10 pockets. Line each pita half with 1 lettuce leaf. Spoon in the chicken mixture, dividing it evenly. Serve at once.

Peach Pita Sandwiches

Who knew a fruity sandwich could be so good?

SERVES 2

2 pita breads

4 curly lettuce leaves

1 cup 1% low-fat cottage cheese

4 tomato slices

4 extra-lean smoked ham slices

1 can (16 ounces) cling peach slices, drained

Cut the pita breads in half, forming 4 pockets. Line each pocket with 1 lettuce leaf. Fill the pockets with the cottage cheese, tomato slices, ham slices, and peach slices, dividing them evenly. Serve at once.

Roast Beef Pita Bread Sandwich with Tomato

The fresh basil in this sandwich is a must have.
The crisp and clean taste will delight the whole family!

SERVES 6

½ cup chopped fresh basil

⅛ cup prepared horseradish

½ cup plain low-fat yogurt

¾ pound delicatessen-style sliced roast beef

1 head butter lettuce, separated into leaves

3 pita breads

1 large tomato, cored and cut into 12 slices

In a large bowl, stir together the basil, horseradish, and yogurt. Spread the horseradish-yogurt mixture on the beef slices and wrap each slice in a lettuce leaf. Cut the pita breads in half, forming 6 pockets. Put the lettuce-wrapped beef and 2 slices of tomato into each half. Serve immediately.

Bruschetta with Basil

Turn this classic Italian appetizer into a full meal by adding soup or salad.

SERVES 16–20

½ pound plum tomatoes, sliced lengthwise

¼ cup diced red onion

1 tablespoon olive oil

2 tablespoons chopped fresh parsley

1 tablespoon chopped fresh basil

1 clove garlic, minced

Salt and pepper to taste

1 sourdough baguette, about 10 ounces, cut on the diagonal into 1-inch slices and lightly toasted

16 to 20 small fresh basil leaves

In a medium bowl, combine the tomatoes, onion, olive oil, parsley, chopped basil, garlic, salt, and pepper. Mix gently. Top each toasted bread slice with about 1 heaping tablespoon of the tomato-avocado mixture. Garnish each with a small basil leaf.

Lemon-Sesame Tuna Sandwiches

This isn't your average tuna sandwich!

SERVES 4

2 tablespoons lemon juice

1 tablespoon soy sauce

1 tablespoon Asian sesame oil

4 tuna fillets, about ⅓ pound each

3 scallions, minced

Pinch of pepper

4 hamburger buns, split and toasted

4 green leaf lettuce leaves

1. In a small bowl, stir together the lemon juice, soy sauce, and sesame oil to form a marinade. Place the tuna steaks on a baking sheet and drizzle the marinade over the fish. Chill for 1 hour.

2. Preheat oven to 400°F. Bake the fish until it is opaque throughout, about 10 minutes, or until done to your liking. Sprinkle with the scallions and pepper and serve on the buns with the lettuce.

Greek Lamb Pita Sandwiches

Pair these sandwiches with a fresh salad
and a light, fruity dessert, for a sure-fire hit.

SERVES 4

½ *pound lean ground lamb*

1 *onion, minced*

3 *cloves garlic, minced*

1 *celery stalk, chopped*

1 *package (10 ounces) chopped*
frozen spinach, thawed and well
drained

1 *teaspoon dried oregano,*
crumbled

Salt and pepper to taste

½ *cup crumbled feta cheese*

4 *pita breads*

8 *lettuce leaves*

1 *tomato, diced*

¼ *cup plain low-fat yogurt*

1. In a large nonstick skillet, combine the lamb, onion, garlic, and celery over medium heat. Sauté until the vegetables are tender, about 5 minutes. Drain off any liquid.

2. Add the spinach, oregano, salt, and pepper, and cook, stirring, for 5 minutes until heated through and the flavors are blended. Remove from the heat and add the feta.

3. Cut each pita bread in half, forming 8 pockets. Slip the lettuce leaves, some tomato, and 1 tablespoon yogurt into each pocket. Spoon the lamb mixture into the pita halves, then serve.

Sweet-and-Sour Turkey Burgers

Another take on the turkey burger—give it a shot!

SERVES 6

1 tablespoon soy sauce

1 tablespoon honey

4 scallions, minced

1 pound ground turkey, lean

6 slices canned pineapple

6 hamburger buns, split and toasted

1. Stir the soy sauce and honey together in a bowl until blended. Add the ground turkey and scallions and mix well. Shape into 4 patties.

2. In a nonstick skillet over medium heat, fry the patties, turning once, until done, about 8 minutes. To serve, place a burger on the base of each bun and top with a pineapple ring.

Mozzarella Sandwiches with Basil and Tomato

*Another classic Italian dish—mozzarella, tomato,
and basil combos are a tradition for a reason!*

SERVES 4

⅔ cup chopped dry-packed sun-dried tomatoes

2 cloves garlic, chopped

¼ teaspoon salt

1 tablespoon olive oil

1 tablespoon lemon juice

¼ teaspoon red pepper flakes

4 black olives, chopped

8 slices sourdough French bread

¼ pound low-fat mozzarella cheese, sliced

Pepper to taste

3 tomatoes, sliced

Salt to taste

2 teaspoons balsamic vinegar

1 cup fresh basil leaves, torn

1. Place the sun-dried tomatoes in a bowl and cover with boiling water. Let stand for 10 minutes. Drain.

2. In a medium bowl, mash together the garlic and salt. Add the oil, lemon juice, and red pepper flakes. Mix well. Add the rehydrated tomatoes and the olives and again mix well. Divide among 4 of the bread slices, spreading evenly. Top with the cheese slices, and sprinkle with the pepper. Place the tomato slices on top and season with salt and vinegar. Top with the basil and then the remaining bread slices. Cut in half to serve.

A Year in Provence Sandwich

Serve these sandwiches at a patio dinner in the
summer and you'll be your friends' favorite host.

SERVES 2

1 teaspoon olive oil

1 onion, chopped

1 teaspoon dried oregano, crumbled

1 teaspoon dried basil, crumbled

1 tablespoon water

¼ cup pitted black olives, sliced

2 tablespoons grated Parmesan cheese

8 to 12 spinach leaves

2 French rolls, split

4 ounces low-fat mozzarella cheese, sliced

2 plum tomatoes, sliced

1. Heat the oil in a large skillet over medium heat. Add onion, oregano, and basil and cook, stirring, for 2 minutes. Add the water, reduce the heat to low, cover, and cook until the onion is tender, about 5 minutes. Remove from the heat and stir in the olives and Parmesan.

2. Arrange 2 or 3 spinach leaves on bottom half of each French roll. Spoon half the onion mixture onto each, top with the cheese slices, and then the tomato slices. Arrange the remaining spinach leaves on top and then the tops of the rolls. Cut in half to serve.

Chicken, Duck, & Turkey

Greek Chicken Stir-Fry

Stir-fry with a twist! These ingredients add spark and great flavor to a typical chicken stir-fry. Serve over steamed rice, instant couscous, or hot cooked noodles.

SERVES 4

1 pound boneless, skinless chicken breasts

Salt and pepper to taste

2 tablespoons olive oil

2 cloves garlic, minced

2 cups frozen bell pepper and onion stir-fry

2 tablespoons lemon juice

½ cup crumbled feta cheese

1. Cut chicken breasts into 1" pieces and sprinkle with salt and pepper. Heat olive oil in wok or large skillet over medium high heat. Add chicken and garlic and stir-fry until chicken is cooked, about 4–5 minutes. Remove chicken and garlic to plate with slotted spoon and set aside.

2. Add frozen vegetables to skillet and stir-fry for 5–6 minutes until hot and crisp tender. Add chicken to skillet and sprinkle with lemon juice. Stir-fry for 1 minute longer. Sprinkle with feta cheese, remove pan from heat, cover, and let stand for 2–3 minutes longer to melt cheese.

Greek Food

Seasonings and ingredients that add a Greek flavor include feta cheese, oregano, olives, spinach, Phyllo dough, pita breads, rice, fresh seafood, grape leaves, lamb, and yogurt. The food is fairly spicy, with some unusual food combinations that include spinach and raisins, and beef and olives.

tip

Chicken Veronique

Sweet and tart grapes complement juicy and tender chicken in this wonderful recipe perfect for entertaining. Make sure to serve it over hot cooked rice to soak up the delicious sauce.

SERVES 4

¼ cup flour

½ teaspoon salt

⅛ teaspoon pepper

½ teaspoon dried marjoram leaves

4 boneless, skinless chicken breasts

¼ cup butter

1 cup chicken stock

½ cup white grape juice

1 cup red grapes, cut in half

1. On shallow plate, combine flour, salt, pepper, and marjoram. Coat chicken breasts in this mixture. In heavy skillet over medium heat, melt butter. Add chicken breasts and cook for 4 minutes. Turn chicken over and cook 3–6 minutes longer until chicken is just done. Remove chicken from pan and cover with foil to keep warm.

2. Add stock and grape juice to pan and bring to a boil, scraping up pan drippings. Boil over high heat for 6–8 minutes until sauce is reduced and thickened. Return chicken to pan along with red grapes, and cook over low heat for 2–3 minutes until grapes are hot and chicken is tender.

Herbed Chicken Breasts

*Serve these well-flavored, tender chicken breasts with a rice pilaf,
a spinach salad, and some oatmeal cookies for dessert.*

SERVES 8

2 tablespoons olive oil

2 tablespoons butter

2 cloves garlic, cut in half

¼ cup lemon juice

2 tablespoons chopped flat leaf parsley

½ teaspoon dried thyme leaves

½ teaspoon salt

⅛ teaspoon white pepper

8 chicken breasts

1. In small saucepan, combine olive oil, butter, and garlic over medium heat. Cook and stir until garlic sizzles; then remove garlic and discard. Add lemon juice, herbs, and salt and pepper to oil and butter in pan, stir, and remove from heat. Let cool for 5 minutes. Loosen chicken skin from the flesh and pour a tablespoon of the lemon herb mixture between the skin and flesh. Smooth skin back over flesh.

2. Place chicken pieces, skin side down, on broiler pan. Brush with lemon mixture. Broil chicken, 4–6" from heat source, for 7–8 minutes, brushing often with the lemon mixture. Turn chicken and broil 6–9 minutes longer, brushing frequently with lemon mixture, until chicken is thoroughly cooked. Discard any remaining lemon mixture.

Chicken Breasts: Boned or Not?

Chicken breasts are sold boneless and skinless, and with bone and skin on. The one you choose depends on what you're cooking. The skin and bone do add more flavor, so in simple broiled recipes bone-in chicken is a good choice. When you want cubed chicken for stir-fries and sandwiches, boneless, skinless breasts are better.

tip

Parmesan Chicken

This simple recipe demands the highest-quality ingredients.
Serve it with some hot cooked couscous, some bakery rolls, and melon wedges.

SERVES 6

6 boneless, skinless chicken breasts

¼ cup lemon juice

1 teaspoon salt

⅛ teaspoon pepper

½ teaspoon dried thyme leaves

¼ cup unsalted butter

½ cup grated Parmesan cheese

1. Cut chicken breasts into 1" pieces. Sprinkle with lemon juice, salt, pepper, and thyme leaves. Let stand at room temperature for 10 minutes.

2. Melt butter in heavy saucepan over medium heat. Sauté chicken until thoroughly cooked, about 5–6 minutes, stirring frequently. Sprinkle cheese over chicken, turn off heat, cover pan, and let stand for 2–3 minutes to melt cheese. Serve over hot cooked rice.

Basil Spinach Risotto

*This recipe does not contain chicken, but it does
use chicken broth to add fabulous flavor.*

SERVES 4

3 tablespoons olive oil

1 onion, finely chopped

1½ cups Arborio rice

½ teaspoon dried basil leaves

4 cups chicken broth

2 cups chopped fresh spinach

1 cup grated Parmesan cheese

1. In heavy saucepan, heat olive oil over medium heat. Add onion; cook and stir for 4–5 minutes until tender. Add rice; cook and stir until rice is opaque and coated. Sprinkle in basil leaves.

2. Meanwhile, in medium saucepan heat chicken broth over low heat. Add ½ cup of the chicken broth to the rice mixture; cook and stir until liquid is absorbed. Continue to add broth, ½ to 1 cup at a time, stirring frequently, until rice is almost cooked and mixture is creamy.

3. Stir in spinach, cover pan, and let stand for 3–4 minutes until spinach is wilted. Remove cover, stir in cheese, and serve.

About Risotto

Risotto is an Italian dish made from short grain rice; Arborio is the most popular type. This rice has a lot of starch, which is released during the cooking and stirring process to thicken the broth. When finished, the rice should be tender but with a tiny bite still left in the middle, and the broth thick and smooth.

tip

Herb-Crusted Chicken Breasts

Soaking chicken in buttermilk, even if just for a few minutes, makes it tender and juicy. You can use white or whole wheat bread in this easy and delicious recipe.

SERVES 6

1 cup buttermilk

1 teaspoon salt

⅛ teaspoon cayenne pepper

6 boneless, skinless chicken breasts

3 slices bread

½ teaspoon dried thyme leaves

½ teaspoon dried basil leaves

½ teaspoon dried tarragon

½ cup grated Parmesan cheese

⅓ cup olive oil

1. Heat oven to 375°F. In large bowl, combine buttermilk with salt and cayenne pepper and mix well. Add chicken breasts, turn to coat, and set aside.

2. Place bread on cookie sheet and bake at 375°F until crisp, about 5–7 minutes. Remove from oven and break into pieces. Place in blender or food processor; blend or process until crumbs are fine. Pour crumbs onto large plate and add herbs and cheese; mix well.

3. Remove chicken from buttermilk mixture and roll in crumb mixture to coat. Set on wire rack. In heavy skillet, heat olive oil over medium heat. Add chicken, two pieces at a time, and cook for 2–3 minutes on each side until browned. Remove to cookie sheet. Repeat to brown remaining chicken. Bake chicken at 375°F for 12–14 minutes or until thoroughly cooked. Serve immediately.

Spicy Chicken Tenders with Creamy Dip

This recipe is reminiscent of Buffalo Chicken Wings, a spicy
appetizer that combines chicken with a creamy blue cheese dip.

SERVES 4–6

1½ pounds chicken tenders

1 teaspoon cayenne pepper

1 tablespoon hot pepper sauce

1 egg, beaten

½ teaspoon salt

1 cup dry bread crumbs

¼ cup olive oil

1 cup creamy blue cheese salad dressing

½ cup chopped celery

1. Spread chicken tenders onto waxed paper. On shallow plate, combine cayenne pepper, hot pepper sauce, egg, and salt and mix well. Place bread crumbs on another plate. Dip chicken tenders, two at a time, into egg mixture then into bread crumbs to coat. Place on wire rack while coating remaining tenders.

2. In small bowl combine salad dressing and celery; cover and chill until ready to serve. Heat olive oil in heavy skillet over medium heat. Fry chicken tenders, 4 or 5 at a time, for 6–9 minutes, turning once, until brown and crisp on the outside and fully cooked. Drain on paper towels as they are finished. Serve hot with the celery dip.

Chicken Tenders

Chicken tenderloin is part of the breast; it is a small thin muscle underneath, next to the bone. Chicken tenders can be made from the tenderloin or just cut from any part of the breast. They cook very quickly and are great for children, because their shape means they easy to pick up, dunk, and eat.

tip

Lemon Chicken en Papillote

Lemon and chicken are perfect partners. The tart lemon tenderizes the chicken and adds great flavor. Serve these 'packages' at the table and let your guests open them.

SERVES 4

4 boneless, skinless chicken breasts

½ teaspoon salt

⅛ teaspoon lemon pepper

1 lemon, cut into thin slices, seeds removed

1 yellow summer squash, thinly sliced

1 zucchini, thinly sliced

¼ cup pine nuts

1. Preheat oven to 425°F. Cut four 12 × 18" pieces of cooking parchment paper. Fold in half, cut into a half-heart shape, then unfold. Place chicken breasts on one side of the fold and sprinkle with salt and lemon pepper. Top with lemon slices.

2. Arrange summer squash and zucchini around chicken and sprinkle pine nuts over all. Fold hearts in half and seal the edges by tightly folding them together twice. Place on cookie sheets and bake at 425°F for 10–15 minutes until chicken registers 170°F on a meat thermometer. Serve immediately.

Green Chile Chicken Burritos

Serve these easy burritos with salsa and guacamole. A mixed fruit salad would be a nice addition to the meal, with a bakery apple pie for dessert.

SERVE 6

2 (9-ounce) packages grilled chicken strips

1 (4-ounce) can chopped green chiles, drained

1½ cups sour cream

¼ teaspoon cayenne pepper

6 flour tortillas

1½ cups shredded Pepper Jack cheese, divided

1. Preheat oven to 400°F. In microwave safe bowl, combine chicken strips and green chiles. Microwave on medium power for 2–3 minutes, stirring once during cooking time, until ingredients are hot. Stir in sour cream and cayenne pepper.

2. Divide mixture among the tortillas. Sprinkle with 1 cup of the cheese. Roll up, folding in sides, to enclose filling. Place in casserole dish and top with remaining cheese. Bake at 400°F for 7–11 minutes until cheese melts and burritos are hot.

Spice It Up

There are lots of ingredients you can use to add spice to your food. Canned chopped green chiles, jalapeño peppers, salsas, taco sauce, and chili powder are all good choices. You can also use cayenne pepper, Tabasco sauce, fresh chiles like habaneros and Anaheim peppers, and ground chile powder.

tip

Turkey and Bean Stir-Fry

*Serve this quick and easy stir-fry over hot cooked rice,
along with a green salad and brownies for dessert.*

SERVES 4–6

1 pound boneless skinless turkey thighs

3 tablespoons flour

1 teaspoon garlic salt

⅛ teaspoon white pepper

2 tablespoons olive oil

2 cups frozen green beans, thawed and drained

1 cup frozen soybeans, thawed and drained

1 cup chicken stock

2 tablespoons cornstarch

1. Cut turkey into 1" pieces. On shallow place, combine flour, garlic salt, and pepper and mix well. Add turkey pieces and toss to coat.

2. In large skillet or wok, heat olive oil over medium high heat. Add turkey; stir-fry for 4–5 minutes until browned. Add beans and soybeans; stir-fry for 3–6 minutes longer until hot. In small bowl, combine chicken stock with cornstarch and mix with wire whisk. Add stock mixture to turkey mixture; cook and stir over medium high heat until liquid bubbles and thickens. Serve immediately.

Frozen Vegetables

You can thaw frozen vegetables by placing them in a colander and running warm water over until thawed. Or you can use the defrost setting on your microwave oven. You can also let the vegetables stand at room temperature for 1 to 2 hours until thawed. Be sure to drain well after thawing so you don't add too much liquid to the recipe.

tip

Spicy Chicken Paillards

Paillards (pronounced pie-YARDS) are thinly pounded pieces of meat, usually chicken or veal, which are coated in flour and spices and quickly sautéed.

SERVES 4

4 boneless, skinless chicken breasts

½ teaspoon salt

Dash white pepper

1 egg, beaten

½ teaspoon Tabasco sauce

2 tablespoons water

⅓ cup flour

1 tablespoon chili powder

⅛ teaspoon cayenne pepper

2 tablespoons cornmeal

3 tablespoons butter

1. Place chicken breasts between two sheets of plastic wrap. Pound gently, starting at the middle and working out, until the breasts are about ⅓" thick. Sprinkle with salt and pepper.

2. In shallow bowl, combine egg, Tabasco sauce, and water and mix well to blend. On shallow plate, combine flour, chili powder, cayenne pepper, and cornmeal. Dip paillards, one at a time, into egg mixture, then into flour mixture to coat.

3. Heat a large skillet over medium high heat. Add butter and heat until sizzling. Add chicken pieces, two at a time, and cook for 2 minutes. Turn and cook for 2–4 minutes longer, until chicken is just done: 170°F on an instant read thermometer. Remove to serving platter and cover with foil to keep warm while you cook the other two Paillards. Serve immediately.

Italian Winter "Fruited" Chicken

*This richly flavored chicken would be best
complimented by a simple rice or risotto dish.*

SERVES 10

3 (1- to 2-pound) whole chickens

3 tart apples

3 pears

3 shallots

½ bulb garlic

3 sprigs fresh thyme

2 tablespoons olive oil

1 cup dry white wine (not
cooking wine)

¼ cup walnuts

¼ cup dried fruit

2 bay leaves

1 cup apple cider

2 cups chicken stock

1. Preheat oven to 350°F. Clean and cut each chicken into 4 serving pieces: 2 breasts and 2 wings, or 2 thighs and 2 legs (reserve backbones for stock).

2. Clean and wedge the apples and pears. Peel and dice the shallots. Peel and mince the garlic. Clean the thyme and remove the leaves from the stems (discard the stems).

3. Heat the oil to medium-high temperature in an ovenproof pan on the stovetop. Brown the chicken pieces on all sides. Add the apples, pears, shallots, and garlic, and sauté for 1 minute. Add the remaining ingredients, and bring to a boil. Cover the pan, and immediately place in the oven.

4. Braise in the oven for 1 hour. Serve hot.

Grilled Turkey Tenderloin

The marinade for this simple recipe is a nice blend of sweet and spicy.
Serve the tenderloin with a mixed fruit salad and some toasted garlic bread.

SERVES 4

1 pound turkey tenderloin

½ cup orange juice

2 tablespoons Dijon mustard

¼ cup honey

2 garlic cloves, minced

½ teaspoon salt

⅛ teaspoon pepper

1. Prepare and preheat grill. Butterfly the tenderloin by cutting it in half lengthwise, being careful not to cut all the way through. Stop about one inch from the other side. Spread the tenderloin open, cover it with plastic wrap, and pound gently with a meat mallet or rolling pin to flatten.

2. For marinade, combine remaining ingredients in a large zip lock plastic bag. Add the turkey, close the bag, and knead the bag, pressing the marinade into the turkey. Let stand at room temperature for 10 minutes.

3. Cook turkey about 6" above medium hot coals for 5 minutes; brush with any leftover marinade. Turn turkey and cook for 4–6 minutes on second side until thoroughly cooked. Discard any remaining marinade.

The Tenderloin

Whether you are cooking beef tenderloin, pork tender, or turkey tenderloin, remember that this popular cut is low in fat and should be cooked quickly. This cut comes from a part of the animal that isn't used much, so it is tender with little connective tissue.

tip

Turkey Cutlets with Pineapple Glaze

Turkey cutlets cook very quickly and are a great choice for a fast meal. Cook them just until done so they stay tender and juicy.

SERVES 4

5 tablespoons olive oil, divided

1 onion, minced

1 (8-ounce) can crushed pineapple, drained

⅓ cup pineapple preserves

1 tablespoon finely minced ginger root

8 turkey cutlets

¼ cup flour

1 teaspoon salt

⅛ teaspoon white pepper

1. In small saucepan, heat 2 tablespoons olive oil over medium high heat. Add onion; cook and stir for 5–6 minutes until onion begins to brown around the edges. Stir in pineapple, pineapple preserves, and ginger root; bring to a boil. Lower heat to medium low and simmer while preparing turkey.

2. Meanwhile, combine flour, salt, and pepper on shallow plate. Dip cutlets, one at a time, into flour mixture. Heat 3 tablespoons olive oil in large skillet over medium high heat. Sauté cutlets, three or four at a time, for 2–3 minutes on each side until browned and thoroughly cooked. Place on serving platter and top with pineapple mixture; serve immediately.

Microwave Salsa Chicken

Serve this delicious dish over couscous, topped with
some sour cream, chopped tomatoes, and diced avocado.

SERVES 4

1½ cups chicken broth

2 tablespoons chili powder

½ teaspoon salt

⅛ teaspoon cayenne pepper

4 boneless, skinless chicken breasts

1 cup chunky salsa

2 tablespoons tomato paste

2 tomatoes, chopped

1. Place chicken broth into a microwave safe dish. Microwave on high for 3–5 minutes until boiling. Meanwhile, sprinkle chili powder, salt, and cayenne pepper on the chicken and rub into both sides. Pierce chicken on the smooth side with a fork. Carefully place in liquid in dish.

2. Microwave the chicken on high power for 8 minutes, then remove dish from oven and carefully drain off chicken broth. Meanwhile, in small bowl combine salsa, tomato paste, and tomatoes and mix well. Turn chicken over, rearrange chicken in dish and pour salsa mixture over. Return to microwave and cook for 2–6 minutes, checking every 2 minutes, until chicken is thoroughly cooked. Let stand for 5 minutes and serve.

Tomato Paste

Tomato paste is a concentrate of fresh tomatoes, sometimes made with seasonings like basil, garlic, and oregano. You can find it in cans or in tubes. Purchase it in tubes and you can add a small amount to dishes and then easily store leftover paste in the refrigerator.

tip

Creamy Chicken over Rice

Serve this easy dish with some steamed asparagus,
a spinach salad, and ice cream sundaes for dessert.

SERVES 4–6

1½ cups Jasmati rice

2½ cups water

3 boneless, skinless chicken breasts

1 teaspoon salt

⅛ teaspoon pepper

3 tablespoons olive oil

1 onion, finely chopped

1 (10-ounce) container refrigerated four cheese Alfredo sauce

1 (3-ounce) package cream cheese, softened

1. In heavy saucepan, combine rice and water; bring to a boil over high heat. Cover, reduce heat to low, and simmer for 15–20 minutes until rice is tender. Meanwhile, cut chicken into 1" pieces and sprinkle with salt and pepper. Heat olive oil in a large saucepan over medium heat. Add onion; cook and stir until crisp tender, about 3–4 minutes. Add chicken; cook and stir until chicken is thoroughly cooked, about 5–6 minutes.

2. Add Alfredo sauce and cream cheese to chicken mixture; cook and stir over low heat until sauce bubbles. When rice is tender, fluff with fork. Serve chicken over rice.

Aromatic Rice Varieties

There are lots of different rice varieties available in the supermarket. Jasmati rice is the American version of Jasmine rice, a fragrant long grain rice that cooks quickly and is always fluffy. You can find Basmati, Texmati, Wehani, Louisiana Pecan, Della, and Jasmine. These rices smell like nuts or popcorn while they cook. *tip*

Grilled Chicken Packets

This one-dish meal is so simple to make. You can make the packets ahead of time and keep them in the fridge until it's time to grill and eat.

SERVES 4

4 boneless, skinless chicken breasts

½ teaspoon salt

⅛ teaspoon pepper

2 cups sliced mushrooms

3 garlic cloves, minced

1 cup pasta sauce

1½ cups shredded Gouda cheese

1. Prepare and heat grill. Tear off four 18 × 12" sheets of heavy duty aluminum foil. Place chicken breasts in center of each sheet and sprinkle with salt and pepper. Divide mushrooms and garlic cloves among foil sheets and top each with pasta sauce. Sprinkle with cheese.

2. Fold foil over ingredients and seal the edges of the foil packets, making double folds on all of the seams. Place over medium coals and cover grill. Cook for 20–25 minutes, rearranging once during cooking time, until chicken is thoroughly cooked. Serve immediately.

Sautéed Chicken Patties

Caramelized onions add great flavor to these tender chicken patties.
Serve them over mashed potatoes to soak up all the sauce.

SERVES 4–6

4 tablespoons olive oil, divided

1 onion, finely chopped

1 teaspoon sugar

1 egg

2 cups panko, divided

½ teaspoon salt

⅛ teaspoon white pepper

1½ pounds ground chicken

1½ cups chicken broth

½ teaspoon dried marjoram
leaves

Panko

Panko, or Japanese bread crumbs, are very light crumbs that make a coating exceptionally crisp and crunchy. You can substitute regular dry bread crumbs if you can't find them, but the coating won't be as crisp. Don't substitute soft bread crumbs, as the texture will be entirely different.

tip

1. Heat 2 tablespoons olive oil in heavy pan over medium heat. Add onion; cook and stir for 3 minutes, then sprinkle with sugar; cook, stirring occasionally, until onion begins to turn light brown, 8–10 minutes.

2. Meanwhile, in large bowl combine egg, ½ cup panko, salt, and pepper and mix well. Add caramelized onions; do not rinse pan. Add ground chicken to egg mixture and mix gently but thoroughly. Form into 6 patties and coat in remaining panko.

3. Add remaining olive oil to pan used to cook onions; heat over medium heat. Add chicken patties, three at a time, and sauté for 4 minutes. Carefully turn patties and sauté for 3–6 minutes longer until thoroughly cooked. Repeat with remaining chicken patties. Remove all chicken patties to serving platter. Add chicken broth and marjoram to saucepan and bring to boil over high heat. Boil for 2–3 minutes to reduce liquid; pour over chicken patties and serve.

Microwave Chicken Divan

This method of cooking chicken breasts in the microwave yields tender, moist chicken. Serve with a spinach salad and some fresh fruit.

SERVES 4

1½ cups chicken broth

4 boneless, skinless chicken breasts

½ teaspoon salt

⅛ teaspoon pepper

½ teaspoon dried marjoram leaves

1 (10-ounce) package frozen broccoli, thawed

1 (10-ounce) container refrigerated four cheese Alfredo sauce

1 cup crushed round buttery crackers

1. Place chicken broth into a microwave safe dish. Microwave on high for 3–5 minutes until boiling. Meanwhile, sprinkle salt, pepper, and marjoram on the chicken and rub into both sides. Pierce chicken on the smooth side with a fork. Carefully place in liquid in dish.

2. Microwave the chicken on high power for 7 minutes, then remove dish from oven and carefully drain off chicken broth. Meanwhile, drain thawed broccoli and combine in medium bowl with Alfredo sauce. Rearrange chicken in dish, turn over, and pour broccoli mixture over; sprinkle with cracker crumbs. Return to microwave and cook for 3–5 minutes, checking every 2 minutes, until chicken is thoroughly cooked. Let stand for 5 minutes and serve.

Quick Chicken Cordon Bleu

Pancetta is Italian bacon that is cured in spices, but not smoked.
The deli department in your supermarket sells it thinly sliced.

SERVES 4

4 boneless, skinless chicken breasts

1 cup grated Parmesan cheese, divided

8 slices pancetta

1 (14-ounce) jar Alfredo sauce

4 slices baby Swiss cheese

1. Preheat oven to 400°F. Place ½ cup Parmesan cheese on a plate and dip chicken breasts into cheese to coat. Wrap pancetta around chicken breasts and place in a 2 quart casserole dish. Bake at 400°F for 10 minutes. In medium bowl combine Alfredo sauce with remaining ½ cup Parmesan cheese.

2. Remove casserole from oven and pour Alfredo sauce mixture over chicken. Return to oven and bake for 10 minutes longer. Top each chicken breast with a slice of cheese and return to the oven. Bake for 5 minutes longer, or until chicken is thoroughly cooked and cheese is melted.

Deconstructing Recipes

One way to make recipes simpler to make is to deconstruct them. Chicken Cordon Bleu is typically made by wrapping chicken around ham and cheese then baking. Wrapping the chicken in pancetta and topping with cheese results in the same taste but is much quicker to make.

tip

Mustard-Glazed Chicken Breasts

When broiling, be sure that you place the food the specified distance from the heat source. This recipe is excellent served with carrots and a lettuce salad.

SERVES 4

4 chicken breasts

½ teaspoon salt

⅛ teaspoon white pepper

¼ cup Dijon mustard, divided

2 tablespoons honey

2 tablespoons mayonnaise

½ teaspoon dried thyme leaves

4 slices Muenster cheese

1. Preheat broiler. Sprinkle chicken with salt and pepper and brush with 2 tablespoons Dijon mustard. Place on broiler pan, skin side down, and broil 6" from heat source for 4 minutes.

2. Meanwhile, combine honey, mayonnaise, thyme leaves, and remaining 2 tablespoons Dijon mustard in small bowl. Turn chicken skin side up and spoon on half of honey mixture. Return to oven and broil 6" from heat source for 4 minutes. Top with remaining honey mixture and place cheese slices on chicken. Return to oven and broil for 2–4 minutes until chicken is thoroughly cooked and cheese is melted and begins to brown. Serve immediately.

Chicken Doneness

Chicken has to be cooked well done. Using a meat thermometer, whole chickens should be cooked to 180°F, chicken breasts to 170°F, ground chicken to 165°F, and chicken thighs to 175°F. Another test is to slice into the chicken; the juice should run clear with no tinge of pink.

tip

Pesto Turkey Cutlets

The sauce for these cutlets is so delicious! Serve this over hot cooked rice or couscous, with steamed broccoli or green beans on the side.

SERVES 6

12 turkey cutlets

⅓ cup flour

1 teaspoon salt

½ teaspoon dried basil leaves

⅛ teaspoon white pepper

¾ cup grated Parmesan cheese, divided

2 eggs, beaten

3 tablespoons olive oil

1 (16-ounce) jar four cheese Alfredo sauce

1 (10-ounce) container refrigerated pesto

1. Place turkey cutlets on work surface. In small bowl, combine flour, salt, basil, pepper, and ¼ cup Parmesan cheese and mix well. Break eggs into shallow bowl and beat well. Dip cutlets into egg, then into flour mixture to coat. Place on wire rack.

2. Heat olive oil in heavy skillet over medium heat. Saute cutlets, four at a time, for 3 minutes, then turn and cook for 2–3 minutes on other side. As cutlets cook, remove to a platter. When all cutlets are cooked, add Alfredo sauce to skillet; bring to a simmer.

3. Add pesto to skillet and stir to mix. Return cutlets to the pan with the sauce and heat for 1–2 minutes. Sprinkle with remaining ½ cup Parmesan cheese and serve immediately.

Classic Chicken Salad

This recipe takes advantage of rotisserie chicken that is available in grocery stores already cooked for you. Serve on a croissant with lettuce or by itself with a fork and carrot sticks.

SERVES 4

1 cold roasted chicken, bones and skin removed

1 cup mayonnaise

¼ cup diced celery

½ cup diced artichoke hearts

½ cup chopped walnuts

Salt and pepper to taste

1. Dice chicken.

2. Combine all ingredients and season with salt and pepper.

Stir-Fried Lettuce Chicken Cups

*The cold crunch of lettuce contrasts the warm, chunky filling of juicy
chicken bits in this recipe once found only in Chinese restaurants.
It is messy to eat, but worth every elbow-licking moment!*

SERVES 4

*8–12 lettuce cups, iceberg or
butter lettuce*

*2 boneless, skinless chicken
breasts, diced*

4 sliced garlic cloves

2 tablespoons peanut oil

1 teaspoon sesame oil

¼ cup sliced green onion

1 teaspoon cornstarch

1 tablespoon soy sauce

¼ cup hoisin sauce

½ cup chicken broth

1 teaspoon sugar

2 teaspoons sherry

¼ cup diced mushrooms

¼ cup diced water chestnuts

¼ cup diced cucumber

¼ cup peas

1 cup sliced toasted almonds

1. Put chicken in a bowl with garlic, sesame oil, green onion, cornstarch, soy sauce, hoisin sauce, sugar, and sherry.

2. Heat wok or sauté pan and add peanut oil. Pour chicken mixture in and stir-fry for a minute. Add chicken broth, mushrooms, water chestnuts and peas.

3. Cook while stirring until chicken is cooked and sauce is thickened.

4. Spoon filling into lettuce cups and sprinkle with almonds.

5. Serve immediately.

Chicken Roulade with Mango

This is a fancy recipe to make for a dinner party using a classic poaching technique. Any filling could be used, such as diced mushrooms or julienned carrots, leeks, and celery. Rice and coconut curry sauce are the perfect complement to the chicken.

SERVES 4

4 boneless, skinless chicken breasts, pounded thin

Salt and pepper

8 fresh spinach leaves

4 slices mango

4 strips roasted red bell pepper

4 cups chicken broth

Coconut Curry Sauce

Combine 1 chopped shallot, 1 13.5-ounce can coconut milk (unsweetened), 1 teaspoon curry powder, and ½ cup chicken broth in a saucepan. Bring to a boil. Add ¼ cup cored, diced apple and ¼ cup diced banana. Turn down the heat and simmer until apples are tender. Puree in a blender, return to the pot, reduce until thickened, and season with salt and white pepper.

tip

1. Lay chicken breasts out on a plastic wrap and sprinkle them with salt and pepper.

2. Lay spinach on the middle of each breast; lay mango and pepper on top of spinach.

3. Roll each breast up so the mango and pepper are in the center. Wrap each breast individually in plastic wrap and foil. Twist the ends to make a tight sausage-like roll.

4. Combine chicken broth and 2 cups water in a 6-quart pot. Bring to a boil, and then reduce heat to simmer.

5. Drop chicken rolls into simmering liquid and poach for 10–15 minutes. Remove from liquid, peel off foil and plastic wrap, and cut each roll diagonally in half. Serve chicken roll cut on the bias to show the vibrant orange, green, and red filling.

Chicken Saltimbocca

*This Italian classic is traditionally made with veal scallops
instead of the chicken in this recipe. Serve this with some
spinach and buttered fettuccine noodles for a complete meal.*

SERVES 4

*4 boneless, skinless chicken
breasts*

4 slices prosciutto

4 fresh sage leaves

2 tablespoons butter

2 tablespoons olive oil

Salt

Pepper

1. Pound the chicken breasts flat so they are
the same thickness throughout.

2. Season chicken with salt and pepper.

3. Lay one sage leaf on each breast and lay
one slice of prosciutto on top of the sage leaf,
covering the whole chicken breast.

4. Heat butter and oil in skillet.

5. Lay chicken in the skillet prosciutto-side
down and sauté until crispy. Turn over and
finish cooking on the other side.

Chicken Parmesan

Serve this chicken parmesan alone or with caesar salad, grilled asparagus, and focaccia for a true Italian meal.

SERVES 4

4 boneless, skinless chicken breasts

½ cup flour mixed with 1 teaspoon salt

1 cup dry bread crumbs

1 cup grated Parmesan cheese

1 tablespoon dried oregano

¼ teaspoon pepper

1 egg

2 cups (1 16-ounce can) tomato sauce

½ cup olive oil

4 slices mozzarella cheese

1. Preheat oven to 350°F. In a large bowl, combine breadcrumbs, Parmesan cheese, oregano, and pepper.

2. In a separate bowl, beat eggs with a whisk or a fork. Put flour into another bowl.

3. Spread half of the tomato sauce on the bottom of a 9 × 13" baking dish.

4. Dip each chicken breast first in flour, then egg, then in the bread crumb mixture.

5. In a large sauté pan, heat the olive oil over medium-high heat. Fry the coated chicken breasts in heated olive oil, turning when bottom side of chicken is golden brown. Place browned chicken breast slices on top of the tomato sauce in the baking dish.

6. Cover chicken breasts with remaining tomato sauce. Top each chicken breast with a slice of mozzarella cheese and bake uncovered for 45 minutes.

Oven-Roasted Whole Chicken

Quartered and served with some potatoes and a green salad this makes a satisfying bistro-style dinner any day of the year.

SERVES 4

1 4-pound roasting chicken, rinsed and insides removed

1 onion, quartered

1 bay leaf

1 tablespoon paprika

1 teaspoon herbs de provence or dried thyme

1 teaspoon each salt and pepper

1. Pre-heat oven to 400°F. Season inside of bird with salt and pepper, then put bay leaf and onion inside. Tuck wings under the front of the bird.

2. Mix together paprika, salt and pepper and rub it all over the skin. Place chicken in a roasting pan

3. Roast chicken uncovered in oven until legs wiggle easily and juices run clear, about 1½ hours.

Cornish Game Hen

This small bird provides a perfect individual presentation for serving one person. It can be stuffed with poultry stuffing or other fillings such as green grapes and shrimp or blueberries.

SERVES 2

2 1½-pound Cornish hens

1 orange, cut in chunks

1 onion, cut in chunks

1 cup leeks, julienne

Salt and pepper

2 tablespoons butter

1. Preheat oven to 400°F. Season inside of hens with salt and pepper, then place orange and onion pieces inside the hens.

2. Scatter leeks on the bottom of a roasting pan and set the hens on top of them. Rub breast skin with butter and season with salt and pepper.

3. Roast until legs wiggle freely and juices run clear, about 40 minutes.

Chicken Fricassee

*This is a comfort food recipe of braised chicken,
smothered in onions and mushrooms.*

SERVES 4

1 3-pound chicken, cut in 8 pieces

1 cup flour, seasoned with salt,
pepper and paprika

1 cup sliced onions

1 cup quartered mushrooms

½ cup white grape juice

2 cups chicken broth

½ cup cream

2 ounces butter

1 bay leaf

Salt and pepper to taste

1. Dredge chicken pieces in seasoned flour then brown them in butter and set them aside on the plate.

2. Sauté the onions in the same pan with more butter if necessary. Pour the chicken broth and grape juice in the pan, stir, then place the chicken back in the pan with the simmering sauce.

3. Add the mushrooms and the bay leaf; cover and simmer for 45 minutes.

4. Take off the lid, remove the bay leaf and stir in the cream.

5. Simmer 5 minutes, then season with salt and pepper to taste.

Duck Leg Confit

*Use this preparation on pizza and salad, in cassoulet, or
warmed and served with parsnip puree, arugula, and prunes.*

SERVES 4

8 duck legs

2 cups kosher salt

¼ cup dried thyme

2 tablespoons pepper

1 tablespoon ground allspice

16 cups duck or pork fat melted

2 bay leaves

2 thyme sprigs

2 juniper berries

1. Mix salt, dried thyme, pepper, and allspice in a bowl.

2. Pack salt mixture over the entire surface of each leg, especially where the bone is, to draw out moisture. Put duck legs in a refrigerator dish, pour remaining salt mixture over them and refrigerate for 24 hours. Turn legs every 6–8 hours.

3. Pre-heat oven to 275°F. Remove the duck legs from the refrigerator and wipe them clean of the salt mixture.

4. Pack legs tightly in a deep baking dish and pour the melted fat over them so they are completely covered with it.

5. Bake until the duck is tender when pierced with a fork, about 1½ hours. Remove duck from the fat and drain. Heat in a 400°F oven to serve for 15 minutes, or take the meat off the bone and serve warm or cold.

Preparation Note

This is a way of cooking and preserving duck in fat so no air can get to the meat, thereby sealing out bacterial growth. If you are not going to save it you don't need to pack it so I have left out the preservation method and just included the cooking method.

tip

170

Pan-Seared Duck Breast

Duck meat is good with fruit, and this recipe uses peaches in the sauce, which is finished in the same pan the duck was cooked in for enhanced duck flavor. Serve with some cabbage and polenta, for a full meal.

SERVES 2

1 boneless duck breast

1 tablespoon butter

1 chopped shallot

1 chopped peach

2 tablespoons rice vinegar

1 tablespoon amaretto liqueur

½ cup chicken broth

Salt and pepper

1. Pre-heat oven to 375°F.

2. Score skin on duck breast, season both sides, and sear skin-side down in a sauté pan over medium-high heat for 3 minutes. Remove duck breast from sauté pan and place skin side up in a baking dish and put in oven to finish cooking for about 5 minutes.

3. In the same sauté pan, cook the shallots in butter for 2 minutes, then add peaches, vinegar and amaretto.

4. Cook to reduce liquid by half, add broth and cook for 5 minutes more. Adjust seasoning in the pan sauce with salt and pepper.

5. Slice the duck breast and fan the slices on a plate then spoon the peach sauce over the meat.

Creamed Turkey Legs

Served on split biscuits, this is comfort food to have when you are missing the warm flavors of Thanksgiving and don't have time to roast a turkey with all the trimmings. Cranberry sauce on the side is a nice tart addition.

SERVES 4

2 turkey legs

2 tablespoons butter

2 tablespoons flour

1 cup milk

1 thyme sprig

½ teaspoon pepper

Salt to taste

1. Roast turkey legs in a pre-heated 350°F oven until internal temperature is 165°F, about 1 hour.

2. Take the meat off the bone and discard the skin and bones. Cut or tear the meat into bite-size pieces.

3. Melt butter in a skillet and add flour, stir and cook for a few minutes, then add milk and thyme and stir until smooth.

4. Add turkey and simmer until thickened. If it becomes too thick, add more milk and cook a little longer.

5. Remove from heat, remove thyme sprig and season with salt and pepper. To serve, spoon over split biscuits or buttered toast points.

Turkey Burgers

Serve these non-red-meat burgers on a bun in the usual manner of a beef burger with a side of your favorite salad—macaroni, potato, green, anything!

SERVES 4

1½ pounds ground turkey

¼ cup sliced green onions

1 tablespoon Dijon mustard

1 clove garlic, minced

1 tablespoon Worcestershire sauce

½ teaspoon salt

¼ teaspoon pepper

½ cup grated Swiss cheese

¼ cup breadcrumbs

1. Combine all ingredients in a bowl mixing thoroughly.

2. Form mixture into 4 patties, taking care not to compress them too much.

3. Grill or sauté burgers until cooked through, about 5 minutes per side.

Serving Suggestion

For a delicious change of pace, these turkey burgers can also be served bun-less as an entrée with vegetables and some sort of cooked potato.

tip

Buffalo Wings

These fiery wings are great to serve on game day or at summertime cookouts. For a cookout, simply grill the wings instead of baking them. If some guests or family members don't like spicy foods, toss half of the wings in barbecue sauce instead.

SERVES 6

3 pounds chicken wings

1 cup butter, melted

1 teaspoon garlic powder

1 tablespoon Worcestershire sauce

½ cup cayenne pepper sauce

1 cup all purpose flour

1 teaspoon salt

1. Preheat oven to 375ºF. Combine the flour and salt in a large bowl. Toss chicken wings in flour mixture.

2. Shake off excess flour and put the wings on a foil-lined cookie sheet. Repeat in batches if all wings do not fit on one cookie sheet.

3. Bake wings for 30 minutes; remove from over. Turn wings over on the cookie sheet and bake another 15 minutes.

4. In a large bowl, combine butter, garlic powder, and Worcestershire sauce and cayenne pepper sauce.

5. Remove cooked wings from over; toss in a large bowl with sauce. Return coated wings to cookie sheet; bake for 15 minutes more.

CHAPTER

6

Pork & Ham

Cuban Pork Chops

Evoke a taste of the tropics with this simple, well-flavored recipe. Serve it with a rice pilaf, spinach salad and some cantaloupe slices drizzled with honey.

SERVES 4

4 boneless pork loin chops

4 garlic cloves, finely chopped

2 teaspoons cumin seed

½ teaspoon dried oregano leaves

½ teaspoon salt

⅛ teaspoon cayenne pepper

2 tablespoons olive oil

¼ cup orange juice

2 tablespoons lime juice

1. Trim excess fat from pork chops. In small bowl, combine garlic, cumin, oregano, salt, and cayenne pepper and mix well. Sprinkle this mixture on both sides of chops and rub into meat. Let stand at room temperature for 10 minutes.

2. Heat olive oil in heavy saucepan over medium heat. Add pork chops and cook for 5 minutes. Carefully turn and cook for 5 minutes on second side. Add orange juice and lime juice and bring to a simmer.

3. Cover pan and simmer chops for 5–10 minutes or until pork chops are tender and just slightly pink in the center, and sauce is reduced. Serve immediately.

Ham Asparagus Wraps

The asparagus has to be cooked in this recipe because it doesn't bake long enough to soften. Use any flavor of cream cheese and bottled Alfredo sauce you'd like!

SERVES 4

4 ¼-inch-thick slices deli ham

½ cup soft cream cheese with garlic

12 spears grilled asparagus

1 10-ounce jar garlic Alfredo sauce

½ cup grated parmesan

1. Preheat oven to 350°F.

2. Place ham on work surface and spread each piece with some of the cream cheese. Top each with three spears of asparagus and roll up.

3. Place in 12 × 8" glass baking dish and pour Alfredo sauce over all. Sprinkle with Parmesan cheese. Bake at 375°F for 15–20 minutes, until ham rolls are hot and sauce is bubbling. Serve immediately.

Pork Chops with Onion Conserve

You'll have three pans cooking on the stove while making this recipe,
but it still takes only 30 minutes!

SERVES 4

½ cup golden raisins

1¼ cups orange juice, divided

¼ cup olive oil, divided

1 red onion, chopped

1 teaspoon sugar

4 center cut boneless pork chops

1 teaspoon salt

⅛ teaspoon pepper

1 teaspoon dried thyme

About Raisins

Raisins are dried grapes, but the way they are dried determines the color. Both golden and dark raisins are made from Thompson variety grapes, but the dark raisins are dried in the sun, while golden raisins are oven dried. The sunlight causes the raisins to darken. Golden raisins may also be treated with sulfur dioxide; read labels carefully!

1. In heavy saucepan, combine raisins and 1 cup orange juice; bring to a simmer over medium heat. Meanwhile, in another heavy saucepan, heat 2 tablespoons olive oil over medium heat. Add red onion; cook over medium heat for 10 minutes, stirring frequently, until onions begin to turn brown. Add sugar to onion mixture; cook for 2 minutes. Add raisin mixture; bring to a boil over high heat, then reduce heat to low and simmer while cooking pork chops.

2. Meanwhile, sprinkle pork chops with salt, pepper, and thyme. Heat remaining 2 tablespoons olive oil in large skillet and add pork chops. Cook over medium heat, turning once, until pork is done, about 10 minutes. Remove pork from pan; cover to keep warm.

3. Add ¼ cup orange juice to drippings remaining in pan; turn heat to high and bring to a boil; reduce heat and simmer for 2–3 minutes until juice is reduced. Return pork chops to pan along with onion mixture. Cover and let stand off the heat for 3 minutes, then serve.

Ham and Asparagus Casserole

Ham and asparagus are natural partners; the sweet saltiness of the ham complements the slight bitterness of the asparagus.

SERVES 4

1 pound asparagus

1½ cups cubed fully cooked ham

1 (10-ounce) container refrigerated Alfredo sauce

1 cup shredded Gruyere cheese

½ teaspoon dried thyme leaves

1 cup bread crumbs

2 tablespoons olive oil

1. Snap ends off asparagus. Place in saucepan and cover with water. Bring to a boil; boil for 3–4 minutes until asparagus is just tender. Drain thoroughly. Place in 2 quart baking dish.

2. In medium saucepan place ham cubes and Alfredo sauce; cook and stir over medium heat until sauce bubbles, about 4–6 minutes. Remove from heat and stir in cheese and thyme until cheese melts and mixture is smooth. Pour over asparagus in casserole.

3. Preheat broiler. In small bowl combine bread crumbs and olive oil and toss to mix. Sprinkle over sauce mixture in casserole. Broil casserole 6" from heat for 4–6 minutes until bread crumbs are toasted. Serve immediately.

Stovetop Lasagna

*Serve this super easy version of lasagna with
a crisp green salad and breadsticks.*

SERVES 6

*1 pound bulk sweet Italian
sausage*

1 onion, chopped

*1 (24-ounce) package frozen
ravioli*

1 (28-ounce) jar pasta sauce

*1 teaspoon dried Italian
seasoning*

*2 cups shredded Italian blend
cheese*

1. In heavy skillet over medium heat, cook sausage and onion, stirring to break up sausage, until meat is browned. Drain thoroughly, and wipe out skillet.

2. Meanwhile, bring large pot of water to a boil and add ravioli; cook until almost tender, about 1–2 minutes. Drain well.

3. In cleaned skillet, spread about 1 cup pasta sauce, then top with layers of sausage mixture, ravioli, and more pasta sauce. Sprinkle each layer with a bit of the dried Italian seasoning. Sprinkle with cheese. Cover and heat over medium heat, shaking pan occasionally, until sauce bubbles, cheese melts, and mixture is hot, about 5–8 minutes. Serve immediately.

Ham and Sweet Potatoes

Sweet potatoes and oranges turn a ham steak into a real feast. This recipe is a good choice for smaller families for Thanksgiving or other holiday dinners.

SERVES 6

1 tablespoon olive oil

1 onion, finely chopped

1½ pound cooked ham steak

½ cup orange marmalade

2 tablespoons reserved sweet potato liquid

¼ teaspoon nutmeg

1 (15-ounce) can sweet potatoes, drained, reserving 2 tablespoons liquid

1 (15-ounce) can mandarin oranges, drained

1. In large skillet, heat olive oil over medium heat. Add onion; cook and stir until crisp tender, about 3 minutes. Add steak to skillet along with marmalade, 2 tablespoons sweet potato liquid, and nutmeg. Cover and simmer for 10 minutes over medium low heat.

2. Turn ham steak, then add sweet potatoes to skillet; cover and simmer for 5 minutes. Stir in mandarin oranges; cover and cook for 2–4 minutes longer until hot. Serve immediately.

Pork and Apricot Skewers

*This recipe is elegant enough for company. Serve with hot cooked
rice and garlic bread, with a spinach salad on the side.*

SERVES 6

*1½ pounds boneless pork
tenderloin*

1 cup apricot preserves

½ cup apricot nectar

12 dried apricots

2 onions

½ teaspoon dried thyme leaves

1. Prepare and heat grill. Cut pork into 1" cubes and place in medium bowl. Top with apricot preserves; let stand while preparing remaining ingredients. In small saucepan, combine apricot nectar and dried apricots; bring to a boil over high heat. Reduce heat and simmer for 3 minutes; drain apricots and set on wire rack to cool; pour nectar over pork cubes. Cut onions into 6 wedges each.

2. Drain pork, reserving marinade, and thread pork cubes, onion wedges, and apricots onto 6 metal skewers. Combine the reserved marinade with the thyme leaves in a small pan and bring to a boil over medium high heat; reduce heat to low and simmer while skewers cook.

3. Grill skewers, covered, over medium coals for 5 minutes. Turn and brush with some of the simmering marinade. Cover and grill for 5–8 minutes longer until pork is slightly pink in center and onions are crisp tender; keep marinade simmering. Serve with the marinade on the side.

Kabobs

When you're making skewers or kabobs there are different materials to choose from. Bamboo skewers must be soaked in water for at least 30 minutes before grilling so they won't burn while the food is cooking. Metal skewers are more durable, but use caution because they get very hot when on the grill.

tip

Basic Italian Pork Sausage

This sausage is commonly known as Italian "sweet" sausage.
Fennel seeds lend the characteristic taste to Italian sweet sausage.

SERVES 10

2½ pounds pork

½–¾ pound pork fat

1 bulb garlic

¼ cup fennel seeds

2 tablespoons dried basil

2 tablespoons dried oregano

Fresh-cracked black pepper

Kosher salt

1. Grind the meat and fat separately. Keep chilled. Peel and mince the garlic.

2. Mix together all the ingredients in a chilled bowl with chilled utensils. If using an electric mixer, be sure not to overblend the meat and fat.

3. Either stuff the mixture into casings or form into patties.

4. Use in desired preparation, or heat a small amount of oil or butter to medium temperature in a large sauté pan. Add the sausage, cover, and cook for about 30 minutes, turning at 5-minute intervals. Uncover and cook for about 10 to 15 minutes, until thoroughly browned.

Grilled Ham Steak

*Ham steak is a fully cooked slice of ham that may or may not contain a bone.
All you have to do is season it if you'd like and heat it.*

SERVES 4

1 cup Texmati rice

2 cups water

¾ cup orange marmalade

2 tablespoons frozen orange juice concentrate

2 tablespoons balsamic vinegar

2 tablespoons water

½ teaspoon dried marjoram leaves

½ teaspoon salt

⅛ teaspoon white pepper

1 (1½-pound) ham steak

1. Prepare and heat grill. In large saucepan combine rice and 2 cups water; bring to a boil over high heat. Reduce heat, cover, and simmer for 15–20 minutes. Meanwhile, in medium saucepan, combine all remaining ingredients except ham and rice and bring to a boil. Reduce heat to low and simmer for about 4 minutes.

2. Place ham steak on grill and brush with some of the glaze. Cover and grill for 4 minutes; turn ham steak and brush with more of the glaze. Cover and grill for 3–5 minutes until ham steak is thoroughly heated. Keep cooking marinade while ham is grilling. Serve with remaining marinade over rice.

Ham and Cheese Penne

This simple one-dish dinner recipe can be made with any frozen vegetable combo. You can even eliminate the pasta if you use a vegetable combo that includes pasta!

SERVES 4

2 cups penne pasta

2 tablespoons olive oil

1½ cups frozen broccoli cauliflower mixture

2 cups cubed ham

1 (10-ounce) container refrigerated four cheese Alfredo sauce

½ cup grated Parmesan cheese

1. Cook penne in rapidly boiling water according to package directions. Meanwhile, heat olive oil in large saucepan over medium heat. Add frozen vegetables; sprinkle with 2 tablespoons water. Cover and cook over medium heat for 4–5 minutes until vegetables are almost hot. Add ham and Alfredo sauce; bring to a simmer.

2. Drain pasta when cooked and add to skillet. Stir gently, then simmer for 2–3 minutes longer until vegetables and ham are hot. Sprinkle with Parmesan cheese and serve.

Al Dente

When cooking pasta, al dente is a term used to indicate doneness. It means 'to the tooth'. Always test pasta by biting into it. When it's tender, but with a firmness to the center, it's done. Look at the pasta: you'll be able to see a small opaque line in the center after you bite it.

tip

Grilled Orange Pork Tenderloin

You can serve this elegant dish to company—add a nice salad
and some breads and you'll be a crowd-pleaser!

SERVES 6–8

2 pounds pork tenderloin

1 teaspoon salt

⅛ teaspoon pepper

⅓ cup frozen orange juice concentrate, thawed

¼ cup honey

¼ cup Dijon mustard

1 tablespoon lemon juice

½ teaspoon dried oregano leaves

1. Prepare and heat grill. Cut pork tenderloins in half crosswise. Then cut the tenderloins horizontally in half, being careful not to cut through to the other side. Spread tenderloin open and place in large casserole dish. Sprinkle both sides with salt and pepper. In medium bowl, combine remaining ingredients and mix well. Spread on all sides of tenderloin and let stand for 10 minutes.

2. Grill tenderloins, covered, turning once, for 14–17 minutes until a meat thermometer registers 160°F. Brush with any remaining marinade after the first turn. Discard remaining marinade. Slice tenderloin across the grain to serve.

Butterflying Meats

Butterflying meats cuts the cooking time almost in half. You can butterfly just about any cut of meat. Use a sharp knife and cut slowly, being sure not to cut all the way through to the other side. Spread the cut meat out and, if desired, use a meat mallet to gently pound it to flatten to an even thickness.

tip

Sausage Stir-Fry

Serve this fresh-tasting stir-fry over hot cooked rice with chopped cashews on the side, along with a gelatin fruit salad.

SERVES 4

1 pound Italian sausage

2 tablespoons olive oil

1 onion, chopped

2 yellow summer squash, sliced

1 cup frozen broccoli florets, thawed

¾ cup sweet and sour sauce

1. In large skillet, cook Italian sausage and water over medium heat for 6–8 minutes, turning once during cooking time, until sausage are almost cooked. Remove sausages to plate and cut into 1" pieces.

2. Drain fat from skillet but do not rinse. Return to medium high heat, add olive oil, then add onion. Stir-fry until onion is crisp tender, 3–4 minutes. Add squash and broccoli; stir-fry for 4–5 minutes longer until broccoli is hot and squash is tender. Return sausage pieces to skillet along with sweet and sour sauce. Stir-fry for 4–6 minutes until sausage is thoroughly cooked and sauce bubbles. Serve immediately.

Cooking Rice

Rice expands to three times its bulk when cooked. Each serving is about ½ cup, so if you want to serve 6 people, cook 1 cup of rice to make 3 cups. Combine 1 cup long grain rice with 2 cups water and a pinch of salt in a saucepan. Cover, bring to a boil, reduce heat to low, and simmer for 15–20 minutes until tender.

tip

Skillet Pork Chops with Cabbage

Serve this hearty German feast with mashed potatoes
and a molded gelatin salad. And don't forget dessert!

SERVES 4

3 tablespoons olive oil

1 red onion, chopped

4 smoked pork chops

3 cups shredded red cabbage

1 Granny Smith apple, peeled
and chopped

1 cup apple juice

½ teaspoon dried thyme leaves

½ teaspoon salt

⅛ teaspoon pepper

1. Heat olive oil in large skillet over medium heat. Add red onion; cook and stir for 3–4 minutes until tender. Add pork chops; brown on both sides for about 3 minutes. Add cabbage and apple to the skillet; cook and stir for 3 minutes.

2. Pour apple juice over all and sprinkle with thyme leaves, salt, and pepper. Bring to a boil, then reduce heat, cover, and simmer for 10–15 minutes until cabbage is crisp tender and pork chops are hot. Serve immediately.

Pork and Bean Tacos

Serve these easy tacos with lots of toppings: sour cream, guacamole, shredded cheese, chopped pickled jalapeño peppers, and chopped tomatoes.

SERVES 4–6

1 (16-ounce) package seasoned pulled pork in BBQ sauce

2 tablespoons oil

2 cups frozen onion and bell pepper mixture

½ cup taco sauce

1 tablespoon chili powder

1 (16-ounce) can seasoned refried beans

8 crisp taco shells

1. Preheat oven to 350°F. Heat pulled pork and BBQ sauce as directed on package. Meanwhile, heat oil in heavy saucepan over medium high heat. Add frozen vegetables, pulled pork, BBQ sauce, taco sauce, chili powder, and refried beans. Bring to a simmer and cook for 6–8 minutes until vegetables and meat are hot.

2. Meanwhile, place taco shells on cookie sheet and heat at 350°F for 4–6 minutes. Fill taco shells with pork mixture and serve.

Italian Crispy Pork Chops

Serve these delicious little pork chops with some rice and greens for a full meal.

SERVES 6–8

8 *thin cut boneless pork chops*

2 *eggs, beaten*

2 *tablespoons water*

½ *cup grated Parmesan cheese*

1 *cup panko*

1 *teaspoon dried Italian seasoning*

½ *teaspoon dried basil leaves*

2 *tablespoons butter*

3 *tablespoons olive oil*

1. Place pork chops between two pieces of plastic wrap and pound with a rolling pin or meat mallet until about ⅓" thick. In shallow bowl, combine eggs and water and beat until blended. On shallow plate, combine cheese, panko, Italian seasoning and basil and mix well. Dip pork chops into egg mixture, then into cheese mixture, pressing the cheese mixture firmly onto the chops. Place on wire rack when coated. Let stand for 10 minutes.

2. Heat butter and olive oil in a large skillet over medium high heat. Fry the pork chops, 2–4 minutes on each side, until brown and crisp and just slightly pink inside. Serve immediately.

Panko Bread Crumb Substitutions

Panko are Japanese bread crumbs that are very light, dry, and rough. If you can't find them, make your own soft bread crumbs from a fresh loaf of bread, spread them on a baking sheet, and bake them in a 350°F oven for 5–8 minutes until dry and crisp.

tip

Sausage Filo Rolls

Serve these crisp little bundles for a brunch along with scrambled eggs, some rolls, and fresh orange juice and hot coffee—for breakfast at dinnertime!

SERVES 4

1 pound bulk pork sausage

1 cup preshredded carrots

1½ cups shredded Colby cheese

6 (12 × 18") sheets frozen filo dough, thawed

½ cup butter, melted

1. Preheat oven to 400°F. In heavy skillet over medium heat, cook sausage until partially done, stirring to break up sausage, about 3–4 minutes. Stir in carrots; continue cooking, stirring frequently, until sausage is done and carrots are crisp tender, 2–3 minutes longer. Drain well if necessary. Remove from heat, sprinkle cheese over sausage mixture, and let stand while preparing filo dough.

2. Place 1 sheet filo dough on work surface and brush with some butter. Continue layering filo with butter. Cut filo into four 6 × 9" rectangles. Stir sausage mixture and divide among rectangles, placing at one 9" edge. Roll up filo, enclosing filling and folding in ends. Brush with more butter.

3. Place on parchment paper lined baking sheets. Bake at 400°F for 20–23 minutes until golden brown.

Filo Dough

You can find filo, or Phyllo, dough in the freezer section of your supermarket near the frozen pie shells. Follow the thawing instructions carefully, and cover the dough that you aren't using with a damp paper towel while you're working with the rest so it doesn't dry out.

tip

Sausage Quesadillas

*These crisp little sandwiches are delicious served
with some fresh tomato salsa for dipping.*

SERVES 4

1 pound bulk pork sausage

1 onion, chopped

1 red bell pepper, sliced

½ teaspoon paprika

½ teaspoon ground cumin

2 teaspoons chili powder

2 cups shredded Cojack cheese

8 (10-inch) flour tortillas

2 tablespoons olive oil

1. Preheat oven to 375°F. In heavy skillet, cook pork sausage with onion over medium heat, stirring to break up sausage, about 4–5 minutes. When browned, drain off most of the fat. Add red bell pepper; cook and stir for 2–3 minutes. Sprinkle with seasonings and remove from heat.

2. Lay four tortillas on work surface. Sprinkle each with ¼ cup cheese and top with one-fourth of the sausage mixture. Sprinkle with remaining cheese and top with remaining tortillas. Place on two cookie sheets and brush quesadillas with olive oil. Bake at 375°F for 7–8 minutes until cheese is melted and tortillas are lightly browned. Cut into wedges and serve.

Tortillas

Tortillas are available in two types, corn and flour. Flour tortillas are usually larger, used for quesadillas and burritos. They can be flavored with spinach, red pepper, garlic, and tomato. Corn tortillas are also available in flavored varieties, as well as the traditional white, yellow, and blue corn flavors.

tip

Knock Bockle

This casserole is so hearty and comforting. Serve it with steamed green beans and a simple green salad, with a chocolate cake for dessert.

SERVES 4–6

1 pound Polish sausage

1 green bell pepper, chopped

1 (18-ounce) jar pasta sauce

1 (16-ounce) package refrigerated mashed potatoes

½ cup grated Parmesan cheese

1. Preheat oven to 425°F. Cut sausages into 1" slices; place in heavy skillet over medium heat and cook, turning several times, until sausage is browned. Add green bell pepper; cook and stir for 2 minutes longer. Drain excess fat if necessary. Add pasta sauce and bring to a simmer.

2. Meanwhile, in medium bowl combine potatoes and Parmesan cheese and mix well. Place sausage mixture into a 2-quart casserole dish and top with spoonfuls of the potato mixture. Bake at 425°F for 15–20 minutes or until potatoes begin to turn light golden brown and sauce bubbles.

Southwest Pork Chops

These spicy pork chops are coated with layers of Tex-Mex flavor. Serve them with hot mashed potatoes, a cooling fruit salad, and a lemon meringue pie for dessert.

SERVES 6

3 tablespoons olive oil

6 (½-inch) boneless pork chops

1 teaspoon salt

⅛ teaspoon cayenne pepper

1 tablespoon chili powder

1 chipotle chile in adobo sauce, minced

2 tablespoons adobo sauce

½ cup salsa

1 (8-ounce) can tomato sauce

1. Place olive oil in heavy skillet and heat over medium heat. Meanwhile, sprinkle pork chops with salt, cayenne pepper, and chili powder and rub into meat. Add pork chops to skillet and cook for 4 minutes.

2. Meanwhile, combine chipotle chile, adobo sauce, salsa, and tomato sauce in a small bowl. Turn pork chops and cook for 2 minutes. Then add tomato sauce mixture to skillet, bring to a simmer, and simmer for 4–5 minutes until chops are cooked and tender.

Pressure Cooker Sausage Risotto

*Your pressure cooker makes the most delicious risotto
in less than half the time of traditional stovetop methods.*

SERVES 4

3 tablespoons olive oil, divided

1 pound bulk sweet Italian sausage

1 onion, finely chopped

2 cups Arborio rice

4 cups chicken stock, warmed

½ teaspoon dried Italian seasoning

½ cup grated Parmesan cheese

1. Turn the pressure cooker to high and add 2 tablespoons of the oil. Cook the sausage until almost done, stirring to break up meat, then add the onion and cook until the sausage is done and the onion is crisp tender. Add remaining olive oil and the rice; cook and stir for 2–4 minutes until the rice is coated and opaque.

2. Add ½ cup of the stock and cook, stirring constantly, for 2–4 minutes until the liquid is absorbed by the rice. Add the remaining stock and Italian seasoning and lock the lid into place. Pressure cook on medium for 8 minutes. Let the pressure release, open the lid, and check the rice. If the rice isn't cooked al dente, lock the lid again and cook for 2–3 minutes longer. Release the pressure, open the lid, and stir in the Parmesan cheese until melted. Serve immediately.

Pressure Cookers

There are two kinds of pressure cookers: those which cook on the stove, and those which are self contained. The newer cookers have more built in safety features and usually have a quick release feature, which lowers the pressure quickly and safely so you can cook a recipe in 30 minutes.

tip

Ham and Cheese Fondue

You'll find packaged fondue in the deli section of your supermarket. Serve this excellent dish with sliced apples, breadsticks, vegetables, and crackers.

SERVES 4

2 tablespoons butter

1 onion, finely chopped

1 cup shredded ham

1 (14-ounce) package premade fondue

French bread cubes

1. In a heavy saucepan, melt butter over medium heat. Add onion; cook and stir until tender, about 5–6 minutes. Add ham and stir. Add fondue and stir to break up.

2. Cook and stir over medium low heat for 15 minutes or until fondue is melted and smooth, stirring almost constantly.

3. Pour into a fondue pot and place over burner. Serve with long forks to spear the bread cubes and dip into the fondue.

Grilled Polish Sausages

This easy recipe is perfect for summer;
serve potato salad and melon wedges on the side.

SERVES 6

6 Polish sausages

1 cup beer

3 cups coleslaw mix

¾ cup coleslaw dressing

6 whole wheat hot dog buns, split

1. Prepare and preheat grill. Prick sausages and place in saucepan with beer. Bring to a boil over high heat, then reduce heat to low and simmer for 5 minutes, turning frequently. Drain sausages and place on grill over medium coals; grill until hot and crisp, turning occasionally, about 5–7 minutes.

2. Meanwhile, combine coleslaw mix and dressing in medium bowl and toss. Toast hot dog buns, cut side down, on grill. Make sandwiches using sausages, coleslaw mix, and buns.

Sausages

Just about any sausage can be substitute for another. Just be sure to read the package to see if the sausages you choose are fully cooked or raw. The fully cooked sausages only need to be reheated, but the raw ones should be cooked until a meat thermometer registers 170°F.

tip

Pork Pinwheels with Apricot Stuffing

Although there are a lot of ingredients for this meal,
the final product is definitely worth the effort!

SERVES 6

1 pork tenderloin, about 1 pound

Stuffing:

⅔ cup reduced-sodium, fat-free chicken broth, heated

⅓ cup snipped dried apricots

2 tablespoons chopped celery

1 small onion, chopped

1 tablespoon buttery light, reduced-fat margarine

⅛ teaspoon ground cinnamon

dash of pepper

2 cups whole-wheat bread cubes

1. Split the tenderloin lengthwise, but do not cut all the way through. Open the tenderloin out flat, as if it were a book. Pound the tenderloin lightly with meat mallet to a 10-by-6-inch rectangle.

2. Preheat broiler.

3. To make the stuffing, place the apricots in a small bowl and pour the broth over them. Let stand for 5 minutes. In a small skillet, melt the margarine over medium heat. Add the celery and onion and sauté until soft but not browned, about 5 minutes. Remove from the heat and stir in the cinnamon and pepper. In a large bowl, mix together the bread cubes, onion mixture, and apricot mixture; toss lightly to moisten.

Pork Pinwheels with Apricot Stuffing

(continued)

Sauce:

1½ teaspoons cornstarch

Dash of ground nutmeg

1 cup apricot nectar

4. Spread the stuffing evenly over the tenderloin. Roll up jelly-roll style, starting from the short side. Secure the roll with wooden toothpicks or tie with kitchen string at 1-inch intervals. Cut the meat roll crosswise into six 1-inch-thick slices. Place the meat slices on a broiler pan, cut side down. Slip under the broiler about 4 inches from the heat source and broil for 12 minutes. Turn the slices over and broil until the meat is cooked through, 11 to 12 minutes. Remove the toothpicks or string and transfer the meat slices to a serving platter.

5. Meanwhile, to make the sauce, combine the cornstarch and nutmeg in a small saucepan. Stir in the apricot nectar and place over medium heat. Cook, stirring, until bubbly, then cook and stir for 2 minutes more. Serve the sauce with meat slices.

Pork Chops Dijon

A somewhat simple pork recipe can go a long, long way!

SERVES 4

1 pound boneless lean pork chops

1 onion, chopped

3 tablespoons Dijon mustard

2 tablespoons low-fat Italian dressing

¼ teaspoon pepper

1. Spray a large skillet with nonstick cooking spray and place over medium-high heat. Add the chops and brown on both sides, turning once. Transfer the chops to a plate and set aside.

2. Add the onions to the skillet and cook and stir over medium heat until soft, about 3 minutes. Push the onions to the side of the skillet and return the chops to the skillet.

3. In a small bowl, quickly stir together the mustard, dressing, and pepper. Spread the mixture over the chops.

4. Cover and cook over medium-low heat until the meat is tender, about 15 minutes. Serve immediately.

Put Down That Fork!

Never use a fork to turn meats. It pierces the meat and allows the flavorful juices to escape. Use a spatula or tongs to gently turn or flip meats.

tip

Pork and Wild Rice Salad with Plums

This savory meal will tempt your family's taste buds with all sorts of flavors!

SERVES 4

1 package (6 ounces) white and wild rice mix

¼ cup herb vinegar

1 tablespoon Dijon mustard

1 tablespoon minced garlic

1 tablespoon honey

2 teaspoons cornstarch

1 cup water

2 tablespoons diced scallions

2 teaspoons dried parsley flakes

¼ teaspoon red pepper flakes

8 cups mixed salad greens

2¾ cups thinly sliced carrots

1½ cups slivered snow peas

10 ounces roast pork, trimmed and thinly sliced

8 plums, pitted and sliced

1. Cook white and wild rice mix as directed on the package. Set aside.

2. In a saucepan over medium heat, combine the vinegar, mustard, garlic, honey, and cornstarch. Stir in the water and cook, stirring, until thickened, about 5 minutes. Remove from the heat and stir in the scallions, parsley, and red pepper flakes. Let cool, cover, and chill.

3. In a bowl, toss together the greens, carrots, and snow peas. Divide among individual salad plates. Spoon the rice into the center of the plates, and top with the pork and plums. Drizzle with the dressing and serve.

Pork and Garbanzo Bean Curry

Curry and pork make a great combination.

SERVES 4

1 pound pork fillets, cut into
1-inch chunks

1 tablespoon olive oil

2 cloves garlic, minced

1 onion, chopped

2 teaspoons peeled and minced
fresh ginger

1 tablespoon all-purpose flour

1 teaspoon curry powder

½ teaspoon ground coriander

½ teaspoon ground cumin

Salt and pepper to taste

2 carrots, grated

2 russet potatoes, peeled and
cubed

½ cup water

1 can (19 ounces) garbanzo
beans, drained and rinsed

1 apple, peeled, cored, and
chopped

1. In a skillet, brown the pork in olive oil over medium heat for 5 minutes. Add the garlic, onion, and ginger and cook for 2 minutes. Stir in the flour, curry powder, coriander, cumin, salt, and pepper. Add the carrots, potato, and water and bring to a boil.

2. Reduce the heat to low, cover, and cook for 10 minutes, adding the ½ cup water if the mixture begins to dry out. Add the garbanzo beans and apple, cover, and cook over medium heat until the vegetables are cooked through, about 10 minutes longer. Serve immediately.

Ham Pinwheels with Ricotta and Almonds

These can be rolled up a day in advance—wrap tightly with plastic wrap and refrigerate. Insert the toothpicks and cut just before serving.

SERVES 4

½ cup ricotta cheese

¼ cup chopped parsley

½ teaspoon seasoned salt

Freshly cracked black pepper

½ pound deli ham, thinly sliced

¼ cup slivered almonds

1. Place the ricotta, half of the parsley, the seasoned salt, and pepper in a bowl and mix until just blended.

2. Place a ham slice on a work surface. Spoon the cheese filling in a line along one side of the slice, about 1 inch from the side nearest to you. Sprinkle with the slivered almonds and lightly press the nuts into the cheese mixture. Starting from the side nearest to you, roll the ham over the filling to form a cylinder. Insert the toothpicks at ½-inch intervals.

3. Just before serving, use a serrated knife to cut through the roll at the midpoint between each toothpick. Arrange the pinwheels on a platter and garnish with the remaining chopped parsley.

Pork Medallions with Jalapeño Mustard

Adjust the amount of jalapeños in this recipe to control the heat, and wear rubber gloves while working with them.

SERVES 2

2 tablespoons Dijon mustard

½ tablespoon honey

1 teaspoon minced garlic

1 tablespoon fresh-squeezed lemon juice

1 tablespoon finely minced jalapeño pepper, seeded (if desired)

Garlic salt, to taste

1 (¾-pound) pork tenderloin, trimmed of excess fat

Salt, to taste

Freshly cracked black pepper

3 tablespoons all-purpose flour

3–5 tablespoons olive oil

1. Combine the Dijon, honey, garlic, lemon juice, jalapeño, and garlic salt in a small non-reactive bowl and mix to combine.

2. Cut the pork tenderloin into 1-inch-thick slices and lightly season with salt and pepper. Place the flour in a shallow bowl. Dredge the pork medallions in the flour, shaking off excess.

3. Heat 3 tablespoons of the oil in a medium-sized nonstick skillet over medium-high heat. Add the pork medallions and cook until both sides are golden brown, about 6 to 7 minutes per side. Add more oil if needed.

4. Add the jalapeño glaze to the pork and stir to coat the medallions. Cook until the pork is firm to the touch and no pink shows in the center, about 2 to 3 minutes. Remove the pan from heat, tent with tinfoil, and let rest for 4 to 5 minutes. Stir to blend the juices, and adjust seasoning to taste. Serve hot.

Chipotle and Pork Tenderloin Medallions

Canned chipotles (dried, smoked jalapeños) are
available in the ethnic section of most major grocers.

SERVES 4

1 (1¼-pound) pork tenderloin,
trimmed of excess fat

Kosher salt, to taste

1 tablespoon minced garlic

2 cups sliced red onions

2 tablespoons olive oil

⅓ cup chipotles in adobo sauce

Hot Peppers

The Scotch bonnet chili is a
small irregular-shaped pepper
that ranges in color from yellow
to orange to deep red. It is one
of the hottest chilies available
and should be used sparingly in
cooking.

1. Preheat oven to 375°.

2. Cut the tenderloin into 8 equal-sized
medallions and gently pat flat with the palm
of your hand. Season with salt and place in
a medium-sized nonreactive bowl. Add the
garlic, 1 cup of the onions, and the oil. Toss
to combine.

3. Cut the chipotles into a fine dice (it is best
to wear gloves when working with hot peppers). Add to the pork and toss to mix.

4. Transfer the pork medallions and
marinade to the rimmed baking sheet of
a shallow broiler pan. Slip the marinated
onion slices under the pork. Bake for 18 to
20 minutes, or until the pork is cooked
through. (Do not overcook; the pork should
be juicy and moist.) Serve with the remaining
1 cup onions on top.

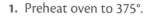

tip

Island Grilled Pork Patties

Make sure you don't overcook the pork—it will get dry and chewy.
Top with your favorite salsa or chutney to finish.

SERVES 4

1 pound lean ground pork

1 tablespoon lime zest

1 teaspoon jerk seasoning

½ teaspoon ground allspice

½ teaspoon cayenne pepper

¼ teaspoon garlic salt

2 tablespoons chopped fresh cilantro

1. Clean and oil grill rack and place it about 4 inches from the heat source. Preheat grill to medium-high. Lightly mix together all the ingredients and form into 4 patties, each about 4 ounces. Grill for 7 to 9 minutes per side, turning once, until cooked throughout. Transfer the burgers to a plate and tent with foil to keep warm. Let rest for 1 to 2 minutes to allow the juices to reabsorb. Serve hot.

Beef Entrées

continued

continued

Greek Tenderloin Steak

Beef tenderloins are also called filet mignon. This method of preparing steak can be varied with different cheeses. Serve with a green salad and corn on the cob.

SERVES 6

6 4-ounce beef tenderloin steaks

½ cup balsamic and oil vinaigrette

1 sweet red onion, chopped

2 cloves garlic, minced

1 tablespoon olive oil

¾ cup crumbled feta cheese with herbs

1. Prepare and preheat grill. Place steaks in baking pan and pour vinaigrette over. Let stand at room temperature for 10 minutes.

2. Meanwhile, in heavy saucepan, cook onion and garlic in olive oil over medium heat until tender and just beginning to brown around the edges, about 6 to 8 minutes. Remove from heat and set aside.

3. Drain steaks and place on grill; cook, covered, 4 to 6 inches from medium heat for 7 minutes. Turn, cover, and cook for 4 to 8 minutes, until desired doneness. Uncover grill and top each steak with some of the feta cheese. Cover grill and cook for 1 minute, until cheese melts. Place steaks on serving plate and top with onion mixture.

Easy Steak Doneness Tests

Put your hand palm up, and touch your thumb and index finger together. Feel the pad at the base of your thumb; that's what rare steaks feel like. Touch your thumb and middle finger together; the pad will feel like a medium-rare steak. Ring finger and thumb is medium, and thumb and pinky feels like a well-done steak.

tip

Beef Stir-Fry

Serve this delicious stir-fry with some hot cooked rice, salad, and a light dessert.

SERVES 4

1 pound sirloin steak

2 tablespoons stir-fry sauce

2 tablespoons oil

1 onion, chopped

1½ cups sugar snap peas

1 red bell pepper, thinly sliced

½ cup stir-fry sauce

1. Thinly slice the steak across the grain. Place in medium bowl and toss with 2 tablespoons stir-fry sauce. Set aside.

2. Heat oil in large skillet or wok over medium-high heat. Add onion; stir-fry for 3 to 4 minutes until crisp-tender. Add peas and bell pepper; stir-fry for 2 to 3 minutes. Add beef; stir-fry for 3 to 4 minutes, until browned. Add stir-fry sauce and bring to a simmer; simmer for 3 to 4 minutes, until blended. Serve over hot cooked rice.

Stir-fry Variations

Once you've learned a stir-fry recipe, you can vary it with many different cuts of meat and lots of vegetables. Just be sure that the veggies are cut to about the same size so they cook in the same amount of time. And experiment with different bottled stir-fry sauces you'll find in the Asian aisle of your supermarket.

tip

Quick Beef and Vegetable Stew

Pre-cooked meats in gravy are a fabulous new product you can find in the meat aisle of your supermarket. You get the rich taste of a slow cooked dinner with almost no work!

SERVES 4

2 tablespoons vegetable oil

1 onion, chopped

2 cloves garlic, minced

1 16-ounce package cooked sirloin tips in gravy

1 10-ounce can beef broth

1½ cups water

1 16-ounce package frozen mixed vegetables

½ teaspoon dried marjoram leaves

⅛ teaspoon pepper

In large saucepan, heat vegetable oil over medium heat. Add onion and garlic; cook and stir for 3 to 4 minutes, until crisp-tender. Stir in sirloin tips and gravy along with beef broth and water. Bring to a simmer over medium heat. Add frozen vegetables, marjoram, and pepper and bring back to a simmer. Simmer for 5 to 7 minutes, until vegetables are hot and stew is slightly thickened. Serve immediately.

Spicy Cube Steaks

This comforting, old-fashioned recipe is delicious served with refrigerated mashed potatoes heated with some sour cream and Parmesan cheese.

SERVES 4

4 cube steaks

3 tablespoons flour

1 tablespoon chili powder

1 teaspoon salt

2 tablespoons olive oil

1 14-ounce can diced tomatoes with green chilies

1 10-ounce can condensed nacho cheese soup

1 cup sliced mushrooms

1. Place cube steaks on waxed paper. In small bowl, combine flour, chili powder, and salt and mix well. Sprinkle half of flour mixture over the steaks and pound into steaks using a rolling pin or the flat side of a meat mallet. Turn steaks, sprinkle with remaining flour mixture, and pound again.

2. Heat olive oil in large saucepan over medium-high heat. Add steaks; sauté for 4 minutes on first side, then turn and sauté for 2 minutes. Remove steaks from saucepan. Pour tomatoes and soup into pan; cook and stir until simmering, scraping up browned bits. Add steaks back to pan along with mushrooms; simmer for 15 to 20 minutes, until tender.

Cube steaks

Cube steaks are typically round steaks that have been run through a machine that pierces the steak all over to break up connective tissue so the meat is more tender. You can pound your own round steaks using the pointed side of a meat mallet.

tip

212

Grilled Steak Kabobs

The combination of barbecue sauce and cola beverage adds nice spice and flavor to these easy grilled kabobs. Serve with hot cooked rice, a green salad, and some breadsticks.

SERVES 4

1 pound sirloin steak

¾ cup barbecue sauce

2 tablespoons cola beverage

¼ teaspoon garlic pepper

8 ounces cremini mushrooms

2 red bell peppers, cut into strips

1. Cut steak into 1-inch cubes and combine with barbecue sauce, cola beverage, and garlic pepper in a medium bowl. Massage the marinade into the meat with your hands; let stand for 10 minutes.

2. Meanwhile, prepare vegetables and prepare and preheat grill. Thread steak cubes, mushrooms, and bell peppers onto metal skewers and place on grill over medium coals. Grill, covered, brushing frequently with remaining marinade, for 7 to 10 minutes, turning frequently, until steak is desired doneness. Discard any remaining marinade.

Grill Temperatures

Check the temperature of the coals by carefully holding your hand about 6 inches above the coals and counting how many seconds you can hold your hand steady before it gets too hot. If you can hold your hand for 5 seconds, the coals are low; 4 seconds, medium; 3 seconds, medium-high; and 2 seconds, high.

tip

Taco Salad

You can use vegetarian chili in place of the beef mixture and refried bean mixture. Top the salad with chopped tomato and chunky salsa, sour cream, or more tortilla chips.

SERVES 4

1 cup sliced cooked beef

1 cup refried beans

1 10-ounce bag mixed salad greens

2 cups blue corn tortilla chips

2 cups shredded Colby cheese

1. In large saucepan, combine beef and refried bean mixture and stir over medium heat until hot.

2. Meanwhile, place salad greens on plates and top with tortilla chips. When beef mixture is hot, spoon over tortilla chips and top with shredded cheese. Serve immediately.

Tortilla Chips

You can make your own tortilla chips. Choose flavored or plain corn or flour tortillas and cut them into wedges using a pizza cutter. Heat 2 cups oil in large pan over medium-high heat and fry tortilla wedges until crisp. Drain on paper towels, sprinkle with salt and seasonings, and serve.

tip

Pesto Steaks

*Pairing pesto and steak might seem a little strange
but it is a very refreshing meal!*

SERVES 4

4 tenderloin steaks

1 teaspoon salt

⅛ teaspoon white pepper

1 cup basil pesto, divided

⅓ cup blue cheese

½ cup fresh basil leaves

1. Prepare and heat grill. Place steaks on a platter; sprinkle both sides with salt and pepper. Using a very sharp knife, cut into the side of each steak, creating a pocket. Be careful not to cut through to the other side. Fill each pocket with about 2 tablespoons pesto.

2. Grill steaks, covered, over medium coals for 5 minutes. Turn steaks, cover again, and cook for 4 minutes. Top each steak with 2 tablespoons of pesto and sprinkle blue cheese on top of the pesto. Cover and grill for 2 to 5 minutes, until desired doneness. Meanwhile, roll basil leaves into a round shape and cut into thin strips, creating a chiffonade. Place steaks on serving platter and sprinkle with basil chiffonade. Let stand 5 minutes, then serve.

Tenderloin Steaks

The tenderloin of beef, or filet mignon, is the most expensive cut of beef available, but it is also economical because there is no waste. The steaks do not need to be trimmed; most of the fat is intramuscular and not visible, but it creates great flavor.

tip

Ginger Meatball Stir-Fry

Serve this excellent quick stir-fry over hot cooked rice,
with a fruit salad on the side. The only work you have to perform
is chopping onions and garlic, then cook for a few minutes.

SERVES 6

1 16-ounce package frozen meatballs

3 tablespoons oil

1 onion, chopped

2 cloves garlic, minced

2 9-ounce boxes frozen Asian vegetables in sesame-ginger sauce

½ cup beef broth

1. Place meatballs in a 12×8" microwave-safe dish and heat on high power for 4 minutes. Rearrange meatballs and heat on high power for 2 minutes longer. Set aside.

2. In heavy skillet or wok, heat oil over high heat. Add onion and garlic; stir-fry for 4 to 5 minutes, until onion is crisp-tender. Add frozen vegetables in sauce and beef broth and bring to a boil over high heat. Cover, reduce heat, and simmer for 5 minutes.

3. Uncover pan and add meatballs. Stir-fry for 3 to 5 minutes longer, until vegetables and meatballs are hot and sauce is slightly thickened. Serve immediately.

Cooking Rice

To cook rice, combine 1 cup long-grain, converted, or Tex-mati rice in a heavy saucepan with 2 cups water or broth and a pinch of salt. Bring to a boil, reduce heat to low, cover, and simmer for 15 to 20 minutes, until liquid is absorbed. Remove from heat and let stand for a few minutes, then fluff with fork and serve. *tip*

Almost Instant Shepherd's Pie

Shepherd's Pie is an old-fashioned recipe that's a great way to use up leftover mashed potatoes. The premade refrigerated type also works very well.

SERVES 6

1 20-ounce package cooked ground beef in taco sauce

1 16-ounce package frozen broccoli, cauliflower, and carrots

¼ cup water

2 9-ounce packages refrigerated garlic mashed potatoes

1 cup sour cream

½ cup grated Parmesan cheese

1. Preheat oven to 400°F. Place ground beef and sauce in a heavy saucepan and heat over medium heat for 5 to 7 minutes, until hot, stirring occasionally.

2. Meanwhile, place frozen vegetables in 2-quart casserole and sprinkle with ¼ cup water. Cover and microwave on high for 5 minutes, stirring once during cooking time; drain well. Then place potatoes in microwave-safe bowl and heat on high for 5 minutes. Remove from microwave, stir, and add ½ cup sour cream; let stand. Add drained vegetables to beef mixture and simmer for 2 to 4 minutes longer.

3. Place hot beef mixture in 2-quart casserole dish. Stir potatoes, add Parmesan cheese, and spread over ground-beef mixture. Bake for 12 to 15 minutes, until casserole is hot and potatoes begin to brown.

Steak Quesadillas

*Serve these spicy little Tex-Mex sandwiches with more salsa,
chopped tomato, sour cream, and guacamole, along with some fresh fruit.*

SERVES 6

*2 cups sliced cooked seasoned
flank steak*

½ cup salsa

*1 4-ounce can diced green chilies,
drained*

*2 cups shredded Pepper Jack
cheese*

12 10-inch flour tortillas

1. Slice steak across the grain and combine in medium bowl with salsa and green chilies. Place six tortillas on work surface and divide steak mixture among them. Top with cheese and remaining tortillas.

2. Heat griddle or skillet over medium high heat. Cook quesadillas, pressing down with spatula and turning once, until tortillas begin to brown and cheese melts, about 4 to 7 minutes. Cut into quarters and serve immediately.

Guacamole

To make your own guacamole, combine 2 mashed avocados with ¼ cup mayonnaise, 2 tablespoons fresh lemon or lime juice, ½ teaspoon salt, dash cayenne pepper, a dash of hot sauce, and 1 chopped tomato. Blend well and put into small bowl. Press plastic wrap onto the surface and refrigerate for 2 to 4 hours before serving. *tip*

Steak and Bean Enchiladas

These hearty enchiladas are wonderful served with Spanish rice made from a mix and a crisp butter lettuce salad with a garlic ranch dressing.

SERVES 4

1 16-ounce flat iron steak

1 teaspoon salt

⅛ teaspoon cayenne pepper

1 tablespoon chili powder

1 teaspoon ground cumin

3 tablespoons oil

2 16-ounce cans pinto beans, drained

1 16-ounce can enchilada sauce

8 10-inch flour tortillas

2 cups shredded Pepper Jack cheese, divided

1. Preheat oven to 400°F. Cut the steak, against the grain, into thin strips. Sprinkle steak with salt, pepper, chili powder, and cumin. Heat a large skillet over medium high heat and add oil; heat until the oil ripples. Add steak; stir-fry for 2 to 4 minutes, until steak is desired doneness. Remove steak from pan using slotted spoon and place in large mixing bowl.

2. Add drained beans and half of enchilada sauce to steak and stir to mix. Divide mixture among the flour tortillas and top with half of the cheese. Roll up tortillas to enclose filling. Place in 3-quart casserole dish. Drizzle with remaining enchilada sauce and sprinkle with rest of the cheese. Bake for 15 to 18 minutes, until heated through.

About Flat Iron Steak

This cut of meat is actually a brand-new cut! It's the top blade steak that has been cut in half to remove some very tough connective tissue that runs through the center of the meat. This steak is inexpensive, tender, and well flavored, especially when quickly grilled or sautéed.

tip

Beef and Tortellini

This simple dish is packed full of flavor. Serve it with some grated Parmesan cheese, a green salad with lots of tomatoes, and some sautéed broccoli.

SERVES 4

1 pound ground beef

1 onion, chopped

1 16-ounce package frozen beef-filled tortellini

1 10-ounce jar four-cheese Alfredo sauce

1 9-ounce container refrigerated pesto

1. Bring a large pot of water to boil over high heat. Meanwhile, in large saucepan, cook ground beef and onion over medium heat, stirring to break up meat, for 4 to 6 minutes, until beef is browned. Drain well. Cook tortellini in boiling water according to package directions, until tender; drain well.

2. Combine beef mixture, cooked and drained tortellini, and Alfredo sauce in large saucepan and cook over medium heat for 5 minutes, stirring occasionally, until mixture is combined and sauce bubbles. Stir in pesto, cover, remove from heat, let stand for 5 minutes, and serve.

Beef Tacos

Tacos are a kid-friendly supper that's very easy, especially when you start with fully cooked ground beef in taco sauce. Serve with all the traditional toppings: guacamole, sour cream, chopped tomatoes, and more taco sauce.

SERVES 4–6

1 16-ounce package cooked ground beef in taco sauce

2 tablespoons olive oil

1 onion, chopped

1 15-ounce can seasoned refried beans

12 crisp taco shells

2 cups shredded Co-Jack cheese

1. Preheat oven to 400°F. Heat beef and sauce according to package directions. Meanwhile, heat olive oil in large skillet over medium heat. Cook onion, stirring frequently, until tender, about 5 to 6 minutes. Stir in refried beans and cook for 3 to 4 minutes longer, until hot.

2. Place taco shells on a baking sheet and heat at 400°F for 4 to 7 minutes, until crisp. Serve the ground-beef mixture along with the refried-beans mixture, the taco shells, and shredded cheese and let diners make their own tacos.

Tacos: Crisp or Soft?

You can make crisp tacos, usually with preformed shells heated in the oven, or soft tacos, made by heating tortillas until softened, then filling and folding to enclose the filling. Soft tacos are essentially the same as burritos, but they aren't fried or baked after filling. Don't worry too much about the nomenclature—just enjoy the food!

tip

Meaty Spaghetti

*Starting with fully cooked meatloaf means this spaghetti is
ready in about 20 minutes; it's also perfectly seasoned.*

SERVES 6

*1 16-ounce package cooked
meatloaf in tomato sauce*

2 tablespoons olive oil

1 onion, chopped

1 28-ounce jar pasta sauce

1 pound spaghetti pasta

1 cup grated Parmesan cheese

1. Bring a large pot of water to a boil over
high heat. Remove meatloaf from package
and crumble. In heavy saucepan, heat olive
oil over medium heat. Cook onion for 4 to
5 minutes, stirring frequently, until crisp-
tender. Add crumbled meatloaf, tomato
sauce from package, and pasta sauce. Bring
to a simmer; cook for 7 to 9 minutes, until
sauce is slightly thickened.

2. Meanwhile, add spaghetti to boiling water
and cook according to package directions,
until al dente. Drain well and place on serving
platter. Top with meat mixture and sprinkle
with Parmesan cheese. Serve immediately.

Recipe Substitutions

You could use leftover meatloaf
in this easy spaghetti recipe, or
use frozen precooked meatballs,
heated according to the package directions, along with one
8-ounce can of tomato sauce.
For more nutrition, add some
preshredded carrots to the pan
when adding the meat-
loaf and let simmer in the
sauce.

tip

Five-Ingredient Chili

Using tomato products seasoned with spices and garlic cuts down on the ingredient list. Serve the chili with sour cream, shredded cheese, and chopped tomato.

SERVES 4–6

1½ pounds ground beef

1 onion, chopped

2 tablespoons flour

1 4-ounce can chopped jalapeños, undrained

2 8-ounce cans tomato sauce with seasonings

2 14-ounce cans diced tomatoes with garlic, undrained

1 cup water

1. In large saucepan, cook ground beef and onion over medium heat, stirring frequently to break up meat, about 4 to 5 minutes. When beef is browned, drain off half of the liquid. Sprinkle flour over beef; cook and stir for 2 minutes.

2. Add remaining ingredients, bring to a simmer, and simmer for 10 to 15 minutes, until flavors are blended and liquid is thickened. Serve immediately.

Five-Way Chili

In Cincinnati, "five-way chili" means chili served with spaghetti, cheddar cheese, beans, and chopped raw onions. If you vary the additions, you'll be serving "two-way" (with spaghetti), "three-way" (spaghetti and cheese), and "four-way" (three-way plus raw onions). "One-way," of course, is plain chili.

tip

Pressure Cooker Beef Goulash

The pressure cooker makes beef tender and delicious in minutes. Serve this hearty dish over hot cooked buttered noodles with a spinach salad.

SERVES 6

2 pounds beef round steak

3 tablespoons flour

1 teaspoon salt

⅛ teaspoon pepper

1 tablespoon sweet paprika

2 tablespoons olive oil

1 onion, chopped

3 russet potatoes, chopped

½ cup water

2 8-ounce cans tomato sauce with roasted garlic

1 cup sour cream

1. Cut steak into 1-inch pieces. In small bowl, combine flour, salt, pepper, and paprika. Sprinkle over beef cubes and rub into meat. Heat olive oil in pressure cooker; add beef and brown on all sides, stirring frequently, about 3 to 5 minutes. Meanwhile, prepare the onion and potatoes.

2. Add onion and potatoes to pressure cooker along with water and tomato sauce. Lock the lid and bring up to high pressure. Cook for 12 minutes, then release pressure using quick-release method. Test to be sure potatoes are tender; if not, lock lid and cook for 2 to 3 minutes longer. Then release pressure, stir in sour cream, and serve over hot cooked noodles or mashed potatoes.

Spicy Grilled Flank Steak

Grill seasoning contains lots of spices, usually including cumin, oregano, pepper, garlic, and sugar. Use it for hamburgers as well as grilled steaks.

SERVES 4–6

3 garlic cloves

1 teaspoon salt

1 tablespoon grill seasoning

¼ teaspoon dry mustard

¼ teaspoon cayenne pepper

2 tablespoons balsamic vinegar

1½ pounds flank steak

1. Prepare and heat grill. On cutting board, mince garlic cloves, then sprinkle with salt. Using the side of the knife, mash garlic and salt together to create a paste. Place in a small bowl and add remaining ingredients except flank steak; mix well. Prick both sides of the steak with a fork and rub the marinade mixture into the steak. Let stand for 10 minutes.

2. Place steak on grill over medium coals and cover. Grill for 5 minutes, then turn steak, cover, and grill for 3 to 5 minutes longer, until medium-rare or medium. Let steak stand for 5 minutes, then slice across the grain to serve.

It's All in the Slicing

Flank steak is a lean, flavorful cut that is tender only if sliced correctly. Look at the steak: you'll see parallel lines running through it. That's called the grain of the steak. When you cut the steak, cut against, or perpendicular to, those lines and the steak will be tender and juicy.

tip

Herbed Steak

The combination of balsamic vinegar and mustard with fresh thyme seasons these tender steaks to perfection. Cook a few more and you can have leftovers tomorrow!

SERVES 6

6 6-ounce strip steaks

1 teaspoon salt

⅛ teaspoon white pepper

2 tablespoons olive oil

2 tablespoons Worcestershire sauce

2 tablespoons fresh thyme leaves

½ teaspoon dried oregano leaves

¼ cup balsamic vinegar

2 tablespoons mustard

1. Prepare and preheat grill. Place steaks in a glass baking dish; pierce all over with a fork. Sprinkle on both sides with salt and pepper. In small bowl, combine remaining ingredients and mix well. Pour over steaks, turning to coat, rubbing marinade into steaks with hands. Let stand for 10 minutes.

2. Place steaks on grill over medium coals and drizzle with any remaining marinade. Cover grill and cook for 5 minutes. Turn steaks and cook for 4 to 6 minutes longer, until desired doneness. Let stand 5 minutes, then serve.

Steak Grilling Temps

An instant-read meat thermometer is always a good utensil to have on hand. When grilling steaks, 140°F is rare, 145°F is medium-rare, 160°F is medium, and 170°F is well done. Be sure to let the steak stand for a few minutes before carving and serving to let the juices redistribute.

tip

Mini Meatloaf

Meatloaves made in muffin tins are cute, fun to make, and fun to eat.
Serve with some ketchup and frozen French fries to give your kids a treat.

SERVES 6

2 eggs

½ teaspoon dried Italian seasoning

½ teaspoon onion salt

⅛ teaspoon garlic pepper

¾ cup soft bread crumbs

¾ cup ketchup, divided

1½ pounds meatloaf mix

1 cup shredded Co-Jack cheese, divided

1. Preheat oven to 350°F. In large bowl, combine eggs, Italian seasoning, onion salt, garlic pepper, bread crumbs, and ½ cup ketchup and mix well. Add meatloaf mix and ½ cup cheese and mix gently but thoroughly to combine.

2. Press meat mixture, ⅓ cup at a time, into 12 muffin cups. Top each with a bit of ketchup and remaining cheese. Bake at 350°F for 15 to 18 minutes, until meat is thoroughly cooked. Remove from muffin tins, drain if necessary, place on serving platter, cover with foil, and let stand 5 minutes before serving.

About Meatloaf Mix

Meatloaf mix is found in the meat aisle of the supermarket. It usually consists of one-third beef, one-third pork, and one-third veal, but read the label to find out what the blend is. The veal lightens the mixture, and the pork adds a slightly different flavor and texture, because meatloaf made with all beef tends to be heavy.

tip

Quick Beef Stroganoff

Beef Stroganoff is an elegant dish that usually takes awhile to make, but using precooked meat products means the dish is ready in about 20 minutes.

SERVES 4

2 tablespoons olive oil

1 onion, chopped

1 16-ounce package fully cooked beef tips with gravy

1 16-ounce package frozen cut green beans, thawed and drained

4 cups egg noodles

1 cup sour cream

1. Bring a large pot of water to a boil. Meanwhile, heat olive oil in large saucepan over medium heat. Add onion; cook and stir for 3 to 4 minutes, until crisp-tender. Add contents of beef package along with green beans. Bring to a simmer; cook for 6 to 7 minutes, until beef and green beans are heated.

2. When water is boiling, add egg noodles. Cook according to package directions, until al dente, about 4 to 5 minutes. Meanwhile, stir sour cream into beef mixture, cover, and remove from heat. When noodles are done, drain well, place on serving platter, and spoon beef mixture over.

Menu Suggestions

Serve this rich entrée recipe with a spinach salad and some carrots. Heated bakery rolls would be a nice addition too, and for dessert, make a berry-inspired dish.

tip

Curried Beef Stir-Fry

Serve this richly seasoned curry on hot cooked rice, with mango chutney and chopped cashews, toasted coconut, and raisins or currants for condiments.

SERVES 4

1 pound strip steak

2 tablespoons oil

1 onion, sliced

3 tablespoons flour

½ teaspoon salt

1 tablespoon curry powder

⅛ teaspoon white pepper

1 12-ounce jar baby corn on the cob, drained

½ cup frozen orange juice concentrate

1 15-ounce can evaporated milk

1. Cut steak into ½-inch pieces across the grain and set aside. Heat oil in a large skillet over medium-high heat. Add onion; stir-fry for 3 to 4 minutes, until crisp-tender. Add steak; stir-fry for 3 to 4 minutes, until steak is browned. Sprinkle with flour, salt, curry powder, and pepper. Stir-fry for 2 to 3 minutes longer.

2. Stir in remaining ingredients; stir-fry over medium heat for 5 to 6 minutes, until liquid is thickened and corn is hot. Serve over hot cooked rice.

Recipe Substitutions

If you can't find baby corn on the cob, you can substitute frozen asparagus cuts, frozen stir-fry vegetables, frozen green beans, frozen sweet corn, or sliced mushrooms in this easy stir-fry. If your family likes spicy foods, increase the curry powder as much as you'd like.

tip

Albuquerque-Style Salisbury Steak

Don't compress the meat so much that the juices
don't have room to cook in the center.

SERVES 4

1½ pounds ground chuck beef

½ cup shredded pepper jack cheese

¼ cup chopped fresh cilantro

1 (4-ounce) can chopped mild green chilies

2 tablespoons minced scallions

2 teaspoons chili powder

1 teaspoon salt

2 tablespoons vegetable oil

Freshly cracked black pepper, to taste

1 cup spicy salsa

Make Steak Ahead

These steaks can be made a day ahead, wrapped in plastic wrap, and refrigerated. Allow the steaks to sit at room temperature for about 15 minutes before cooking for better control of internal temperatures.

tip

1. Combine the beef, cheese, cilantro, chilies, scallions, chili powder, and salt in a medium-sized mixing bowl. Gently combine with a fork or your hands. Compress very lightly into 4 oval patties, about ¾ inch thick. Sprinkle with pepper.

2. Heat the oil in a nonstick skillet over medium-high heat. Add the steaks and cook until brown on both sides, about 6 minutes per side for medium-rare. Transfer the steaks to a plate and tent with tinfoil to keep warm. Let rest for 4 to 5 minutes to allow the juices to reabsorb.

3. To serve, place a steak on each serving plate and add a portion of the salsa on the side. Serve hot.

Beef Tenderloin and Mushroom Stir-Fry

*Fillets may be expensive, but the convenience of no prep and
no waste makes them a great one-skillet dinner that's delicious.*

SERVES 1

1 (5-ounce) beef tenderloin fillet,
1 inch thick

Garlic salt, to taste

Freshly cracked black pepper

2 tablespoons olive oil, divided

1 teaspoon grainy mustard

4 ounces sliced mushrooms

¼ cup sherry wine

1 teaspoon chopped fresh thyme

1. Trim any visible fat from the fillet and cut into 5 even-sized chunks. Season the fillet with garlic salt and pepper. Heat 1 tablespoon of the oil in a small nonstick skillet over medium-high heat. Add the mustard and fillet pieces and stir-fry to desired temperature, about 7 minutes total for medium-rare. Transfer the meat to a plate and tent with tinfoil to keep warm.

2. Heat the remaining oil and add the mushrooms, and stir-fry for about 3 minutes. Add the sherry and simmer until reduced by half, about 3 minutes. Add the thyme, and adjust seasoning to taste. Spoon mushroom sauce over the fillet pieces and accumulated juices. Serve hot.

Grilled Pepper Steak with Gorgonzola

If you don't have a grill, broiling the steaks works just as well.
Use the convenience of the salad bar for the onions and peppers.

SERVES 1

1 (5-ounce) beef tenderloin fillet

⅛ teaspoon Kosher salt

Freshly cracked pepper

2 tablespoons olive oil

⅛ cup sliced yellow onion

¼ cup bell pepper strips, assorted colors (thin strips)

1 clove garlic, minced

¼ cup beef or chicken stock

1 tablespoon Gorgonzola crumbles

Cleaning Tip

If you use a garlic press to mince garlic, use an old toothbrush to clean the grid. The small head of the toothbrush makes it easy to get into hard-to-reach areas. Pop the toothbrush into the dishwasher to clean it.

1. Preheat grill or oven broiler to medium-high; lightly oil the grill or broiler rack. Season the fillet with salt and pepper.

2. Heat the oil in a small nonstick skillet over medium-high heat. Add the onions and pepper strips and cook for about 4 minutes, stirring frequently. Add the garlic and cook for about 30 seconds, stirring to prevent the garlic from scorching. Remove from heat and set aside.

3. Grill or broil the fillet, about 4 minutes per side for medium-rare. While the fillet is cooking, reheat the pepper mixture over medium heat and add the stock. Bring to a simmer and cook for about 2 minutes to allow the flavors to meld.

4. Transfer the steak to a warm plate and let rest for about 4 to 5 minutes before serving. To serve, ladle the pepper mixture over the steak and top with the Gorgonzola crumbles. Serve hot.

Tuscan-Style Strip Steaks

The basting sauce enhances the flavors and melds with the natural pan juices to create a simple Tuscan-inspired sauce for the steaks.

SERVES 4

5 tablespoons extra-virgin olive oil

1 tablespoon lemon juice

2 garlic cloves, minced

1 tablespoon chopped parsley

1 tablespoon chopped oregano

Seasoned salt, to taste

Ground black pepper, to taste

1 tablespoon vegetable oil

2 pounds boneless strip steak (1 to 1¼ inches thick), trimmed of visible fat and cut into 4 pieces

3 ounces Parmesan cheese, cut into thin shavings

1. In a medium-sized bowl, mix together the olive oil, lemon juice, garlic, parsley, oregano, salt, and pepper. Add the steaks and turn to coat evenly.

2. Heat the vegetable oil in a medium-sized nonstick skillet over medium-high heat. Remove the steaks from the marinade and cook until starting to brown, about 8 minutes per side. Baste with the remaining marinade during the cooking process.

3. Transfer the steaks to a plate and tent with tinfoil to keep warm. Let rest for 5 minutes to allow the juices to reabsorb. To serve, place a steak on each plate, drizzle any accumulated juices over the steaks, and garnish with Parmesan shavings.

Storing Extra Cheeses

While freezing is not recommended for storing cheeses, most can be frozen without much loss of flavor and texture. To freeze cheese, wrap individual portions airtight in a double layer of plastic wrap. Only thaw what you'll be consuming in one sitting as many defrosted cheeses develop a bitter aftertaste after a day.

tip

Pan-Seared Veal Chops with Spinach

*Use packaged baby spinach leaves, available in the
produce section of your grocer, to save a prep step.*

SERVES 4

3 tablespoons extra-virgin
olive oil

4 bone-in rib veal chops, 1 to 1¼
inches thick, trimmed of excess fat

Salt, to taste

Ground black pepper, to taste

2 teaspoons vegetable oil

1 teaspoon minced garlic

2 teaspoons fresh-squeezed
lemon juice

1 teaspoon lemon zest

2 tablespoons minced parsley

8 cups baby spinach leaves

Types of Salt

Table salt is a fine-grained refined salt with additives that allow it to flow freely. Iodized salt is table salt with added iodine. Kosher salt is an additive-free coarse-grained salt. Sea salt is available in fine grain and coarse grain and is manufactured by evaporating seawater. Rock salt is gray in color and comes in large crystals.

tip

1. Heat the olive oil in a large nonstick skillet over high heat. Season the chops with salt and pepper. Cook the chops until golden on the underside, about 7 minutes. Turn the chops and cook until golden, another 6 to 7 minutes for medium. Transfer the chops to a plate and tent with tinfoil to keep warm.

2. Add the vegetable oil to the pan and heat through, about 1 minute. Add the garlic and cook for about 30 seconds, stirring to prevent scorching. Add the lemon juice, lemon zest, and parsley; sauté for 1 minute, stirring. Add the spinach and cook until just wilted, about 2 minutes. Season with salt and pepper.

3. To serve, equally divide the spinach between 4 warmed serving plates. Top the spinach with a veal chop and drizzle any accumulated juices over the chop.

Lemon-Garlic Venison

Thaw frozen venison in your refrigerator overnight.
This recipe is much simpler than most recipes for game.

SERVES 4

1 tablespoon minced garlic

¼ cup finely chopped fresh parsley

1 teaspoon lemon zest

1 teaspoon freshly cracked pepper

2 tablespoons olive oil

¼ teaspoon salt

4 (4- to 5-ounce) venison tenderloin steaks

1. Combine the garlic, parsley, lemon zest, and pepper in a small bowl. Pat the steaks dry with a paper towel. Rub both sides of the steaks with the parsley mixture and let stand for several minutes at room temperature.

2. Heat the oil in a medium-sized nonstick skillet over medium-high heat. Sprinkle the salt over the oil. Add the steaks to the skillet and cook for 6 to 8 minutes per side for medium-rare. Transfer the steaks to a plate and tent with tinfoil to keep warm. Let the steaks rest for 5 to 6 minutes to allow the juices to reabsorb. Serve hot with any accumulated pan juices.

Quick Tip

Use a mini–food processor to mince garlic. Always mince a little (or a lot) extra and store in a ramekin under a thin layer of olive oil. Refrigerate and use as needed.

tip

Beef Tenderloin with a Trio of Mustards

*Serve with a hearty salad and simple vegetable
and you have a great couples' dinner party.*

SERVES 6

6 (6-ounce) filet mignons

¼ teaspoon kosher salt

Freshly cracked black pepper

2 tablespoons butter

1 tablespoon vegetable oil

¼ cup dry white wine

2 tablespoons Dijon mustard

2 tablespoons yellow mustard

2 tablespoons whole-grain mustard

1 cup heavy cream, at room temperature

1. Season the steaks with salt and pepper. Heat the butter and oil in a medium-sized heavy skillet over medium-high heat. Add the filets in a single layer, with space between each. Cook the steaks for 5 minutes, turn, and cook for another 5 minutes for medium-rare. Transfer the steaks to a plate and tent with tinfoil to keep warm.

2. Pour out and discard any accumulated fat in the skillet. Add the wine and bring to a simmer, stirring and scraping the bottom of the pan to loosen any browned bits. Add the mustards and stir to combine. Slowly add the cream, stirring constantly to combine. Simmer for 2 minutes, until reduced slightly. Taste and adjust seasoning as desired.

3. To serve, place each filet on a serving plate and drizzle with equal amounts of any accumulated juices. Spoon equal portions of the sauce over the filets and serve hot.

Filet Mignon with Horseradish Cream

The extra dollop of horseradish is for those who like a little more zest with their steaks. Prepare the sauce in advance to save time.

SERVES 2

¼ cup sour cream

2 tablespoons mayonnaise

1 teaspoon lemon juice

1 tablespoon bottled horseradish, slightly drained

Dash hot pepper sauce

1 teaspoon chopped parsley

Pinch seasoned salt

Freshly cracked pepper

1½ tablespoons olive oil

2 (6-ounce) filet mignons

Additional horseradish, for garnish

Cut to the Chase

Always put a damp cloth or nonskid plastic mat under your cutting board. Sliding cutting boards are one of the main causes for accidental knife cuts.

1. Mix together the sour cream, mayonnaise, lemon juice, horseradish, pepper sauce, parsley, salt, and pepper. Set aside.

2. Heat the oil in a small nonstick skillet over high heat. Season the filets with salt and pepper. Cook, searing quickly over high, until the underside is browned, about 4 to 5 minutes for medium-rare. Flip the filets and cook for another 4 to 5 minutes.

3. Transfer the filets to a plate and tent with tinfoil to keep warm. Let rest for 4 to 5 minutes to allow the juices to reabsorb.

4. To serve, place the steaks on serving plates and dollop the sauce on top. Garnish with additional horseradish, if desired.

tip

Grilled Rib-Eye Steaks with Chipotle Butter

Rib-eyes are one of the most flavorful cuts for grilled steaks.
The chipotle butter adds a nice amount of heat and flavor.

SERVES 4

4 (8-ounce) rib-eye steaks, about ¾ inch thick

2 tablespoons olive oil

Salt, to taste

Freshly cracked black pepper

¼ cup butter, softened

1 tablespoon chipotles in adobo sauce

1. Clean and oil grill rack. Preheat grill to medium-high.

2. Pat the steaks dry with paper towels and brush both sides with the oil. Season the steaks with salt and pepper. Grill the steaks over medium-high heat until grill marks are evident, about 4 minutes per side for medium-rare. Transfer the steaks to a plate and tent with tinfoil to keep warm. Let rest for 4 to 5 minutes to allow the juices to reabsorb.

3. Combine the butter and chipotles in a small food processor and blend until evenly mixed.

4. To serve, place the steaks on serving plates and drizzle with any accumulated juices. Top each steak with a dollop of the chipotle butter, and serve hot.

Beef Wellington

Beef Wellington is thought to be named after the first Duke of Wellington, Arthur Wellesley, who became a British war hero after defeating Napoleon at Waterloo in 1815. He loved a version of this tasty dish made with pâté and Madeira wine.

SERVES 4

4 filets mignon

Salt and pepper

4 tablespoons butter

1 sheet puff pastry

1 cup mushroom duxelles

2 ounces pâté de foie gras

Egg wash (egg beaten with about 2 tablespoons of water)

1. Season filets with salt and pepper and sauté them in butter until they are browned but still pink inside (medium). Chill filets.

2. Roll out and cut puff pastry into 4 squares. Spread ¼ cup duxelles in the middle of each pastry square. Place a chilled filet on top of the duxelles. Spread pâté evenly divided on top of the filets. Wrap the pastry around the filet, sealing with egg wash to make a package. Chill until ready to bake.

3. Preheat oven to 400°F. Brush Wellingtons with egg wash, and bake for 35 minutes.

Duxelles

Duxelles is a mushroom stuffing traditionally used in the classic dish Beef Wellington. Chopped mushrooms are twisted in a tea towel to squeeze out excess moisture. Then they are sautéed in butter with shallots, seasoned with parsley, salt, and pepper, and cooled. It can be added to rice pilaf, stirred in sauces, or spread on toasts.

tip

Classic Meatloaf

Meatloaf can be cooked with a variety of toppings, such as ketchup, barbecue sauce, brown sugar, mustard, onions, or beef broth. Serve it with mashed potatoes, gravy, and green beans. Leftovers can be turned into hot or cold sandwiches.

SERVES 4

⅔ pound ground beef

⅓ pound ground pork

¼ cup shredded carrots

¼ cup minced onion

½ teaspoon celery salt

1 tablespoon Dijon mustard

1 tablespoon ketchup

1 teaspoon Worcestershire sauce

1 egg

1 tablespoon chopped fresh parsley

Salt and pepper

¼ cup oatmeal

¼ cup bread crumbs

3 slices bacon

1. Preheat oven to 350°F.

2. In a bowl, using your hands, combine all ingredients except for the bacon.

3. Shape into a loaf and press into a loaf pan.

4. Line the top of the meatloaf with bacon slices.

5. Bake until meat thermometer inserted in the center of the meatloaf reads 160°F, which should be after about 1¼ hours.

Steak with Red Wine Sauce

*This sauce is a quicker version of the French classic Steak Bordelaise,
also known as Wine Merchant's Steak. It is made in the same pan
the steak was seared in to utilize the browned flavor bits left behind.*

SERVES 2

2 filet mignon steaks

1 tablespoon olive oil

2 tablespoons butter

1 shallot, minced

1 cup red wine (Bordeaux style)

1 tablespoon beef broth

1 teaspoon ketchup

1 dash Worcestershire sauce

Salt and pepper to taste

2 steak-sized croutons made out
of toasted bread rounds

1. Preheat oven to 400°F. Sear steaks on both sides in a sauté pan with oil and 1 tablespoon of the butter. Transfer steaks to a baking dish and cook them in the oven while you are making the sauce in the pan; about 8 minutes.

2. Sauté shallots in pan for a few minutes, then add wine, broth, ketchup, and Worcestershire sauce. Cook to reduce by half. Season with salt and pepper.

3. Put one crouton on each plate and top it with the steak.

4. Swirl remaining butter in the pan sauce to make it glossy, and pour sauce over steak.

Teriyaki Flank Steak

Take advantage of bottled teriyaki sauce and add different flavors to it to personalize your marinade. Corn on the cob and mashed potatoes round out the meal, and a warm apple crisp with vanilla ice cream makes a good ending.

SERVES 4

1 cup teriyaki sauce

1 flank steak

1 tablespoon honey

1 tablespoon peeled, grated fresh ginger root

½ cup sliced whole green onions

1 clove garlic, minced

½ teaspoon sesame oil

1. Combine ½ cup of the teriyaki sauce with all ingredients except the steak.

2. Marinate the steak for 1 hour (up to overnight) before grilling.

3. Grill both sides of flank steak, basting with remaining teriyaki sauce (not the marinade).

4. Serve sliced thin and on the diagonal.

Pot Roast

This recipe is a basic meat-and-potatoes version that can be expanded on with whatever flavor elements you like. Use the leftover meat for sandwiches, or turn the meat and vegetables into potpie.

SERVES 4

1 large onion

1- to 2-pound beef roast

3 carrots, peeled

2 celery stalks

2 large potatoes, peeled

1 cup beef broth

½ teaspoon salt

¼ teaspoon pepper

1 tablespoon chopped parsley

1. Preheat oven to 325°F.

2. Cut onion into large chunks and scatter them on the bottom of a roasting pan.

3. Put the meat on top of the onions.

4. Cut the carrots, celery, and potatoes into 2-inch chunks and scatter them around the meat. Pour the broth over the meat. Sprinkle the salt, pepper, and parsley over the meat and vegetables.

5. Cover and roast in the oven for 2–2½ hours.

Italian Pot Roast

Make your pot roast with tomato juice and red wine instead of beef broth and add canned diced tomatoes, oregano, and basil. Poke holes in the meat with a paring knife and insert garlic slices before cooking. Serve sliced pot roast and vegetables over creamy polenta.

tip

243

Orangey Beef and Broccoli Stir-Fry

This zesty treat is much better than takeout!

SERVES 6

3 oranges

3 tablespoons reduced-sodium soy sauce

1 tablespoon rice wine or dry sherry

1 tablespoon cornstarch

½ teaspoon sugar

3 teaspoons sesame oil

1 pound lean beef sirloin, trimmed of fat and sliced against the grain into ⅛-inch slices

2 tablespoons minced garlic

2 tablespoons minced fresh ginger

6 to 8 small dried red chiles

2 pounds broccoli, broken into small florets (6 cups)

⅓ cup water

1 red bell pepper, seeded and sliced

½ cup sliced scallion greens

1. With a small sharp knife or vegetable peeler, carefully pare wide strips of zest from one of the oranges. Cut zest into 1-inch lengths and set aside. Squeeze juice from all the oranges into a small bowl (about ¾ cup). Add soy sauce, rice wine (or sherry), cornstarch, and sugar; stir to combine and set aside.

2. In a wok or large skillet, heat 1 teaspoon of the oil over high heat until almost smoking. Add beef and stir-fry just until no longer pink on the outside, about 1 minute. Transfer to a plate lined with paper towels and set aside.

3. Add the remaining oil to the pan and heat until very hot. Add garlic, ginger, chiles, and reserved orange peel. Stir-fry until fragrant, about 30 seconds. Add broccoli and water. Cover and simmer, stirring occasionally, until water has evaporated and broccoli sizzles, about 3 minutes. Add bell peppers and stir-fry for 1 minute more.

4. Stir the reserved orange sauce and pour into the wok. Bring to a boil, stirring; cook until sauce has thickened slightly, 1 to 2 minutes. Add scallions and reserved beef, toss to coat with sauce, and heat through.

Italian Meatloaf

This version of meatloaf, layered with spinach and mashed potatoes, is a bit more elegant and complex than standard meatloaf.

SERVES 10

1 teaspoon olive oil

3 pieces basic Italian flatbread

1 yellow onion

1 shallot

4 cloves garlic

¼ cup pecans

3 sprigs fresh thyme

1½ pounds ground beef

1 egg, lightly beaten

¼ cup dried currants

1 teaspoon ground cinnamon

¼ teaspoon red pepper flakes

1½ cups garlic mashed potatoes

2 cups steamed spinach

1. Preheat oven to 375°F. Grease a loaf pan with the oil. Soak the flatbread in 2 cups water, then squeeze out liquid. Peel and chop the onion and shallot. Peel and mince the garlic. Chop the pecans. Clean the thyme and remove the leaves (discard the stems).

2. Mix together the flatbread, onions, shallot, garlic, pecans, thyme, beef, egg, currants, cinnamon, and pepper flakes.

3. Layer the smashed potatoes, spinach, and beef mixture in the prepared pan. Press firmly.

4. Bake for 45 minutes, uncovered. Drain off excess grease, and let cool slightly. Remove from loaf pan, slice, and serve.

Meat Ravioli

These can be made larger and called tortelli. Ravioli or tortelli
can be stuffed with numerous different ingredients.

SERVES 10

6 cloves fresh garlic

1 fresh shallot

¼ bunch fresh oregano

4 thick slices crusty Italian bread

¾ pound lean ground beef

¾ pound lean ground pork

¼ cup fresh-grated Asiago,
Parmesan, or Romano cheese

Fresh-cracked black pepper

1 recipe Basic Pasta (see below)

Basic Homemade Pasta

Sift together 3 cups of durum wheat flour and ⅛ of a teaspoon of iodized salt in a large mixing bowl. In another bowl, whisk 3 eggs, ¼ cup of olive oil, and ¼ cup of water. Make a well in the center of the flour and pour the egg mixture in. Mix together with your hands, or a dough hook, until the dough forms a ball. Wrap the dough in plastic wrap and refrigerate for at least an hour, and no longer than one day.

tip

1. Peel and mince the garlic and shallot. Clean and dry the oregano, and chop the leaves (discard the stems). Soak the bread (stale or toasted) in water, then squeeze out all excess water.

2. In a large mixing bowl, mix together the beef, pork, cheese, pepper, garlic, shallot, oregano, and bread.

3. Roll out the pasta dough on a floured surface into a sheet about ⅛ to ¼ inch thick. Cut into 3-inch squares.

4. Place 1 to 1½ teaspoons of the meat mixture in the center of each square. Lightly wet the edges with water using a small pastry brush or your finger. Fold over 1 corner to form a triangle, and seal together the edges.

5. Bring a large pot of water to a slow boil. Add the pasta, and cook for about 20 minutes. Drain, and serve as desired.

Chuck Steak Pot Roast

This hearty winter dish goes wonderfully with bread or some other type of starch. The combination creates quite a feast!

SERVES 10

4 yellow onions

1 pound carrots

1 bunch celery

4 tomatoes

1 bunch fresh parsley

3 sprigs fresh thyme

1 tablespoon olive oil

1 (4–pound) beef chuck roast

1 cup Cabernet Sauvignon

1 gallon beef stock

1 bay leaf

1. Preheat oven 375°F. Peel and roughly chop the onions and carrots. Clean and roughly chop the celery and tomatoes. Clean and chop the parsley and thyme leaves.

2. Heat the oil to medium-high temperature in a heavy-bottomed ovenproof pot with a tight-fitting lid (such as a Dutch oven). Sear the meat on all sides. Add the onions, carrots, celery, and sauté for 5 minutes. Add the tomatoes.

3. Pour in the wine, and reduce by ½ the volume. Add the stock. Reduce heat to medium, and bring to a simmer. Cover the pan, and place in the oven. Braise for 4 hours.

4. Add the parsley, thyme, and bay leaves. Simmer for 30 more minutes with lid ajar. Serve.

"Sweating" Onions

Sweating onions means to cook them in a small amount of oil or butter over moderate heat, covered. This cooking method breaks down the rigid cell walls and allows the juices to escape without burning, which releases the full flavor of the onions. Many Italian recipes include this step.

tip

Beef and Polenta Casserole

*Similar to lasagna, the ingredients in this dish
are spread between layers of polenta.*

SERVES 10

2 tablespoons olive oil, divided

2 Vidalia onions

1 shallot

1 bulb garlic

4 tomatoes

3 sprigs basil

1½ pounds lean ground beef

½ recipe Basic Polenta (see below)

1 bunch steamed escarole

½ cup ricotta

Black pepper (optional)

¼ cup fresh-grated Romano cheese

2 tablespoons melted unsalted butter

Basic Polenta

Heat 5 cups of water and ¼ cup of unsalted butter to a simmer over medium to high heat in a saucepan. Slowly whisk 1¼ cup cornmeal into the pan, stirring constantly. Reduce heat to low and cook for 20 minutes, stirring often. Season with salt and pepper if you wish.

tip

1. Preheat oven to 350°F. Lightly grease a large casserole dish with 1 tablespoon of the oil. Peel and dice the onions. Peel and mince the shallot and garlic. Clean and slice the tomatoes. Clean and gently chop the basil leaves.

2. Heat the remaining oil to medium temperature in a skillet. Add the onions, shallots, garlic, and beef. Sauté for 10 to 15 minutes, until the beef is browned. Drain off excess grease.

3. Spread a thin layer of the polenta in the bottom of the prepared casserole dish. Spread layers of the beef, tomatoes, escarole, ricotta, basil, and pepper on top. Top with the remaining polenta. Sprinkle with the cheese. Drizzle with the butter.

4. Bake for 20 minutes, and serve.

Vegetarian Dishes

Spicy Vegetarian Chili

You can use this chili in so many ways: from the topping for taco salad, to filled stuffed baked potatoes, and as the base for enchiladas and burritos.

SERVES 4–6

2 15-ounce cans spicy chili beans, undrained

1 14-ounce can diced tomatoes with green chilies, undrained

1 12-ounce jar tomato salsa

1 tablespoon chili powder

1 green bell pepper, chopped

1 cup water

In a heavy saucepan, combine all ingredients. Bring to a boil, then reduce heat and simmer for 15 to 20 minutes, stirring occasionally, until peppers are crisp-tender and mixture is heated and blended. Serve immediately, topped with sour cream, grated cheese, and chopped green onions, if desired.

Canned Tomatoes

There are several different types of flavored tomatoes in the market. Fire-roasted tomatoes are broiled or roasted until the skins blacken, then chopped or diced. Tomatoes can be packed with garlic, with green chilies; there are Mexican-seasoned tomatoes and Italian-seasoned tomatoes. Stock up on several kinds to add kick to your recipes.

tip

Vegetarian Curry Stir-Fry

You can increase the amount of curry powder you use, depending on your preferences. Serve this delicious curry over some hot cooked basmati rice.

SERVES 4

2 tablespoons olive oil

1 onion, sliced

2 green bell peppers, sliced

2 teaspoons curry powder

3 tablespoons flour

½ teaspoon salt

¼ teaspoon red pepper flakes

1 pound firm tofu, cubed

1 14-ounce can coconut milk

1. In heavy saucepan over medium-high heat, add olive oil. Cook onion and green bell peppers for 4 to 5 minutes, stirring frequently, until crisp-tender.

2. In small bowl, combine curry powder, flour, salt, and red pepper flakes. Sprinkle over onion mixture. Cook and stir for 3 to 4 minutes, until bubbly. Add tofu and coconut milk to the saucepan. Cook, stirring occasionally, over medium heat for 5 to 8 minutes, until sauce is thickened and tofu is hot. Serve immediately.

About Tofu

There are two different types of tofu available in the supermarket: regular and silken. Regular tofu is firmer than silken tofu. Firm or extra-firm regular tofu can be sliced or cut into cubes; it's perfect for stir-fries and grilling. Silken tofu is usually used for dressings or puddings.

tip

Cheese Omelet

Add any of your favorite vegetables to this easy omelet recipe.
Serve it with a fresh fruit salad and some croissants from the bakery.

SERVES 3–4

1 tablespoon olive oil

3 tablespoons butter

8 eggs

⅓ cup heavy cream

2 teaspoons chopped freeze-dried chives

Salt and pepper to taste

1¼ cups shredded Fontina cheese

¼ cup grated Parmesan cheese

1. Place olive oil and butter in a large non-stick skillet and heat over medium heat. Meanwhile, beat eggs, cream, chives, salt, and pepper in large bowl until foamy. Add eggs to skillet and cook over medium heat for 5 to 8 minutes, lifting edges of the omelet as it cooks to allow uncooked egg mixture to flow underneath.

2. When egg is cooked but still glossy, sprinkle cheeses on top. Cover and let stand for 2 to 3 minutes off the heat. Uncover pan and fold omelet out onto heated serving plate. Serve immediately.

Cream or Water?

Believe it or not, a battle is raging over whether to add cream, milk, or water to eggs when making an omelet or scrambled eggs. Cream makes the eggs soft and fluffy; water makes the eggs fluffy but doesn't add any fat, so the eggs are not as creamy. All three additions work well; it's your choice.

tip

Vegetable Pancakes

You can make this recipe ahead of time and refrigerate. When ready to serve, microwave the crepes at 70 percent power for 4–7 minutes until hot.

SERVES 4

8 crepes

2 tablespoons olive oil

1 cup refrigerated hash brown potatoes

1 cup frozen baby peas

½ teaspoon dried tarragon leaves

½ teaspoon salt

⅛ teaspoon pepper

1 cup sour cream, divided

1½ cups shredded Gruyère cheese

Crepes

You can find prepared crepes in the supermarket's produce section. If not, they're easy to make. Combine 1 cup milk, 2 eggs, ½ cup flour, 3 tablespoons melted butter, and ½ teaspoon salt in a blender. Blend until smooth. Heat 8" pan over medium heat. Cook ¼ cup batter, rotating the pan so it covers the bottom.

tip

1. Prepare crepes or defrost if frozen. In medium saucepan, heat olive oil over medium heat. Add potatoes and peas; cook and stir until vegetables are hot and potatoes begin to brown. Remove from heat and sprinkle with tarragon, salt, and pepper.

2. Add half of the sour cream and mix well. Fill crepes with this mixture; roll to enclose filling. Place in microwave-safe baking dish. Spread crepes with remaining sour cream and sprinkle with cheese.

3. Microwave, covered, for 3 to 6 minutes on 70 percent power, rotating once during cooking time, until cheese is melted and crepes are hot. Serve immediately.

Pesto Pasta

This simple recipe is bursting with the flavors of summer.
You must make it only when tomatoes are ripe, sweet, and tender.

SERVES 4

1 pound linguine

2 tomatoes, seeded and chopped

1 10-ounce container basil pesto

½ cup toasted pine nuts

½ cup grated Parmesan cheese

1. Bring large pot of water to a boil and cook linguine according to package directions.

2. Meanwhile, in serving bowl, place tomatoes and pesto. When linguine is cooked al dente, drain well and add to serving bowl. Toss gently to coat pasta with sauce. Sprinkle with pine nuts and cheese and serve.

Tomatoes and Pierogi

You can use canned whole tomatoes in this recipe if the fresh ones are not in top condition. Drain well and cut the tomatoes in half; add when directed in recipe.

SERVES 4

1 cup vegetable broth

½ teaspoon dried thyme leaves

1 16-ounce package frozen pierogies

2 cups frozen baby peas

3 tomatoes, cut into wedges

In heavy saucepan, combine vegetable broth and thyme. Bring to a boil over high heat. Add pierogies, bring to a simmer, lower heat to medium, and cover. Simmer for 5 to 7 minutes, until pierogies are almost hot. Add baby peas and tomatoes, cover, bring to a simmer, and cook for 3 to 5 minutes longer, or until pierogies are heated through and vegetables are hot. Serve immediately.

Pierogies

Pierogies are large pasta half rounds that are stuffed with mashed potatoes and seasonings, usually onion and cheese. They are a Polish or Hungarian specialty that are sold individually frozen. They cook in only a few minutes and can be dressed with any pasta sauce.

tip

Broccoli Frittata

A frittata is an open-faced omelet that is usually finished under the broiler. Serve it with some orange juice, whole wheat toast, and grapefruit halves. Who doesn't love breakfast for dinner?

SERVES 4

2 tablespoons olive oil

1 onion, finely chopped

1½ cups frozen broccoli florets, thawed

6 eggs, beaten

⅓ cup whole milk

½ teaspoon garlic salt

⅛ teaspoon white pepper

Dash red pepper flakes

1 cup shredded Gouda cheese

1. Preheat broiler. In large ovenproof skillet, heat olive oil over medium heat. Add onion; cook and stir for 3 to 4 minutes, until crisp-tender.

2. Meanwhile, drain broccoli thoroughly and press between paper towels to remove more liquid. Add broccoli to skillet; cook and stir for 2 to 3 minutes, until hot. In large bowl, beat eggs with milk, garlic salt, white pepper, and red pepper flakes to taste. Pour into skillet.

3. Cook over medium heat, covered, for 4 to 5 minutes. Remove cover and run spatula under eggs to loosen; cook until edges are puffed and center is almost set. Sprinkle with cheese. Place skillet under broiler and broil for 2 to 4 minutes, until eggs are set and cheese is melted.

Flavored Salt and Pepper

There are quite a few flavored salts and peppers that add great flavor with no extra work. Garlic salt, onion salt, seasoned salt, celery salt, and lemon-garlic salt are popular flavors. Lemon pepper, garlic pepper, and seasoned pepper are also good items to keep on hand in your pantry.

tip

Veggie Burritos

Burritos are made from flour tortillas rolled around a spicy seasoned filling. Serve plain, or place in a baking pan, cover with enchilada sauce, and bake until bubbly.

SERVES 4

2 tablespoons olive oil

1 onion, chopped

½ teaspoon crushed red pepper flakes

2 cups frozen broccoli and cauliflower combo, thawed

1 15-ounce can black beans, rinsed and drained

1½ cups shredded Pepper Jack cheese

4 10-inch flour tortillas

1. Heat large skillet over medium heat. Add olive oil and onion; cook and stir for 3 to 4 minutes, until crisp-tender. Sprinkle with red pepper flakes; cook and stir for a minute. Drain the vegetable combo well, then add to the skillet; cook and stir for 3 to 5 minutes, until hot. Stir in black beans, cover, and let simmer for 3 to 4 minutes.

2. Meanwhile, warm tortillas by layering in microwave-safe paper towels and microwaving on high for 1 to 2 minutes. Spread tortillas on work surface, divide vegetable mixture among them, sprinkle with cheese, and roll up, folding in sides. Serve immediately.

Frozen Vegetable Combos

Browse through your grocer's freezer aisle and you'll find almost endless combinations of frozen vegetables to add nutrition to your recipes in just one step. The combos range from broccoli, cauliflower, and carrots to baby corn, red peppers, and peas. They'll keep for a year in your freezer, so stock up!

tip

Mushroom Risotto

Risotto is a creamy, rich dish of short-grain rice and vegetables. Cooking constantly while stirring releases starch from the rice, which makes the mixture thick.

SERVES 4–6

3 tablespoons olive oil

1½ cups assorted fresh mushrooms, sliced

½ teaspoon dried thyme leaves

1 cup Arborio rice

4 cups vegetable stock

1 cup grated Parmesan cheese

2 tablespoons butter

1. Place olive oil in large saucepan over medium heat. When hot, add the mushrooms and thyme. Cook and stir until mushrooms give up their liquid and the liquid evaporates, about 6 to 8 minutes. Then stir in rice; cook and stir for 3 to 4 minutes, until rice is opaque.

2. Meanwhile, heat vegetable stock in another saucepan; keep over low heat while making risotto. Add the stock to the rice mixture about one cup at a time, stirring until the liquid is absorbed.

3. When all the stock is added and rice is tender, remove from the heat, stir in cheese and butter, cover, and let stand for 5 minutes. Stir and serve immediately.

Fresh Mushrooms

The variety of fresh mushrooms is staggering. In the regular grocery store, you can find portobello, cremini, button, chanterelle, shiitake, and porcini mushrooms. Use a combination for a rich, deep, earthy flavor in just about any recipe. Just brush them with a damp towel to clean, then slice and cook.

tip

Potato Curry

This rich dish uses refrigerated prepared potatoes to save time.
Serve it with a fruit salad and some whole wheat breadsticks.

SERVES 6–8

1 15-ounce package refrigerated
hash brown potatoes

3 tablespoons olive oil

1 onion, chopped

3 cloves garlic, minced

1–2 tablespoons curry powder

1 teaspoon salt

⅛ teaspoon red pepper flakes

2 cups frozen baby peas

1 cup sour cream

1. Drain potatoes well, if necessary. Spread on paper towels to dry. Meanwhile, in large skillet, heat olive oil over medium heat. Add onion and garlic; cook and stir for 3 to 4 minutes, until crisp-tender. Sprinkle curry powder, salt, and red pepper flakes into skillet; cook and stir for 1 minute longer.

2. Add potatoes to skillet; cook and stir for 8 to 10 minutes, until potatoes are hot and tender and browning around the edges. Stir in peas and cook for 2 to 3 minutes longer.

3. Remove from heat and stir in sour cream. Cover and let stand for 3 minutes, then serve immediately.

Artichoke Stir-Fry

Be sure to purchase artichoke hearts that have been packed in water, not marinated. Serve this dish over hot cooked couscous with snap peas.

SERVES 4

1 14-ounce can artichoke hearts

3 tablespoons olive oil

2 cups cremini mushrooms, sliced

3 cloves garlic, minced

½ teaspoon salt

⅛ teaspoon pepper

½ teaspoon dried thyme leaves

1 15-ounce can cannellini beans, rinsed and drained

¼ cup reserved artichoke liquid

¼ cup grated Romano cheese

1. Drain artichoke hearts, reserving ¼ cup liquid; cut artichoke hearts in thirds and set aside. In large skillet, heat olive oil over medium heat. Add mushrooms; cook and stir for 4 to 5 minutes, until tender. Sprinkle with garlic, salt, pepper, and thyme leaves; cook and stir for 1 minute longer.

2. Add drained artichoke hearts and cannellini beans along with reserved artichoke liquid. Cook and stir for 4 to 5 minutes, until ingredients are hot. Sprinkle with Romano cheese, cover pan, remove from heat, and let stand for 4 minutes. Stir and serve immediately.

Complete Proteins

When planning vegetarian menus, it's important to consider complete proteins. Your body needs complete proteins to heal injuries and keep your body healthy. Beans and grains are a common combination that provides these proteins. You don't need to fulfill all the requirements in one day; balancing over a two-day period is just fine.

tip

Tortellini in Wine Sauce

This elegant recipe is perfect for a spur of the moment dinner party. You can keep all of these ingredients on hand and dinner will be on the table in under 15 minutes.

SERVES 4

1 14-ounce package frozen cheese tortellini

2 tablespoons olive oil

3 cloves garlic, minced

½ cup white wine or vegetable broth

2 cups frozen baby peas

¼ teaspoon onion salt

¼ cup chopped flat-leaf parsley

1. Bring a large pot of water to a boil and cook tortellini as directed on package. Meanwhile, in a large saucepan, heat olive oil over medium heat. Add garlic; cook and stir for 2 minutes, until garlic just begins to turn golden. Add wine, peas, and salt and bring to a simmer.

2. Drain tortellini and add to saucepan with wine. Cook over low heat for 4 to 5 minutes, until mixture is hot and slightly thickened. Add parsley, stir, and serve.

Pasta with Spinach Pesto

*Adding spinach to prepared pesto turns the color a bright green
and adds flavor and nutrition, in addition to lowering the fat content.*

SERVES 8

½ cup frozen cut spinach

¾ cup grated Parmesan cheese,
divided

1 10-ounce container prepared
basil pesto

2 tablespoons lemon juice

1 16-ounce package campanelle
or farfalle pasta

1. Thaw spinach by running under hot water; drain well and squeeze with your hands to drain thoroughly. Combine in food processor or blender with ¼ cup Parmesan cheese, pesto, and lemon juice. Process or blend until mixture is smooth.

2. Meanwhile, cook pasta as directed on package until al dente. Drain well, reserving ½ cup pasta cooking water. Return pasta to pan and add pesto mixture and ¼ cup pasta cooking water. Toss gently to coat, adding more pasta cooking water if needed to make a smooth sauce. Serve with remaining ½ cup Parmesan cheese.

Pasta Shapes

There are thousands of different pasta shapes on the market. Campanelle, which means "bellflowers," is a crimped and ruffled pasta that holds onto thick sauces. Farfalle, or butterfly-shaped pasta, is a good substitute, as is penne rigate or mostaccioli. Browse through the pasta aisle in your supermarket for more ideas.

tip

Linguine with Tomato Sauce

The combination of basil, tomatoes, and Brie cheese with hot pasta is simply sensational. This recipe can only be made when tomatoes are in season.

SERVES 4–6

5 large beefsteak tomatoes

⅓ cup olive oil

1 12-ounce box linguine pasta

½ teaspoon salt

¼ cup chopped fresh basil

1 6-ounce wedge Brie cheese

1. Cut tomatoes in half and squeeze out seeds. Coarsely chop tomatoes and combine in large bowl with olive oil.

2. Bring a large pot of water to a boil and cook linguine pasta as directed on package. Meanwhile, add salt and basil to tomatoes and toss gently. Cut Brie into small cubes and add to tomatoes.

3. Drain pasta and immediately add to tomato mixture. Toss, using tongs, until mixed. Serve immediately.

Soft Cheeses

Soft cheeses include Brie, Camembert, and Reblochon. These cheeses have a tangy flavor and very soft texture, making them difficult to work with. When you need to slice or grate these cheeses, place them in the freezer for about 15 minutes. The cheese will harden, making it easier to handle.

tip

Linguine with Peas

This recipe is so simple, yet packed full of flavor. You can make it with
spaghetti or fettuccine as well; just make sure to serve it as soon as it's cooked.

SERVES 4–6

1 pound linguine pasta

¼ cup olive oil

1 onion, chopped

3 cups frozen baby peas

½ cup toasted pine nuts

1 cup cubed Gouda cheese

1. Bring a large pot of salted water to a
boil and cook pasta according to package
directions.

2. Meanwhile, heat olive oil in a heavy saucepan over medium heat and add onion. Cook
and stir for 5 to 7 minutes, until onions are
tender. Add peas; cook and stir for 2 to
4 minutes longer, until peas are hot. Turn
off heat and add pine nuts and Gouda
cheese; cover and let stand while you drain
pasta. Toss pasta with pea mixture and
serve immediately.

Cooking Pasta

Pasta must be cooked in a large
amount of salted, rapidly boiling water. The proportions are
1½ quarts of water for every 3
ounces of dried pasta. When fin-
ishing a dish by adding the pasta
to a sauce, slightly undercook
the pasta. Some of the residual
heat from the sauce will continue to cook the pasta in
the last few seconds.

tip

Black Bean Spaghetti

*A combination of salty fermented black beans and canned black beans is a delicious
topping for spaghetti. Serve it with a simple green salad and a fresh fruit salad.*

SERVES 4

1 pound spaghetti

3 tablespoons fermented black
beans

1 15-ounce can black beans

¼ cup olive oil

5 cloves garlic, minced

1. Bring a large pot of water to a boil and add
the spaghetti. Cook according to package
directions until al dente.

2. Meanwhile, place fermented black beans
in a strainer and rinse; drain on paper towels. Drain the black beans and rinse, then
drain again. Heat olive oil in large skillet over
medium heat. Add garlic; cook and stir for
3 to 4 minutes, until garlic is fragrant. Do not
let it burn.

3. When pasta is cooked, drain thoroughly
and add to skillet along with fermented
black beans and plain black beans. Toss until
heated and mixed and serve immediately.

About Fermented Black Beans

Fermented black beans are
actually black soybeans that
are marinated in a mixture of
garlic, salt, and spices. They are
very strongly flavored and add a
nice spicy kick to Asian dishes. If
using more than 1 tablespoon,
rinse them briefly to cut down
on the salt.

tip

Pasta Frittata

Leftover pasta can be made into this simple main dish. Just reheat it in boiling water for about 30 seconds, drain well, then continue with the recipe.

SERVES 4

1 handful linguine pasta

8 eggs, beaten

¼ cup heavy cream

½ teaspoon dried Italian seasoning

½ teaspoon garlic salt

⅛ teaspoon garlic pepper

2 tablespoons olive oil

1 cup chopped mushrooms

1 cup grated Cotija or Parmesan cheese

1. Heat a large stockpot filled with water until boiling. Break linguine in half and add to pot. Cook linguine until almost al dente, about 5 to 7 minutes; drain well. Meanwhile, in large bowl, beat eggs with cream, Italian seasoning, garlic salt, and garlic pepper.

2. Preheat broiler. Heat olive oil in heavy ovenproof skillet over medium heat. Add mushrooms; cook and stir for 3 to 4 minutes, until almost tender. Add egg mixture to skillet along with drained pasta; arrange in an even layer. Cook over medium heat for 4 to 7 minutes, until eggs are almost set, lifting egg mixture occasionally to let uncooked mixture flow to bottom.

3. Sprinkle frittata with cheese and place under broiler for 3 to 5 minutes, until eggs are cooked and cheese is melted and beginning to brown. Serve immediately.

Menu Ideas

A frittata is a wonderful dish for a late-night supper. Serve it with a spinach salad made with sliced red and yellow bell peppers, croutons, and a creamy Italian salad dressing, and some garlic bread.

tip

Black Bean Unstructured Lasagna

Lasagna in under 15 minutes! Serve this wonderful dish with a fresh green salad drizzled with Italian dressing, some crisp breadsticks, and ice cream for dessert.

SERVES 6–8

2 tablespoons olive oil

1 red bell pepper, chopped

1 28-ounce jar pasta sauce

½ cup water

1 24-ounce package frozen ravioli

1 15-ounce can black beans, rinsed and drained

1½ cups shredded pizza cheese

Preheat broiler. Heat olive oil in large oven-proof skillet over medium heat. Add bell pepper; cook and stir for 2 to 3 minutes, until crisp-tender. Add pasta sauce and water; bring to a boil. Add ravioli, stir, bring to a simmer, and cook for 4 to 8 minutes, until ravioli are hot. Add beans and stir. Sprinkle with cheese, place under the broiler, and broil until cheese is melted and begins to brown. Serve immediately.

Modifying Equipment

If you don't have ovenproof pans or skillets, use heavy-duty foil to protect the handles. Wrap two layers of the foil around the handles and you can use the pans under the broiler. Foil can also be used to make a large pan smaller; just use it to build walls for the size pan you want. Fill the empty space with dried beans.

tip

Baked Vegetable Casserole

*This is a truly customizable dish. You can
substitute nearly any vegetable for those listed.*

SERVES 10

1 large eggplant

3 red bell peppers

2 yellow onions

1 pound fresh spinach

3 cloves garlic

1½ cups ricotta cheese

*¼ cup fresh-grated Parmesan
cheese*

*½ cup shredded mozzarella
cheese*

1 egg

Fresh-cracked black pepper

¼ cup olive oil

Eggplant

When selecting eggplant (*mela-nazana*) in the market, look for
firm ones with a smooth texture.
Whenever a recipe calls for
eggplant slices to be breaded or
coated in flour and then fried,
you can choose to bake them on
a baking sheet instead for less
mess and much less fat.

1. Preheat a grill or broiler to medium-high
temperature. Cut the eggplant lengthwise
into ½-inch-thick slices. Cut the bell peppers in half. Peel and cut the onions into
½-inch-thick slices. Clean the spinach. Peel
and mince the garlic.

2. Combine the ricotta, ½ of the Parmesan
cheese, ½ of the mozzarella, the egg, garlic,
and pepper. Preheat oven to 350°F. Grease a
loaf pan with 1 tablespoon of the oil.

3. Toss the vegetables in the remaining oil.
Grill the vegetables for 2 minutes on each
side, until just tender (al dente).

4. In the prepared pan, alternate layers of
the vegetables and thin layers of the cheese
mixture, starting with a layer of eggplant.
Grind pepper over each layer and repeat until
all the ingredients are used. Top with the
remaining mozzarella and Parmesan, and finish with another grinding of black pepper.

5. Cover, and bake for 20 to 25 minutes, until
thoroughly heated and the cheese is melted.
Serve hot.

Wilted Kale with Dried Currants and Walnuts

*The slightly bitter taste of the kale is offset by the sweetness
of the currants. The nuts create a nice crunchy texture.*

SERVES 10

3 bunches fresh kale (or substitute any other fresh green)

2 cups balsamic vinegar

1 cup dried currants

1 cup chopped walnuts

¼ cup honey

¼ cup extra-virgin olive oil

Kosher salt

Fresh-cracked black pepper

1. Rinse the kale in cold water and pat dry.

2. Place the kale, vinegar, currants, and walnuts in a large stockpot Cover, and bring to low simmer. Cook for 5 to 10 minutes or until the greens are just wilted.

3. Immediately remove from heat and drizzle with the honey and oil. Sprinkle with salt and pepper, and serve.

Pasta, Pizza, & Risotto

continued

continued

Pasta Marinara

This is a tomato sauce that does not cook for very long, so it retains the garden-fresh flavor of the tomatoes and herbs in it.

SERVES 4

½ chopped onion

2 cloves garlic, minced

¼ cup olive oil

1 28-ounce can crushed tomatoes

¼ cup chopped fresh basil leaves

Pinch sugar

Salt and pepper to taste

1. On medium-low heat, sauté the onions and garlic in oil until soft.

2. Add tomatoes and cook for about 5 minutes.

3. Add basil, sugar, salt, and pepper and cook for 10 minutes.

4. Adjust seasoning with salt and pepper if necessary.

5. Add this marinara sauce to your favorite pasta for a simple, fresh-tasting meal.

Pasta Bolognese (Meat Sauce)

This is a tomato-based sauce with ground beef in it. The meaty flavor permeates the sauce because the meat is simmered in it. Serve this sauce on ravioli or spaghetti for a classic pasta meal.

SERVES 4

½ *large onion, chopped*

2 *cloves garlic, minced*

2 *tablespoons olive oil*

1 *pound ground beef*

1 *28-ounce can crushed tomatoes*

1 *teaspoon dried oregano*

1 *teaspoon dried basil*

1 *teaspoon salt*

½ *teaspoon pepper*

1. Sauté onions and garlic in olive oil until soft.

2. Add ground beef to the pan and cook, stirring occasionally, until brown.

3. Pour in the crushed tomatoes and bring to a simmer.

4. Stir in the herbs, salt, and pepper, and then simmer uncovered for an hour.

5. Adjust seasoning with salt and pepper.

Ravioli

Ravioli are usually square pasta pillows stuffed with various fillings. Two perennial favorites are ricotta cheese and ground beef. Other pasta shapes are circles and half-moons, and other fillings can be pumpkin, spinach, prosciutto, and even raw egg yolks.

tip

Pesto Pasta

Basil sauce is traditionally made using a mortar and pestle to pound it into a paste. This recipe uses a food processor for easier preparation, but you could also use a blender. Pesto can be used as a pasta sauce, a sandwich spread, or a stuffing enhancement.

SERVES 4

2 cloves garlic

⅓ cup pine nuts or walnuts

2 cups packed fresh basil leaves

½ cup olive oil

¼ cup grated Parmesan cheese

½ teaspoon salt

1 teaspoon plain yogurt

1. Preheat oven to 350°F. Lay the pine nuts or walnuts out in an even layer on an ungreased baking sheet pan; bake for 10 minutes. Set aside.

2. In a food processor, chop the garlic and nuts together to make a paste.

3. Add the basil and 2 tablespoons of the oil to the food processor and process with the nuts and garlic.

4. With the processor running and the pour hole on the top open, pour the rest of the oil in a thin stream into the basil mixture to form a purée.

5. Add the Parmesan cheese and salt, and process to blend.

6. Store with a teaspoon of plain yogurt stirred into the pesto to prevent it from turning black.

Creamy Tomato Sauce with Meatballs

*This **wonderful 20-minute recipe** is great for a last-minute supper or to serve for unexpected company. Use freshly grated Parmesan cheese for the best flavor.*

SERVES 6–8

1 16-ounce package frozen meatballs

1 28-ounce jar pasta sauce

1 16-ounce package linguine pasta

1 cup whipping cream

1 cup grated Parmesan cheese

1. Bring a large pot of water to a boil. Bake meatballs as directed on package until hot and tender. Meanwhile, place pasta sauce in large saucepan; heat over medium heat until it comes to a simmer. Simmer for 4 to 5 minutes.

2. Cook pasta according to pasta directions until al dente; drain well. Meanwhile, remove meatballs from oven and add to pasta sauce in saucepan along with whipping cream. Bring back to a simmer and cook over medium heat for 4 to 6 minutes, stirring occasionally. Serve over cooked and drained pasta with Parmesan cheese on the side.

About Frozen Meatballs

There are several types of frozen meatballs in your grocer's freezer section. You can find plain meatballs, beef meatballs made with wild rice, chicken meatballs, and meatballs seasoned with Italian spices. Keep a selection in your freezer and you'll have the makings for dinner in minutes.

tip

Meaty Mostaccioli

There are many varieties of jarred pasta sauce; you can find it with lots of vegetables, with meat, or just plain. Pick your favorite for this easy recipe.

SERVES 4–6

3 cups uncooked mostaccioli pasta

1 pound ground beef

1 onion, chopped

1 28-ounce jar pasta sauce

½ cup grated Parmesan cheese

1. Bring a large pot of water to boil and cook pasta according to package directions. Meanwhile, in heavy saucepan, cook ground beef with onion until beef is browned, stirring frequently to break up meat. Drain well, if necessary.

2. Add pasta sauce to ground beef mixture and bring to a simmer. When pasta is cooked al dente, drain and place on serving plate. Cover with pasta sauce mixture, sprinkle with cheese, and serve.

Pasta Alfredo

This creamy sauce is most commonly served with fettuccine noodles. Dress it up by adding sautéed shrimp or sliced, grilled chicken to the finished pasta and sauce. Green spinach fettuccine noodles are delicious with this sauce, and the colors look nice.

SERVES 4

2 *cloves garlic, minced*

4 *tablespoons butter*

2 *tablespoons olive oil*

1 *tablespoon all-purpose flour*

1 *cup milk*

½ *cup heavy cream*

1 *cup grated Parmesan cheese*

Salt and pepper to taste

1. In a 12" sauté pan garlic in butter and olive oil for 1 minute, then sprinkle with flour.

2. Stir and cook for 1 minute; then add milk and cook, stirring constantly, until sauce thickens and is bubbling.

3. Add cream and cook for a minute or two.

4. Add Parmesan cheese and stir to make a smooth creamy sauce.

5. Season sauce with salt and pepper. Serve over pasta.

Manicotti

The Italian word *manicotti* means "little sleeves" in English. In pasta it refers to a stuffed tube of cooked pasta that is covered with sauce and baked. Ricotta cheese is the usual filling.

tip

Pasta Carbonara

This recipe is very rich, and although you wouldn't want to eat it every day, it is worth the occasional indulgence. Pancetta is an Italian bacon that is cured but not smoked. Regular bacon may be substituted for the pancetta.

SERVES 4

6 *slices pancetta, chopped*

1½ *cups heavy cream*

4 *eggs*

1 *cup Parmesan cheese*

¼ *cup frozen peas*

4 *cups cooked linguini noodles*

Salt and pepper to taste

2 *tablespoons chopped fresh parsley*

1. Cook the pancetta in a sauté pan until crisp. Add cream and turn off the heat while you do the next step.

2. Separate egg whites from egg yolks by straining the white through your cupped fingers over a bowl. The bowl will catch the white, leaving the yolk in your fingers. Whisk the 4 egg yolks and Parmesan cheese together in a bowl; discard egg whites.

3. Ladle about ½ cup of the warm cream from the pan into the egg yolk mixture to temper it. This will bring the yolks to a temperature closer to the cream and bacon so the yolks will not curdle when you add them.

4. Pour the yolk mixture into the pan with the bacon and cream and stir to combine. Add peas and cook for a few minutes while stirring, then add cooked linguini and toss to coat with sauce.

5. Remove from heat, season with salt and pepper, and toss in chopped parsley.

Pasta Primavera

Primavera **means "spring" in Italian. This dish is loaded with fresh vegetables available in spring. A light cream sauce (compared to Alfredo or Carbonara) is the vehicle for the veggies. Serve it with farfalle (bow-tie-shaped pasta) for a pretty presentation.**

SERVES 4

½ cup diced onion

½ cup diced carrot

¼ cup diced red bell pepper

2 tablespoons olive oil

½ cup chicken broth

1 cup fresh asparagus spears, cut into 1" pieces

1 cup broccoli florets

½ cup heavy cream

½ cup frozen peas

½ cup grated Parmesan cheese

Salt and pepper to taste

1. In a 6-quart soup pot, sauté onions, carrots, and red bell pepper in oil until tender.

2. Add chicken broth, asparagus, and broccoli. Simmer uncovered for 5 minutes.

3. Add cream and peas; simmer for 5 minutes more.

4. Stir in Parmesan cheese and remove from heat.

5. Season with salt and pepper. Serve sauce over cooked pasta.

Cannelloni

The Italian term *cannelloni* loosely translates to "hollow canes." It refers to either a pasta sheet or crepe that is rolled into a tube around a filling of meat or cheese or any combination of meat and cheese.

tip

Pasta Putanesca

*This is a spicy and pungent tomato-based sauce made with capers,
black olives, and anchovies. Serve it over cooked pasta such as spaghetti,
linguini, or fettuccine, along with a green salad and crusty bread.*

SERVES 4

2 cloves garlic, minced

¼ cup olive oil

1 28-ounce can crushed
tomatoes

1 teaspoon dried crushed red
pepper

½ teaspoon dried oregano

1 cup oil-cured black olives,
chopped coarse

5 anchovies, chopped

Salt and pepper to taste

2 tablespoons drained capers

2 tablespoons chopped fresh
parsley

1. In a 6-quart soup pot, sauté garlic in oil for a few minutes.

2. Add tomatoes, red pepper, and oregano, and cook over medium heat for 10 minutes.

3. Add capers, black olives, and anchovies and cook for another 5 minutes.

4. Season sauce with salt (if necessary) and pepper.

5. Toss cooked pasta in the sauce, and top with chopped fresh parsley.

Pasta Aglio Olio

This is the simplest of all pasta dishes.

SERVES 4

5 cloves garlic, minced

¼ cup olive oil

½ cup homemade or panko bread crumbs

1 pound spaghetti, cooked

Salt and pepper to taste

2 tablespoons grated Parmesan cheese

2 tablespoons chopped fresh parsley

1. Sauté garlic in oil for a few minutes. Add bread crumbs and lightly brown them in the garlic oil over medium heat for about 5 minutes.

2. Toss cooked spaghetti with the garlic mixture; season with salt and pepper to taste.

3. Serve with Parmesan cheese and parsley sprinkled on top.

Bread Crumbs

The quality of bread crumbs matters, so try to make your own if possible by processing chunks of Italian or French bread in a food processor until you have breadcrumbs. Lay them out on a baking sheet pan to air dry for one hour. They may also be toasted in a preheated 350°F oven for 10–15 minutes.

tip

Gnocchi

Gnocchi are little pasta dumplings made from potatoes. They need to be cooked in boiling water for 5–10 minutes. Serve with any sauce (tomato, Alfredo, pesto) or a mixture of melted butter and dry bread crumbs.

SERVES 4

1 large potato (about 1 pound), baked

¾ cup all-purpose flour

½ teaspoon salt

1 egg, beaten

1. Scoop the cooked potato flesh out of the skin and put it through a potato ricer or food mill (or just mash it with a fork or potato masher).

2. In a bowl, lightly toss the flour and salt with the riced potatoes.

3. Make a well in the center of the potato mixture and put the egg in it. Gradually incorporate the potato mixture into the egg to make a dough that comes together. Roll dough into 1-inch-thick logs, and cut 1-inch pieces off the logs. These are your gnocchi dumplings ready to be boiled.

Tortellini

Tortellini are circles of pasta that have been topped with a meat or cheese filling, folded in half and then pinched into a ring. They resemble little belly buttons.

tip

Lasagna

This is a crowd-pleaser, full of meat and cheese. For a complete meal, serve with a green salad and garlic bread. Leftovers can be wrapped in individual portions and frozen for 1 month.

SERVES 12

5 cups tomato sauce

1 pound ground beef, browned and drained

1-pound box lasagna noodles

3 eggs

16 ounces ricotta cheese

2 cups shredded mozzarella cheese

½ cup chopped fresh parsley

½ cup grated Parmesan cheese

Salt and pepper to taste

1. Preheat oven to 350°F. Oil a lasagna (baking) pan and spread 1 cup tomato sauce on the bottom. Mix the remaining tomato sauce with the cooked ground beef. Set aside.

2. Cook the lasagna noodles in boiling water. Take them out before they are completely done —about 1 minute before package instructions suggest—so they don't overcook when you bake the lasagna. Place one layer of noodles over the sauce layer in the pan.

3. In a bowl combine the eggs, ricotta, and 1 cup mozzarella cheese until well blended. Stir in the parsley and salt and pepper to taste.

4. Spread half of the ricotta mixture over the noodles in the pan. Top the ricotta with a layer of noodles. Ladle 2 cups of the meat sauce over the noodles; top with another layer of noodles.

5. Spread the remaining ricotta mixture over the noodles. Top with the last of the noodles. Ladle the remaining meat sauce over noodles.

6. Scatter the remaining mozzarella cheese over the sauce; sprinkle it with the Parmesan cheese. Bake for 1 hour and 25 minutes.

Spaghetti and Meatballs

This is a recipe for a favorite comfort food for all ages.
The meatballs can also be used to make meatball sandwiches.

SERVES 4

4 cups tomato sauce

1 pound ground beef

1 egg

1 slice white bread, torn into pieces

¼ cup chopped onion

2 tablespoons chopped fresh parsley

2 cloves garlic, minced

¼ cup grated Parmesan cheese

1 pound spaghetti, cooked

1. In a large pot, heat the tomato sauce to a simmer while assembling the meatballs.

2. To make the meatballs: Combine ground beef in a bowl with the remaining ingredients (except for the spaghetti).

3. Shape meat mixture into 2-inch balls and drop them into the simmering sauce.

4. Simmer uncovered for 1½ hours, stirring gently from time to time.

5. Serve over cooked spaghetti.

Penne

Penne is dried tubular pasta, usually with ridges, that has been cut diagonally so each piece has pointed ends like a quill pen tip. They are perfect for baking with sauce because they hold up and don't get mushy.

tip

Pasta Dough

This is a recipe for homemade fresh pasta.
It needs only a brief 3–5 minutes of cooking time in boiling water.
A pasta machine is best for rolling this dough thin enough.

SERVES 2

½ cup semolina flour

½ cup all-purpose flour

½ teaspoon salt

1 egg, beaten

2 teaspoons water

1. Combine flours and salt in a large bowl. Using your fingers, make a well in the center.

2. Combine egg with water and pour into the well in the flour mixture. Gradually bring the flour into the egg with a fork to form the dough. When dough comes together, press it together with your hands to form a ball and transfer it to a lightly floured surface. Knead dough for 10 minutes by folding dough and pressing it down with your hands, adding flour sparingly if dough is too sticky. Wrap in plastic.

3. Let dough rest 45 minutes before rolling as thinly as possible with a pasta machine or rolling pin. If you're using a rolling pin, slice pasta thinly with a sharp knife when your dough is about 1⁄16" thick.

4. Cook pasta in salted boiling water for 3–5 minutes. You will know it is done when the pasta floats to the top of the water.

Herb Pasta Dough

This is fresh pasta dough with fresh herbs added. The flavor is subtle and delicious. Use any herb you want instead of or in addition to the rosemary in this recipe.

SERVES 2

½ cup semolina flour

½ cup all-purpose flour

½ teaspoon salt

2 teaspoons minced fresh rosemary

1 egg, beaten

2 teaspoons water

1. In a bowl, combine flours, salt, and rosemary. Using your fingers, make a well in the center of the mixture.

2. Combine egg with water and pour into the well in the flour mixture. Gradually bring the flour into the egg with a fork to form the dough. When dough comes together, press it together with your hands to form a ball and transfer it to a lightly floured surface. Knead dough for 10 minutes by folding dough and pressing it down with your hands, adding flour sparingly if dough is too sticky. Wrap in plastic.

3. Let dough rest 45 minutes before rolling as thinly as possible with a pasta machine or rolling pin. If you're using a rolling pin, slice pasta thinly with a sharp knife when your dough is about 1/16" thick.

4. Cook pasta in salted boiling water for 3–5 minutes. You will know it is done when the pasta floats to the top of the water.

Classic Pizza

Pizza is not nearly as difficult to make as you may imagine, and makes for a quick meal that will satisfy your whole family. Experiment with toppings like feta cheese, spinach, broccoli, cooked sausage, or grilled chicken.

SERVES 4

½ recipe Pizza Dough (see below)

1 tablespoon olive oil

1 10-ounce can tomato sauce

4 cups shredded mozzarella cheese

1. Preheat oven to 475°F. Lightly flour a large surface. Using a rolling pin, roll the pizza dough out into a 12" circle, flipping the dough over occasionally so that it does not stick to your surface.

2. Transfer the circle of dough onto a lightly oiled pizza pan or cookie sheet.

3. Use a ladle or spoon to spread tomato sauce over the dough. Leave a 1" border of dough for the crust.

4. Sprinkle the cheese evenly over the sauce.

5. Bake for 15 minutes, or until cheese is melted and bubbly and the crust is lightly browned.

Pizza Dough

Combine 1 package of yeast with 3 ounces of warm water, ½ teaspoon of sugar, and a ½ cup of flour. Let sit for 10 minutes. Add 2 tablespoons of olive oil, ½ cup of cool water, 1 ½ teaspoons of salt, and 1 more cup of flour and combine with a wooden spoon. Add even one more cup of flour and knead dough on a floured board for 5 minutes. Place this dough in an oiled bowl and let rise for 1 hour in a warm place. Divide the dough in half and let each ½ rise, covered, for 1 hour. Then it is ready to roll out or stretch into pizza!

tip

Hawaiian Pizza

While the idea of serving ham and pineapple on a pizza may seem odd, the combination makes for a delicious blend of flavors. Both the pineapple and the ham are slightly sweet and work well with the saltiness of the cheese.

SERVES 4

½ recipe Pizza Dough
(see page 288)

1 tablespoon olive oil

1 10-ounce can tomato sauce

3 cups shredded mozzarella cheese

4 slices ham, chopped

½ cup pineapple chunks

¼ cup sliced red onion

¼ cup diced green pepper

1. Preheat oven to 475°F. Lightly flour a large surface. Using a rolling pin, roll the pizza dough out into a 12" circle, flipping the dough over occasionally so that it does not stick to your surface.

2. Transfer the circle of dough onto a lightly oiled pizza pan or cookie sheet.

3. Use a ladle or spoon to spread tomato sauce over the dough. Leave a 1" border of dough for the crust.

4. Sprinkle the cheese evenly over the sauce.

5. Cover the cheese with the ham, pineapple, red onion and green pepper.

6. Bake for 20 minutes, or until cheese is melted and bubbly and the crust is lightly browned.

Chicago Pan Pizza

This recipe is for a style of pizza made famous by the city of Chicago. The Chicago-style deep-dish pan pizza, which originated in Chicago in the 1940s, is a pizza with a deep crust surrounding layers of sauce, cheese, and plenty of toppings.

SERVES 4

½ recipe Pizza Dough (see page 288)

¼ cup cornmeal

¼ cup olive oil

½ cup (half of one 8-ounce can) canned tomato sauce

1 10-ounce can diced tomatoes, drained

2 cups shredded mozzarella cheese

½ cup sliced pepperoni

1. Preheat oven to 425°F. Coat the bottom of a 9" cake pan with half of the olive oil and all of the cornmeal.

2. Press dough in pan to cover the bottom and go all the way up the sides, like a pie crust.

3. Cover the bottom of the dough with cheese.

4. Cover the cheese with pepperoni.

5. Put tomato sauce on the pepperoni. Cover the top with the diced tomatoes. Drizzle with the rest of the olive oil.

6. Bake for 35 minutes, or until cheese is melted and bubbly and the crust is lightly browned.

Penne with Chicken, Broccoli, and Rosemary

This simple meal combines great flavors. Rich and refreshing at the same time, this dinner is sure to be a family favorite!

SERVES 4

1 tablespoon olive oil

1 clove garlic, minced

2 shallots, minced

½ teaspoon dried rosemary, crumbled

¾ pound skinless chicken breast meat, cut into bite-sized strips

2 cups broccoli florets, separated into bite-sized pieces

½ cup reduced-sodium, fat-free chicken broth

¼ cup dry white wine

2 tablespoons fresh parsley, chopped

½ pound penne

Salt and pepper to taste

2 tablespoons grated Parmesan cheese

1. In a large, deep skillet, heat the oil over medium heat. Add garlic, shallots, and rosemary and cook for 1 minute. Add the chicken and sauté, tossing well, until lightly browned, about 3 minutes. Add the broccoli, broth, wine, and parsley. Simmer to heat through.

2. Meanwhile, cook the penne in boiling salted water until al dente. Drain.

3. Add the penne to the skillet with the chicken. Raise the heat to high and boil, stirring, until the liquid reduces enough to glaze the pasta lightly. Season with salt and pepper.

4. Transfer to a warmed platter, sprinkle with the Parmesan, and serve.

Summer Vegetable Spaghetti

What's better in the summer than an easy, quick meal?
One that uses fresh vegetables to celebrate the season!

SERVES 8

2 cups small onions, cut into eighths

2 cups peeled and chopped tomatoes

1 cup thinly sliced yellow squash

1 cup thinly sliced zucchini squash

1½ cups green beans, cut into ½-inch lengths

⅔ cup water

2 tablespoons minced fresh parsley

1 clove garlic, minced

½ teaspoon chili powder

¼ teaspoon salt

⅛ teaspoon pepper

1 can (6 ounces) tomato paste

1 pound spaghetti

½ cup grated Parmesan cheese

1. In a large saucepan, combine all the ingredients except the tomato paste, spaghetti, and cheese. Place over low heat and cook, stirring often, for 10 minutes, then stir in the tomato paste. Cover and cook gently, stirring occasionally, until the vegetables are tender, about 15 minutes.

2. Meanwhile, cook the spaghetti in boiling unsalted water until al dente. Drain and place in a large bowl. Spoon the sauce over the spaghetti and then sprinkle the Parmesan over the top. Serve immediately.

Broccoli-Pasta Toss

*Although this sounds like a game rather than a dinner, the tossed pasta
means that the dressing touches each bite—ensuring a delightful dinner!*

SERVES 6

2 cups broccoli florets

¼ pound eggless fettuccine,
broken up

1 tablespoon olive oil

3 tablespoons grated Parmesan
cheese

1 teaspoon sesame seeds, toasted

⅛ teaspoon garlic powder

Pepper to taste

1. In a large saucepan, cook the broccoli and
pasta in boiling salted water until the pasta
is al dente, stirring once or twice. Drain and
place in a bowl.

2. Add the oil to the pasta mixture and toss
well. Add the cheese, sesame seeds, garlic
powder, and pepper. Toss gently to coat.
Serve immediately.

Pasta Shells with Zucchini

*Crisp zucchini and soft pasta come together in this
great dish, perfect for any time of the year.*

SERVES 4

2 teaspoons butter

1 clove garlic, minced

4 zucchini, sliced

1 teaspoon dried rosemary,
crumbled

Salt and pepper to taste

1 pound large pasta shells

2 tablespoon chopped fresh
parsley

⅓ cup grated Parmesan cheese

1. In a large skillet or shallow saucepan, melt the butter over medium heat. Add the garlic and zucchini and cook until crisp-tender, about 5 to 7 minutes. Add the rosemary and season with salt and pepper. Raise the heat and cook for a few minutes to blend the flavors. Remove from the heat.

2. Meanwhile, cook the pasta in boiling salted water until al dente. Drain thoroughly and add to the zucchini mixture. Return the pan to the heat and toss until the shells are well coated with sauce, 2 to 3 minutes. Add the parsley and cheese and toss again. Serve at once.

California Fettuccine

Enjoy this California favorite all over the country!

SERVES 4

½ *pound eggless fettuccine*

½ *avocado, pitted, peeled, and cut into chunks*

1 can (8 ounces) marinated artichoke hearts, drained

1 large tomato, diced

2 cloves garlic, minced

1 tablespoon olive oil

2 scallions, thinly sliced

½ *pound cooked shrimp*

2 tablespoons grated Parmesan cheese

1. Cook the fettuccine in boiling salted water until al dente. Drain and place in a bowl. Add all the remaining ingredients except the Parmesan cheese and toss well.

2. Serve warm or chilled. Top with the Parmesan just before serving.

3. *Variations:* Chopped fresh basil or coriander or toasted sesame seeds are nice additions to this dish.

Italian-Style Pistachio Pasta

You don't have to be Italian to love their rich and romantic foods.

SERVES 4

1 tablespoon butter or buttery light, reduced-fat margarine

1 onion, cut into thin wedges

¼ cup finely diced green bell pepper

¼ cup finely diced yellow bell pepper

¼ cup finely diced red bell pepper

2 tablespoons minced garlic

¼ pound prosciutto, sliced ⅛ inch thick and then diced

1 cup pistachios, coarsely chopped

1½ teaspoons dried rosemary, crumbled

3 tablespoons extra-virgin olive oil

1 pound penne

1. In a skillet, melt the butter or margarine over low heat. Add the onion and sauté until nearly tender. Add all the bell peppers, the garlic, prosciutto, pistachios, rosemary, and olive oil. Continue to cook, stirring, until thoroughly heated.

2. Meanwhile, cook the penne in boiling salted water until al dente. Drain and place in a bowl. Spoon the hot sauce over the top and serve.

Pasta with Sautéed Artichokes

Artichokes aren't as hard to get at as they look! If you take a little time and get the "meat" out of them, it'll be well worth the effort!

SERVES 1

1 artichoke

1 lemon, halved

2 tablespoons olive oil

1 cup sliced mushrooms

2 tablespoons dry white wine

¼ cup thinly sliced scallions

½ teaspoon dried basil, crumbled

Salt to taste

¼ pound mostaccioli

1 tablespoon grated Parmesan cheese

Cracked pepper to taste

1. Bend back the outer leaves of the artichoke until they snap off easily near base. Edible portion of the leaf should remain on the artichoke base or heart. Snap off and discard the thick, dark leaves until central core of pale green leaves is reached. Cut off the top 2 inches of artichoke; discard. Cut off the stem; reserve. Using a paring knife, trim the dark green outer layer from the artichoke bottom and the stem. Rub all cut surfaces with a lemon half to prevent discoloration. Quarter the artichoke lengthwise. Scoop or cut out the prickly center petals and choke and discard. Rub again with a lemon half. Cut the artichoke and stem lengthwise into very thin slices.

2. In a large skillet, heat the oil over medium heat. Add the artichoke and mushrooms and sauté for 2 minutes. Add the wine, scallions, and basil; cover and simmer until the liquid has evaporated and the artichokes are tender, about 5 minutes. Season with salt.

3. Meanwhile, cook the pasta in boiling salted water until al dente. Drain and place in a bowl. Spoon the sauce over the pasta and sprinkle with Parmesan and pepper.

Savory Pastitsio

Savory for sure.

SERVES 10

1 teaspoon olive oil

1 large onion, finely chopped

1½ pounds lean ground beef or ground turkey

1 cup water

¾ cup dry white wine

1 can (6 ounces) tomato paste

½ cup bulgur

¾ teaspoon cinnamon

¾ teaspoon nutmeg

¾ teaspoon allspice

1½ teaspoons salt, plus more to taste

½ teaspoon black pepper, plus more to taste

2 cups 1% cottage cheese

2 tablespoons all-purpose flour

1 cup reduced-sodium, fat-free chicken broth, cold

1 can (12 ounces) evaporated skim milk

¾ cup plus 2 tablespoons freshly grated Parmesan cheese

1. In a large nonstick skillet, heat oil over medium heat; add onion and sauté until softened, about 5 minutes. Add ground meat, breaking it up with a wooden spoon, until no longer pink, about 5 minutes. Drain off fat.

2. Add water, wine, tomato paste, bulgur, spices, 1 teaspoon of the salt, and ½ teaspoon of the pepper. Simmer, uncovered, over low heat, stirring occasionally, until the bulgur is tender, about 20 minutes. Taste and adjust seasonings.

3. In a food processor or blender, purée cottage cheese until smooth. Set aside. In a bowl, stir together flour and ¼ cup chicken broth until smooth. In a heavy saucepan, combine evaporated skim milk and the remaining chicken broth. Heat over medium heat until scalding. Stir the flour mixture into the hot milk mixture and cook, stirring constantly, until thickened, about 2 minutes.

4. Remove from heat and whisk in puréed cottage cheese and the ½ cup of grated cheese. Season with salt and pepper. To prevent a skin from forming, place wax paper or plastic wrap over the surface and set aside.

Savory Pastitsio

(continued)

1 pound elbow macaroni

1 teaspoon olive oil

2 tablespoons chopped fresh parsley (optional)

5. In a large pot of boiling salted water, cook macaroni until al dente, 8 to 10 minutes. Drain and return to the pot. Toss with ¼ cup of the grated cheese, oil, and ½ teaspoon of the salt.

6. Preheat oven to 350°F. Spray a 9 x 13-inch baking dish with nonstick cooking spray. Spread half of the pasta mixture over the bottom of the prepared dish. Top with one third of the cream sauce. Spoon all of the meat sauce over, spreading evenly.

7. Cover with another third of the cream sauce. Top with the remaining pasta mixture and cover with the remaining cream sauce. Sprinkle with the remaining 2 tablespoons of the grated cheese. Bake for 40 to 50 minutes, or until bubbling and golden. Sprinkle with parsley, if using, and serve.

Fusilli with Chicken and Coriander Pesto

This peppery treat will wake you up and tease your senses.

SERVES 4

2 *whole chicken breasts, halved*

3 *ounces cilantro*

4 *cloves garlic, cut up*

½ *cup slivered blanched almonds*

4 *serrano chile peppers, seeded*

2 *tablespoons olive oil*

1 *cup low-fat mayonnaise*

1 *pound fusilli pasta, cooked, drained, and chilled*

1. Preheat oven to 375°F. Place the chicken breasts in a baking pan. Bake until cooked through and tender, 15 to 20 minutes. Remove from the oven and let cool. Remove and discard the skin and bones and shred the meat. Place in a bowl, cover, and chill.

2. In a food processor or blender, combine the cilantro, garlic, almonds, and chiles. Process until finely chopped. With the motor running, add the oil in a thin, steady stream, processing until the pesto is the consistency of a thick paste.

3. Place the pesto in a bowl. Whisk in the mayonnaise.

4. In a large bowl, combine the chilled pasta, shredded chicken, and the pesto. Stir to mix well. Cover and chill for 1 hour before serving.

Pasta Salad Niçoise

You can have this light, classic dish any time of year!

SERVES 4

¼ cup low-fat Italian dressing

¼ cup chopped fresh basil

2 cloves minced garlic

¼ teaspoon red pepper flakes

2 cups small shell pasta, cooked, drained, and chilled

1 can (6 ounces) water-packed albacore tuna, drained and flaked

¾ cup diced tomato

½ avocado, peeled and diced

¼ cup thinly sliced red onion

2 tablespoons chopped black olives

4 lettuce leaves

1. In a small bowl, stir together the dressing, basil, garlic, and red pepper flakes to form a dressing. In a large bowl, combine the pasta, tuna, tomato, avocado, red onion, and olives. Add dressing and toss well. Line 4 plates with the lettuce leaves. Spoon the pasta mixture on the lettuce, dividing evenly. Serve at once.

Jumbo Shells Stuffed with Cheese

Great for large families, a particularly hungry night, or a cold wintery night, these Jumbo Shells will be a huge hit for your clan.

SERVES 6

12 jumbo pasta shells

2 tablespoons grated Parmesan cheese

¼ teaspoon chili powder

1½ cups low-fat cheddar cheese, shredded

2 cloves garlic, pressed

1 tablespoon chopped fresh parsley

¼ cup low-fat sour cream

¼ cup chopped black olives

1. Cook the pasta shells in a large pot of boiling salted water until al dente. Drain into a colander and let stand for at least 10 minutes, or until completely drained. (Shells may be prepared in advance and stored in a covered container in the refrigerator.)

2. In a shallow bowl, mix together the Parmesan cheese and chili powder. Roll the pasta shells in the mixture. In a mixing bowl, combine cheddar cheese, garlic, parsley, sour cream, and olives. Mix well.

3. Stuff the shells with the cheese mixture. The shells can be eaten as they are, or you can bake them. To do the latter, preheat an oven to 400°F. Arrange the shells on a baking sheet, propping their open ends up with crumpled foil so the filling won't run out during baking. Bake until the cheese is melted, 8 to 10 minutes. Serve hot.

Linguine Stir-Fry with Asparagus and Garlic

Smooth linguine finds its perfect match with the crisp taste of asparagus and a zesty garlic bite.

SERVES 4

1 pound linguine

2 tablespoons olive oil

1 pound skinless chicken breast meat, slivered

1 pound asparagus, trimmed and cut on the diagonal into 1-inch lengths

2 red bell peppers, diced

4 cloves garlic, minced

¼ cup teriyaki sauce

1 cup reduced-sodium, fat-free chicken broth

1. Cook the linguine in boiling salted water until al dente.

2. Once the water is put on to boil, in a wok or large, deep skillet, heat 1 tablespoon of the oil over high heat. Add the chicken and stir-fry until firm and cooked through, about 4 minutes. Remove the chicken and set aside.

3. Add the remaining tablespoon oil to the pan. When it is hot, add the asparagus and bell pepper and stir-fry until crisp-tender, about 5 minutes. Add the garlic and stir-fry for 30 seconds. Stir in the teriyaki sauce and the broth.

4. As the pasta finishes cooking, return the chicken to the wok and heat through. Drain the pasta and toss with the chicken and sauce. Transfer to a warmed platter and serve at once.

Basic Italian Risotto

Riso **is the Italian word for "rice."** *Risotto* **refers more to a cooking method in which rice is first "toasted" with oil and onions and then liquid is added a little at a time.**

SERVES 10

½ bulb garlic

2 shallots

2 tablespoons olive oil

2 cups arborio rice

½ cup dry white wine (not cooking wine)

5½ cups chicken stock

¾ cups fresh-grated Parmesan cheese

Fresh-cracked black pepper

1. Peel and mince the garlic and shallots. Heat the oil in a large saucepan over medium heat. Add the garlic and shallots. Sauté for about 3 minutes, then add the rice. Stir constantly.

2. Add the wine and stir until fully absorbed. Add the stock ½ cup at a time, stirring frequently and allowing each addition to be completely absorbed before adding the next. Continue until all the stock is absorbed and the rice is tender.

3. Remove from heat and add the cheese and pepper. Stir, and serve.

The Perfect Pan

Risotto should always be cooked in a heavy saucepan with a large, flat bottom so that the flame underneath can be evenly distributed. If the heat is not evenly distributed throughout the risotto, the grains of rice will cook at different rates, leaving you with the occasional crunchy grain.

tip

Roasted Carrot Risotto

When entertaining, to save time, the carrots can be
prepared the day before and refrigerated until ready to use.

SERVES 10

1 pound fresh carrots

3 large yellow onions

4 large sprigs rosemary

3 tablespoon olive oil, divided

2 cups arborio rice

½ cup dry white wine (not cooking wine)

5½ cups vegetable stock

Fresh-cracked black pepper

1. Preheat oven to 375°F. Peel and thickly dice the carrots and onions. Clean and remove the leaves from the rosemary.

2. Toss the carrots and onions with 2 tablespoons of the oil and ½ of the rosemary. Spread out in an even layer on a baking sheet and roast for about 15 minutes. Set aside.

3. Heat the remaining oil to medium temperature in a large saucepan. Add the rice and stir for 1 minute. Add the wine and stir until fully absorbed.

4. Add the stock ½ cup at a time, stirring frequently and allowing each addition to be completely absorbed before adding the next. Continue until all the stock is absorbed and the rice is tender.

5. Remove from heat. Add the roasted carrots and the remaining rosemary, and season with pepper. Serve in a heated bowl.

Grilled Broccoli Raab and Alfredo Risotto

The classic Alfredo sauce gives this risotto a rich and creamy taste.
The bright green of the broccoli raab mounded on the creamy rice contrasts
nicely with the white sauce, making for a beautiful presentation.

SERVES 10

2 pounds broccoli raab

5 tablespoons olive oil, divided

Fresh-cracked black pepper

2 shallots

2 cloves garlic

2½ cups arborio rice

½ cup dry white wine (not cooking wine)

6 cups stock of choice

1½ cups cream

¼ cup cold unsalted butter

¼ cup shredded fontina cheese

Rice for Risotto

The best variety of rice for making risotto is arborio rice—an imported Italian rice. Other types of rice cannot absorb as much liquid or hold their shape throughout the constant stirring required when making risotto.

1. Preheat grill. Clean and dry the broccoli raab, toss in 4 tablespoons of the olive oil, and sprinkle with black pepper. Grill for 2 minutes on each side.

2. Peel and mince the shallots and garlic. Heat the remaining oil to medium temperature in a saucepan. Sauté the shallots and garlic for 5 minutes. Add the rice, and stir for 2 minutes.

3. Add the wine, and stir until completely absorbed. Add the stock ½ cup at a time, stirring frequently and allowing each addition to be completely absorbed before adding the next. Continue until all the stock is absorbed and the rice is tender.

4. Prepare the Alfredo sauce by heating the cream to medium-high temperature in small saucepan until reduced by half the volume. Add the cold butter a bit at a time, and stir to incorporate before adding more. Remove from heat and stir in the cheese.

5. To serve, mound the rice in a serving bowl, top with the broccoli raab, and drizzle with the sauce.

tip

Browned Risotto Patties

*The Italian version of "potato pancakes," these
patties are a great way to use up leftover risotto.*

SERVES 10

2 tablespoons olive oil, divided

1 large yellow onion

½ cup cold unsalted butter

2 cups arborio rice

6 cups stock of choice

¼ cup shredded fontina cheese

Fresh-cracked black pepper

1. Preheat broiler. Lightly grease a baking sheet with 1 tablespoon of the oil and finely chop the onion. Cut the butter into pats.

2. Heat the remaining oil to medium temperature in large saucepan. Sauté the onion for about 2 minutes. Add the rice, and stir for 2 minutes. Add the stock ½ cup at a time, stirring frequently and allowing each addition to be completely absorbed before adding the next. Continue until all the stock is absorbed and the rice is tender.

3. Remove from heat and stir in the cheese. Let cool, then form into ½-cup patties.

4. Place the patties on the prepared baking sheet pan, place a pat of butter on top of each patty, and brown lightly under the broiler. Serve.

Tomato and Parmesan Risotto

This dish is like baked ziti but with risotto instead of pasta.

SERVES 10

1 large yellow onion

½ bulb garlic

¼ bunch fresh basil

¼ bunch fresh oregano

¼ bunch fresh parsley

1 tablespoon olive oil

2 cups arborio rice

6 cups chicken stock

4 cups Old World Gravy
(see facing page)

½ cup fresh ricotta

½ cup shredded fresh mozzarella cheese

Fresh-cracked black pepper

1. Preheat oven to 350°F. Peel and dice the yellow onion. Peel and mince the garlic. Clean and chop the basil, oregano, and parsley leaves.

2. Heat the oil in to medium temperature in a large saucepan. Sauté the onions and garlic for 3 minutes. Add the rice, and stir for 1 minute. Add the stock ½ cup at a time, stirring frequently and allowing each addition to be fully absorbed before adding the next. Continue until all the stock is absorbed and the rice is tender.

3. Pour 2 cups Old World Gravy into a large baking dish. Spoon the risotto on top in an even layer. Place dollops of the ricotta all over the risotto, and sprinkle with the shredded mozzarella and ½ of the fresh herbs. Ladle the remaining Old World Gravy over the top. Cover with foil, and bake for 10 minutes. Uncover, and bake for 5 more minutes.

4. Sprinkle with black pepper and the remaining herbs, and serve.

Old World Gravy

Also known as Long-Cooking Tomato Sauce, this sauce is a great complement to all types of pasta dishes.

SERVES 10

3 *Vidalia onions*

1 *bulb of garlic*

6 *pounds of plum tomatoes*

1 *bunch of fresh basil*

½ *bunch of fresh oregano*

½ *bunch of fresh parsley*

1 *tablespoon olive oil*

2½ *pounds of pork spare ribs*

1 *pound of Italian sausage (casings removed)*

8 *cups stock of your choice*

1. Peel and dice the onions. Peel and mince the garlic. Clean and roughly chop the plum tomatoes. Clean and gently chop the herbs.

2. Heat the olive oil to medium-high temperature in large stockpot. Add the pork spare ribs and Italian sausage and brown for 10 minutes.

3. Add the onions and garlic. Sauté for 5 minutes, then add the tomatoes and stock. Reduce heat to low and simmer for 3 hours, uncovered, stirring occasionally.

4. Add the herbs and spices, and simmer for a minimum of 3 more hours, uncovered and stirring occasionally.

5. Adjust seasonings to taste, and serve or store as desired. Store in sealed containers and refrigerate for up to 5 days or freeze for up to 3 months.

Spicy Risotto

*This spicy risotto is great on its own, though it makes
a great accompaniment to any roast or meatloaf.*

SERVES 10

5 *Italian peppers*

2 *fresh plum tomatoes*

2 *large yellow onions*

½ *bulb fresh garlic*

4 *sprigs fresh marjoram or
oregano*

1 *tablespoon olive oil*

2 *cups arborio rice*

½ *cup pinot noir or other red
drinking wine of choice*

5½ *cups chicken stock*

1 *cup Old World Gravy
(Long-Cooking Tomato Sauce)
(see page 309)*

⅓ *cup Parmesan cheese*

Fresh-cracked black pepper

1 *tablespoon red pepper flakes*

1. Clean and finely dice the peppers and tomatoes. Peel and dice the onions. Peel and mince the garlic. Clean and gently chop the marjoram leaves.

2. Heat the oil to medium temperature in a large frying pan. Lightly sauté the peppers, onion, garlic, and rice for 2 minutes. Pour in the wine, and stir until absorbed. Add the stock ½ cup at a time, stirring frequently and allowing each addition to be completely absorbed before adding the next. Continue until all the stock is absorbed and the rice is tender.

3. Add the Old World Gravy, tomatoes, and marjoram. Remove from heat and sprinkle with cheese, red pepper flakes, and black pepper. Serve.

Seared Filet Mignon Risotto

Keeping the meat cold in the refrigerator until just ready
to broil or grill helps the meat to sear better.

SERVES 10

½ *bulb garlic*

3 *tablespoons olive oil*

Fresh-cracked black pepper

1¼ *pounds filet mignon (or other tender beef)*

2 *cups arborio rice*

½ *cup robust red wine (not cooking wine)*

5½ *cups beef stock*

¼ *cup fresh-grated Romano cheese*

2 *tablespoons cold unsalted butter*

1. Preheat grill to medium-high heat. Peel and mince the garlic. Mix together half the oil, half the garlic, and some pepper. Rub the mixture onto the meat and place in the refrigerator until ready to cook.

2. Heat the remaining oil in a large saucepan to medium-high temperature. Add the remaining garlic and the rice, and stir for 1 minute. Pour in the wine, and stir until absorbed. Stir in the stock ½ cup at a time, stirring frequently and allowing each addition to be completely incorporated before adding the next. Continue until all the stock is absorbed and the rice is tender.

3. Stir in the cheese, butter, and pepper to taste. Keep covered and warm until ready to serve.

4. Approximately 10 minutes before the risotto is done, sear the meat on the hot grill to desired doneness. Slice thinly, and fan over the rice. Serve immediately.

Stewed Veal Risotto

You can prepare the veal ahead of time and reheat when ready to serve.

SERVES 10

3 *large yellow onions*

6 *cloves fresh garlic*

2 *stalks celery*

1 *pound fresh plum tomatoes*

2 *large carrots*

2 *tablespoons olive oil*

1 *pound veal stew meat*

1 *tablespoon dried oregano*

1 *tablespoon dried thyme*

1 *bay leaf*

1 *cup hearty red wine*

6 *cups water*

2 *cups arborio rice*

5½–6 *cups beef stock*

¼ *cup fresh-grated Parmesan cheese*

¼ *cup fresh-grated Romano cheese*

Fresh-cracked black pepper

1. Peel and slice the onions and garlic. Clean and chop the celery and tomatoes. Peel and chop the carrots.

2. Heat 1 tablespoon of the oil to medium temperature in a large Dutch oven. Brown the meat, onions, garlic, celery, and carrots for about 4 minutes. Reduce heat to medium-low. Add the tomatoes, oregano, thyme, bay leaf, ½ cup of the wine, and 6 cups of the water. Cover, and simmer for 3 to 4 hours, until the veal is fork-tender.

3. Heat the remaining oil to medium temperature in a large saucepan. Add the rice, and sauté for 1 minute. Add the remaining wine, and stir until absorbed. Stir in the stock ½ cup at a time, stirring frequently and allowing each addition to be completely absorbed before adding the next. Continue until the rice is fork-tender. Before adding the last ½ cup of stock, add the veal.

4. Remove from heat. Stir in the cheeses and black pepper. Keep warm.

5. Ladle the veal into serving bowls and top with the risotto.

Braised Veal and Pepper Risotto

Although a little more complex in preparation than most dishes,
this fragrant and delicious veal and pepper mix is worth the extra
effort and makes a great dish for a cold winter weekend.

SERVES 10

Veal:

1½ pounds veal meat (keep chilled)

6 green bell peppers

3 large yellow onions

½ bulb garlic

½ pound fresh parsnips or carrots

½ bunch fresh parsley

1 tablespoon olive oil

4 cups beef stock

2 cups gravy

Risotto:

½ bunch fresh parsley

1 tablespoon olive oil

1½ cups arborio rice

4½ cups beef stock

½ cup fresh-grated Asiago cheese

Fresh-cracked black pepper

1. *To prepare the veal:* Preheat oven to 350°F. Cut the veal into 2½ inch cubes. Clean and cut the peppers into large wedges. Peel and chop the onions. Peel and mince the garlic. Peel and chop the parsnips. Clean and chop the parsley. Heat a Dutch oven (or other heavy-bottomed ovenproof pot with a lid) to medium-high temperature, then add the cold veal. Sear, until browned on all sides. Add the peppers, onions, garlic, and parsnips, and sauté for 3 to 4 minutes. Add the wine and reduce by ½ the volume. Add the stock and sauce. Bring to simmer, add the parsley, and cover. Transfer the pot to the oven and cook for 2 hours.

2. *To prepare the risotto:* Clean and mince the parsley. Heat the oil to medium temperature in a large saucepan. Add the rice, and toss in the oil for 1 minute. Add the stock ½ cup at a time, stirring frequently and allowing each addition to be completely absorbed before adding the next. Continue until all the stock is absorbed and the rice is tender. Remove from heat. Stir in the cheese and parsley. Serve in bowls with the veal mixture.

Seafood Risotto

*Chock-full of juicy shrimp, lobster, and scallops,
this dish impresses guests and family alike.*

SERVES 10

*1½ pounds cooked shrimp,
scallops, and lobster (or any
seafood combination of choice)*

2 leeks

1 bunch fresh parsley

*2 tablespoons cold unsalted
butter*

1½ tablespoons olive oil

1½ cups arborio rice

*½ cup dry white wine (not
cooking wine)*

4½ cups fish stock

½ cup fresh-grated Asiago cheese

Fresh-cracked black pepper

1. Clean, shell, and cut the seafood into bite-sized chunks. Thoroughly clean the leeks and cut into small dice, using both the white and green parts. Clean and gently chop the parsley.

2. Heat the oil to medium temperature in a large saucepan. Add the leeks, and sauté for 2 minutes. Add the rice, and stir for 1 minute.

3. Pour in the wine, and stir until fully absorbed. Add the stock ½ cup at a time, stirring frequently and allowing each addition to be completely absorbed before adding the next. Continue until all the stock is absorbed and the rice is tender.

4. Remove from heat, and stir in the seafood, cheese, and butter. Serve on a heated platter, sprinkled with the parsley and pepper.

Risotto Patties

Don't throw away your leftover risotto. This can be mixed with eggs and grated Parmesan cheese, formed into patties, and fried for a quick and tasty side dish. Risotto patties make a great accompaniment to roasted meat dishes.

tip

Seafood

Halibut Bruschetta

Bruschetta is an Italian appetizer of toasted bread slices topped with a fragrant tomato salad. In this recipe, halibut replaces the bread for an easy and elegant main dish.

SERVES 4

4 halibut fillets

3 tablespoons olive oil, divided

Salt and pepper to taste

2 cups chopped, seeded tomatoes

⅔ cup pesto sauce

½ cup grated Parmesan cheese

1. Preheat broiler. Place fillets on broiler pan and brush with half of the olive oil; sprinkle with salt and pepper. In small bowl, combine tomatoes, remaining olive oil, pesto, and Parmesan cheese; season with salt and pepper to taste.

2. Broil halibut fillets for 8 to 12 minutes or until fish flakes easily when tested with a fork. Top with tomato mixture and broil for 1 to 2 minutes longer. Serve immediately.

Other Fish Choices

You can use other mild fish fillets in this easy, nutritious, and beautiful recipe. Think about using orange roughy, tilapia, or cod. This topping would also be wonderful on salmon or swordfish fillets or steaks. Cook all of these fish just until the fish flakes when you insert a fork and twist it.

tip

Shrimp Scampi Kabobs

Lemon and garlic are the main seasonings in Shrimp Scampi.
This is an easy way to make scampi on your grill. Serve with hot cooked rice.

SERVES 6

3 lemons

¼ cup olive oil

4 cloves garlic, minced

1 teaspoon dried thyme leaves

½ teaspoon salt

⅛ teaspoon white pepper

1¼ pounds large raw shrimp, cleaned

18 large mushrooms

2 yellow squash, cut into 1-inch pieces

1. Prepare and preheat grill. Using lemon zester, remove peel from 1 of the lemons. Place in medium bowl. Squeeze juice from the peeled lemon and add to peel in bowl. Cut remaining lemons into 6 wedges each and set aside. Add oil, garlic, thyme, salt, and pepper to lemon mixture in bowl and mix well. Add shrimp and let stand for 10 minutes.

2. Drain shrimp, reserving marinade. Place shrimp, mushrooms, squash pieces, and lemon wedges alternately on twelve 8"-long metal skewers. Brush skewers with marinade, then grill 4 to 6 inches from medium-hot coals for 8 to 14 minutes, turning once, until shrimp are curled and pink and vegetables are tender. Brush skewers often with marinade. Discard any remaining marinade.

Cleaning Shrimp

If the shrimp you buy still have the shell and tail on them, you must clean them before use. Cut a shallow slit along the back; remove the shell, tail, and legs; then rinse out the dark vein running along the shrimp, using your fingers to remove it if necessary.

tip

Crab Burritos

You can make these excellent burritos with two pouches of boneless skinless salmon, 12 ounces of cooked small or medium shrimp, or 2 cups of flaked and cooked fish.

SERVES 6

2 6-ounce cans crabmeat, drained

1 cup frozen pepper and onion stir-fry mix

1 10-ounce container refrigerated four-cheese Alfredo sauce

1½ cups shredded Monterey Jack cheese

12 6-inch spinach-flavored flour tortillas

1. Preheat oven to 350°F. Drain crabmeat well, pressing with paper towel to absorb excess moisture. Place in medium bowl. Thaw pepper and onion mix in microwave on 30 percent power for 2 to 3 minutes; drain well and add to crabmeat. Stir in half of the Alfredo sauce and ½ cup Monterey Jack cheese.

2. Fill tortillas with 2 tablespoons crabmeat mixture and roll up. Place in 13×9" glass baking dish. Top each filled burrito with some Alfredo sauce and sprinkle with remaining Monterey Jack cheese. Bake for 10 to 16 minutes until burritos are hot and cheese is melted. Serve immediately.

Broiled Cod Montauk

Mayonnaise helps keep the fish moist while it cooks. Serve this simple dish with a lettuce and vegetable salad and some soft breadsticks.

SERVES 6

½ cup mayonnaise

1 teaspoon Dijon mustard

1 tablespoon lemon juice

2 tablespoons grated Parmesan cheese

½ teaspoon dried tarragon leaves

6 6-ounce cod fillets

1. Preheat broiler. In small bowl, combine mayonnaise, mustard, lemon juice, cheese, and tarragon, and mix well.

2. Place cod on broiler rack. Broil 4 to 6 inches from heat source for about 4 minutes. Remove from oven, turn fillets, and spread mayonnaise mixture over each fillet. Return pan to oven and broil for 3 to 5 minutes longer, until fish flakes when tested with fork and mayonnaise mixture begins to bubble and brown. Serve immediately.

Mayo: Low-Fat or Regular?

You can find mayonnaise in low-fat, no-fat, and regular versions; they all taste pretty much the same. You can use any type in most cooking recipes, salad dressings, and sandwich spreads. In baking, however, you should use full-fat mayonnaise unless the recipe says otherwise.

tip

Poached Salmon with Alfredo Sauce

You can find jarred Alfredo and other cheese sauces by the pasta sauces in the supermarket; they are a good substitute for the refrigerated sauces.

SERVES 4

4 6-ounce salmon fillets

½ cup water

½ cup white wine or fish stock

1 tablespoon olive oil

1 onion, finely chopped

1 10-ounce container refrigerated Alfredo sauce

½ teaspoon dried basil leaves

½ cup grated Parmesan cheese

1. In shallow saucepan large enough to hold fillets in a single layer, place water and wine. Bring to a boil over medium heat and add salmon. Reduce heat to low, cover pan, and cook for 8 to 10 minutes or until fish is opaque and flakes easily when tested with fork.

2. Meanwhile, in heavy saucepan, heat olive oil over medium heat. Add onion and cook until tender, about 4 to 5 minutes. Add Alfredo sauce and basil; cook and stir over low heat until sauce bubbles.

3. Place salmon on serving plates; cover with sauce and sprinkle with Parmesan cheese. Serve immediately.

Poaching

Poaching is cooking meat or fruit in a liquid that is just below the boiling point. This method retains and concentrates the flavor of the food, and the results are juicy and tender. Fish is usually poached because the delicate flesh cooks gently with this method and does not dry out.

tip

Shrimp and Rice

*There are so many variations on this simple shrimp and
rice meal—but this signature dish is always a hit.*

SERVES 4

2 tablespoons olive oil

1 onion, finely chopped

1 cup Texmati rice

1½ cups chicken broth

1 14-ounce can diced tomatoes
with green chilies, undrained

1½ pounds medium raw shrimp,
cleaned

½ teaspoon dried oregano leaves

⅛ teaspoon cayenne pepper

1. In large saucepan, heat olive oil over medium heat. Add onion; cook and stir until crisp-tender, about 3 to 4 minutes. Add rice and stir to coat. Add chicken broth, bring to a boil, then cover, reduce heat, and simmer for 15 minutes.

2. Add tomatoes to rice mixture and bring to a simmer. Add shrimp, oregano, and pepper, and simmer for 4 to 6 minutes, until rice is tender and shrimp are pink and curled. Serve immediately.

Jamming Seafood Jambalaya

Jambalaya is a festive Southern dish that usually takes hours to make. Serve this easy version with some melon wedges, croissants, and ice cream sundaes for dessert.

SERVES 4

1 8-ounce package yellow rice mix

2 tablespoons olive oil

1 onion, chopped

1 14-ounce can diced tomatoes with green chilies

1 8-ounce package frozen cooked shrimp, thawed

2 grilled sausages, sliced

1. Prepare rice mix as directed on package.

2. Meanwhile, in large saucepan, heat olive oil over medium heat. Add onion; cook and stir for 4 to 5 minutes, until tender. Add tomatoes, shrimp, and sliced sausages; bring to a simmer, and cook for 2 to 3 minutes.

3. When rice is cooked, add to saucepan; cook and stir for 3 to 4 minutes, until blended. Serve immediately.

Frozen Shrimp

You can buy frozen shrimp that has been shelled, deveined, and cooked. To thaw it, place in a colander under cold running water for 4 to 5 minutes, tossing shrimp occasionally with hands, until thawed. Use the shrimp immediately after thawing.

tip

Shrimps de Jonghe

The bread crumb mixture for this elegant dish can be prepared ahead of time.
Purchase cooked, shelled, and deveined shrimp from your butcher.

SERVES 6

3 cloves garlic, minced

½ teaspoon salt

½ cup butter, softened

1½ cups fine bread crumbs

¼ teaspoon dried marjoram leaves

¼ teaspoon dried tarragon leaves

⅛ teaspoon white pepper

2 pounds cooked, shelled shrimp, thawed if frozen

¼ cup lemon juice

1. Preheat oven to 425°F. In medium bowl, mash garlic with salt to form a paste. Add butter and beat until combined. Add bread crumbs, marjoram, tarragon, and white pepper and mix well.

2. Butter a 2-quart casserole dish. In large bowl, combine shrimp and lemon juice; toss to coat, then drain shrimp. Layer shrimp and bread crumb mixture in prepared casserole dish. Bake for 15 to 20 minutes, until hot and bread crumbs begin to brown.

Purchasing Shrimp

You can find cooked, shelled, and deveined shrimp in the meat aisle of the grocery store. This product is also stocked in the freezer section of the meat aisle; thaw according to package directions. Fresh cooked shrimp should be used within two days. It should smell sweet and slightly briny; if there is any off odor, do not buy it.

tip

Salmon Steaks with Spinach Pesto

This elegant dish is perfect for company. Serve it with pasta,
bread, and some greens, with a bakery cake for dessert.

SERVES 6

¼ cup lemon juice, divided

2 tablespoons oil

½ teaspoon dried basil leaves

6 salmon steaks

1 10-ounce container refrigerated pesto

½ cup frozen chopped spinach, thawed and drained

¼ cup chopped salted cashews

1. In glass baking dish, combine 2 tablespoons lemon juice, oil, and basil leaves. Add salmon steaks, turn to coat, and let stand for 10 minutes at room temperature.

2. While steaks marinate, combine pesto, spinach, and remaining 2 tablespoons lemon juice in a blender or food processor. Process or blend until mixture is smooth. Place in small bowl and stir in cashews.

3. Remove steaks from marinade and place on broiler pan. Broil 4 to 6 inches from heat source for 5 minutes, turn steaks, and broil for 5 to 8 minutes longer, until fish flakes when tested with fork. Top each with a spoonful of the pesto mixture and serve.

Spark up Pesto

Adding spinach and lemon juice to prepared pesto makes the sauce a bright green color and perks up the flavor. And adding more nuts, whether pine nuts, cashews, or walnuts, makes the sauce a bit crunchy. Spinach also adds more nutrition and helps cut the fat, and it doesn't alter the flavor.

tip

Shrimp Pesto Ravioli

You can use fish fillets, cut into cubes, in place of the shrimp, or substitute bay scallops. Serve this easy dish with some breadsticks and a fruit salad.

SERVES 4

1 tablespoon olive oil

1 red bell pepper, chopped

1 pound shelled, deveined large raw shrimp, thawed if frozen

1 9-ounce package refrigerated cheese ravioli

1½ cups water

¾ cup pesto sauce

½ cup grated Parmesan cheese

1. In heavy skillet, heat oil over medium heat. Add red bell pepper and stir-fry for 3 to 4 minutes, until crisp-tender. Add shrimp; cook and stir for 4 to 6 minutes, until shrimp curl and turn pink. Remove shrimp and peppers from skillet.

2. Add ravioli and water to skillet and bring to a boil over high heat. Reduce heat to medium-high, cover, and simmer for 4 to 6 minutes, until ravioli are hot, stirring occasionally. Drain off excess liquid and return shrimp and pepper to skillet. Cook and stir over medium-high heat, stirring occasionally, until shrimp are cooked and mixture is hot. Stir in pesto, place in serving dish, sprinkle with cheese, and serve.

Honey Mustard Salmon

Honey and mustard make an irresistible flavor combination with rich and savory salmon fillets. You can multiply this recipe for a larger crowd; marinating and cooking times remain the same.

SERVES 4

⅓ cup honey mustard salad dressing

2 tablespoons honey

½ teaspoon dill seed

2 tablespoons butter, melted

4 6-ounce salmon fillets

1. In shallow casserole dish, combine salad dressing, honey, dill seed, and butter and mix well. Add salmon fillets and turn to coat. Cover and let stand at room temperature for 10 minutes.

2. Prepare and preheat grill or broiler. Remove salmon from marinade and place, skin-side down, on grill or broiler pan. Cover and grill, or broil, 6 inches from heat for 8 to 12 minutes, until salmon is cooked and flakes when tested with a fork, brushing with remaining marinade halfway through cooking time. Discard remaining marinade. Serve immediately.

Menu Ideas

Any fish dish is delicious served with a salad made from baby spinach. Toss together spinach, sliced water chestnuts, sliced mushrooms, and red bell pepper, and drizzle with some creamy garlic salad dressing. Top it with croutons or Parmesan shavings. Add some ready-to-bake breadsticks and your meal is complete.

tip

Garlic Mussels

This is such a beautiful dish; the shiny black mussel shells contrast with the red pepper and the creamy beige flesh. Serve it with fresh fruit and crusty bread.

SERVES 3–4

½ pound spaghetti pasta

4 pounds cleaned mussels

¼ cup olive oil

6 cloves garlic, minced

1 red bell pepper, cut into strips

½ teaspoon dried oregano leaves

1½ cups dry white wine

Salt and pepper to taste

1. Bring a large pot of water to a boil; cook spaghetti pasta according to package directions. Meanwhile, place mussels in a colander; pick over them to remove any opened mussels; rinse well and set aside.

2. In large stockpot big enough to hold the mussels, heat olive oil over medium high heat. Add garlic; cook and stir until fragrant, 1 to 2 minutes. Add red bell pepper; cook and stir for 3 to 4 minutes, until crisp-tender. Sprinkle with oregano and pour wine into pot; bring to a boil. Add salt and pepper, then add mussels.

3. Cover pot and turn heat to medium-low. Cook, shaking pan frequently, for 4 to 7 minutes or until all mussels open. (Discard any mussels that do not open.) Remove mussels and bell peppers from pot and place in serving bowl. Strain liquid and pour half over mussels. Combine remaining liquid with cooked and drained spaghetti; serve immediately with the mussels.

About Mussels

Mussels used to be difficult to prepare because they needed to be cleaned, debearded, and scrubbed. Now you can buy them precleaned, with the beards off; just rinse and use. Be sure to discard open mussels and those with broken shells before cooking, and discard mussels that aren't open after cooking.

tip

327

Fruity Tuna Steaks

Curry powder, orange juice, and apricot jam add great flavor to tender tuna steaks. Because the steaks are simmered in the sauce, they pick up more flavor.

SERVES 4

2 tablespoons olive oil

1 onion, chopped

2 teaspoons curry powder

⅓ cup frozen orange juice concentrate

2 tablespoons water

¼ cup apricot jam

Salt and pepper to taste

4 6-ounce tuna steaks

1. In heavy skillet, heat olive oil over medium heat. Add onion; cook and stir for 2 minutes. Sprinkle curry powder over onions; cook and stir for 2 to 3 minutes longer, until onions are crisp-tender.

2. Add orange juice concentrate and water to skillet along with apricot jam and salt and pepper. Bring to a boil, then reduce heat to a simmer and add tuna. Cook for 8 to 10 minutes per inch of thickness, turning tuna once during cooking time, until fish flakes when tested with fork. You can serve tuna medium-rare if you'd like.

3. Place tuna on serving plate. If necessary, reduce sauce by turning heat to high and simmering until thickened, 3 to 4 minutes. Pour sauce over tuna and serve.

Steamed Spicy Scallops

A peppery wine sauce finished with butter coats these tender scallops that are steamed to perfection.

SERVES 4–6

2 tablespoons olive oil

4 cloves garlic, minced

1 serrano pepper, minced

1 cup dry white wine

2 pounds sea scallops

1 teaspoon salt

⅛ teaspoon cayenne pepper

2 tablespoons butter

1. In large saucepan, heat olive oil over medium heat. Add garlic and serrano pepper; cook and stir for 2 to 3 minutes, until fragrant. Add wine, reduce heat to low, and simmer while cooking scallops.

2. Meanwhile, place water in the bottom of a steamer and bring to a boil over high heat. Sprinkle scallops with salt and cayenne pepper and place in steamer top. Place over boiling water, cover, and steam scallops for 2 minutes. Gently stir scallops, cover again, and steam for 2 to 5 minutes, until scallops are opaque.

3. Remove serrano pepper sauce from heat and swirl in butter until melted. Place scallops on serving plate and top with sauce. Serve immediately.

Scallops

There are three kinds of scallops available. Sea scallops are the largest, about 30 to the pound, and are white, sometimes with an orange tint. Bay scallops are smaller, about 50 to the pound, are sweet and white with a hint of pink. And calico scallops, the smallest of all, are darker in color and not as tender.

tip

Shrimp Omelet

This fluffy omelet filled with shrimp, bell pepper, and cheese is perfect for brunch-lovers at dinnertime. Serve with caramel rolls and a citrus salad for a real treat.

SERVES 3–4

3 tablespoons butter

1 red bell pepper, finely chopped

8 eggs

2 tablespoons water

½ teaspoon salt

⅛ teaspoon white pepper

1 pound cooked shrimp

1½ cups grated Havarti cheese

1. In large nonstick skillet, melt butter over medium heat. Add bell pepper; cook and stir for 3 to 4 minutes, until crisp-tender. Meanwhile, in large bowl, beat eggs with water, salt, and pepper.

2. Add egg mixture to pan. Cook for 2 minutes. Continue cooking, lifting egg mixture to allow uncooked portion to flow underneath. When eggs are almost set but still glossy after about 4 minutes longer, top with shrimp and cheese. Cover and cook for 2 more minutes, until cheese melts. Fold omelet and serve immediately.

Scallop Tacos

These pretty tacos are sweet, spicy, and crunchy.
Serve them with a pineapple and melon salad for a cooling contrast.

SERVES 4

2 tablespoons olive oil

1 onion, chopped

1 pound scallops

½ teaspoon salt

2 teaspoons chili powder

½ teaspoon cumin

¼ teaspoon red pepper flakes

8 taco shells

1 cup mango salsa

2 cups finely shredded cabbage

1. Preheat oven to 375°F. In a heavy skillet, heat olive oil over medium-high heat. Add onion; cook and stir until tender, about 4 to 5 minutes. Meanwhile, sprinkle scallops with a mixture of salt, chili powder, cumin, and red pepper flakes. Add to skillet; cook for 2 minutes, then turn scallops and cook until opaque, about 2 to 4 minutes.

2. While scallops are cooking, put taco shells on a baking sheet and heat in the oven until crisp, about 5 to 7 minutes. Combine mango salsa and cabbage in medium bowl.

3. Make tacos with cabbage mixture, heated taco shells, and scallop mixture and serve immediately.

Salsa

There are so many types of salsa available today. You can find mango salsa, black bean salsa, vegetable salsa, and plain old tomato salsa in any supermarket. They range in spiciness from mild to extra hot. Be sure to read labels carefully to make sure you're buying the flavor and heat intensity you want.

tip

Salmon Florentine

Jarred four-cheese Alfredo sauce is a great timesaver. Find it near the pasta in the regular grocery store; stock up, because you can make many recipes with it.

SERVES 4

4 6-ounce salmon fillets

1 teaspoon salt

⅛ teaspoon white pepper

½ teaspoon dried Italian seasoning

2 tablespoons olive oil

1 10-ounce jar four-cheese Alfredo sauce

1 cup frozen chopped spinach, thawed and well drained

½ cup grated Parmesan cheese

1. Preheat broiler. Sprinkle salmon with salt, pepper, and Italian seasoning and drizzle with olive oil. Place on broiler pan and let stand for 5 minutes.

2. In large skillet, heat Alfredo sauce over medium-low heat until bubbly. Place salmon fillets under broiler 4 to 6 inches from heat source for 5 minutes. Stir spinach into Alfredo sauce and let simmer over low heat. Turn salmon fillets and broil for 3 to 4 minutes longer, until salmon is almost done.

3. Place salmon on ovenproof serving platter and top with Alfredo sauce mixture. Sprinkle with Parmesan cheese. Broil for 2 to 4 minutes, until cheese melts and begins to brown. Serve immediately.

Red Snapper en Papillote

Parchment paper not only holds in the steam to cook this delicate fish to perfection, it makes a beautiful presentation too.

SERVES 4

4 6-ounce red snapper fillets

½ teaspoon salt

⅛ teaspoon white pepper

½ teaspoon dried thyme leaves

1 lemon

2 cups sliced mushrooms

2 cups sliced yellow summer squash

⅓ cup dry white wine

1. Preheat oven to 400°F. Cut four 12×18" rectangles from parchment paper and trim each into a large heart shape. Fold in half, then unfold and place one fillet in the center of each heart half. Sprinkle with salt, pepper, and thyme leaves. Thinly slice lemon and place on fillets.

2. Arrange vegetables around the fish and sprinkle everything with the wine. Fold the other half of the parchment paper over the food and crimp the edges together to seal. Place on cookie sheets and bake for 12 to 16 minutes or until fish flakes when tested with a fork. Place parchment packages on plates to serve.

Parchment or Foil?

You can use parchment paper or foil to cook food *en papillote*. The parchment paper makes a prettier presentation at the table, but the foil is a better choice when the recipe cooks longer than 15 minutes, because the paper can burn. Let your guests open their packages at the table; warn them to be careful of the steam.

tip

Mussels in Spicy Broth

*Serve the broth on the side after straining for another course;
top with some minced parsley, cilantro, or chopped green onions.*

SERVES 3–4

4 pounds fresh mussels, cleaned

2 oranges

2 tablespoons olive oil

1 cup sliced mushrooms

1 jalapeño pepper, minced

2 cups fish stock

½ teaspoon salt

⅛ teaspoon red pepper flakes

1. Pick over mussels, discarding any that stay open when tapped and those with broken or cracked shells. Rinse and set aside. Remove 1 teaspoon orange zest from oranges and squeeze juice; set aside.

2. In a large stockpot, heat olive oil over medium heat and add mushrooms and jalapeño pepper. Cook and stir for 4 to 5 minutes, until mushrooms begin to brown. Remove mushrooms with slotted spoon and set aside. Add fish stock, orange juice and zest, salt, and red pepper flakes; bring to a boil.

3. Add mussels, cover pot, and cook until the mussels open, about 4 to 7 minutes, shaking pot frequently and rearranging mussels once during cooking time. Transfer mussels to serving bowl. Serve broth with mushrooms as a separate course.

Fish Stock

If you can't find fish stock in cans or boxes, you can make your own. In a large pot, combine 1 pound fish trimmings (not salmon) with 1½ quarts water; a bay leaf; a quartered onion; 3 garlic cloves; 2 stalks celery, chopped, including leaves; and 1 teaspoon salt. Simmer for 20 to 30 minutes, strain broth, and freeze.

tip

Microwave Shrimp Scampi

This dish can be multiplied to serve more people. You must proportionally increase the microwave cooking time: if you double the shrimp, double the cooking time.

SERVES 4

1 cup jasmine rice

2 cups chicken broth

2 lemons

½ cup butter

1½ pounds medium raw shrimp, cleaned

¼ teaspoon garlic powder

⅛ teaspoon garlic pepper

½ teaspoon garlic salt

1. Combine rice and chicken broth in medium saucepan and bring to a boil over high heat. Cover pan, lower heat to medium low, and simmer for 15 minutes.

2. Meanwhile, grate lemon zest from lemons and squeeze juice. Combine the zest, juice, and butter in microwave-safe dish. Microwave on high for 2 minutes. Sprinkle shrimp with garlic powder, garlic pepper, and garlic salt and add to butter mixture; toss to coat shrimp. Cover and microwave on high for 2 minutes. Uncover dish, stir shrimp, cover, and microwave on high for 1 to 3 minutes longer, until shrimp curl and turn pink.

3. Let shrimp stand, covered, for 2 to 3 minutes. Fluff rice with a fork. Serve shrimp and sauce over rice.

Quick-Cooking Rice

You don't have to use instant rice when you want some in a hurry. Read labels at the grocery store. There are some kinds of rice, including Texmati and Jasmine, that cook in only 15 minutes. As a bonus, those rice varieties are fragrant and full of flavor.

tip

Pan-Seared Sea Scallops

Sea scallops are a sweet, creamy delight when cooked properly. Take care not to overcook them, or they will become rubbery. This recipe for scallops in a light, lemony cream sauce is best served with linguine or fettuccine.

SERVES 4

½ cup all-purpose flour

1 teaspoon salt

1 teaspoon lemon pepper

16 sea scallops

1 tablespoon olive oil

2 tablespoons butter

1 shallot, chopped

¼ cup chopped leeks (white and light green parts only—discard dark green part)

2 tablespoons diced red bell pepper

¼ cup white wine or white grape juice

¼ cup heavy cream

½ teaspoon grated lemon zest

Salt and pepper to taste

1. Mix together the flour, salt, and lemon pepper.

2. Dip the scallops in the flour to coat both sides, shaking off excess (a process called "dredging"). Heat a large sauté pan over medium-high heat.

3. Add oil to preheated sauté pan, then add the scallops. Sear the scallops in oil for about 3 minutes per side; they should get a nice crust on them.

4. Remove the scallops from pan to warmed plates.

5. In the same pan, sauté shallots, leeks, and red bell pepper in the leftover oil in the pan. Add wine or juice, and simmer to reduce liquid by half. Add cream and lemon zest; and reduce by half again. Season with salt and pepper. To serve, pour sauce over scallops.

Lemon-Scented Bay Scallops

Tender bay scallops are baked in gratin dishes in this easy and delicious recipe. Serve with rice pilaf and some peas.

SERVES 4

2 tablespoons butter

2 pounds bay scallops

2 tablespoons lemon juice

Salt and pepper

½ cup dry bread crumbs

1 tablespoon grated lemon zest

2 tablespoons chopped fresh parsley

1. Preheat oven to 400°F.

2. Butter 4 individual gratin dishes with ½ tablespoon butter each.

3. Arrange ½ pound scallops in each gratin dish, then sprinkle them with lemon juice. Season scallops with salt and pepper.

4. Combine bread crumbs with lemon zest and parsley; sprinkle scallops with bread-crumb mixture.

5. Bake gratin dishes in the oven for 12 minutes.

Tartar Sauce

Tartar sauce is traditionally served with fish. It is a mayonnaise-based cold sauce with lemon and diced pickles or pickle relish.

tip

Shrimp Tempura

Serve these crunchy morsels as an entrée with vegetables and rice.
Some vegetables, such as asparagus, green beans, and carrot slices,
can be cooked in the same way as the shrimp in this recipe.

SERVES 4

¾ cup beer

¾ cup all-purpose flour

¾ teaspoon salt

4 cups vegetable oil for
deep-frying

24 large uncooked shrimp,
shelled

1. Whisk beer into flour until smooth. Stir in salt.

2. Heat 4 cups vegetable oil in a 6 quart soup pot or a deep fryer to 375°F.

3. Dip shrimp individually in batter. Let excess batter drip off, and then carefully drop the shrimp into the hot oil.

4. Cook battered shrimp about 3 minutes. Remove from oil using tongs or a slotted spoon.

5. Drain on paper towels or brown paper; serve immediately.

Fried Calamari

Calamari (squid) can be bought cleaned and frozen for this recipe. All you need to do is thaw them, cut them into rings (if they are still in their tubular shape), and flash fry them. Serve with an aioli or tomato sauce.

SERVES 4

1 cup flour

1 teaspoon salt

1 teaspoon paprika

½ teaspoon pepper

4 cups vegetable oil for deep-frying

2 pounds thawed calamari, cut into rings

Lemon wedges

1. Mix flour with salt, paprika, and pepper.

2. Heat 4 cups vegetable oil in a 6 quart soup pot or a deep fryer to 365°F.

3. Toss a handful of calamari in flour mixture and shake off excess.

4. Deep fry until golden brown, about 3 minutes. Drain on paper towels.

5. Repeat with remaining calamari. Serve immediately with lemon wedges to sprinkle calamari with lemon juice.

Remoulade Sauce

Remoulade is a traditional French sauce that is served with fish and seafood. It is similar to tartar sauce, but also contains hardboiled egg, capers, Dijon mustard, parsley, and cayenne pepper.

tip

Citrus Shrimp Brochettes

This recipe can be served on salad greens that have been dressed with citrus vinaigrette, or as an entrée with rice and vegetables.

SERVES 4

¼ cup orange juice

¼ cup lemon juice

¼ cup lime juice

¼ cup olive oil

1 teaspoon orange zest

1 teaspoon lemon zest

1 teaspoon lime zest

Salt and pepper to taste

24 uncooked shrimp, peeled

8 bamboo skewers, presoaked in water

1. Combine juices, oil, zests, salt, and pepper in a bowl or plastic bag.

2. Marinate shrimp in juice mixture for at least an hour.

3. Thread 6 shrimp onto two parallel skewers, so that 2 skewers go through each shrimp. Repeat 3 more times.

4. Grill skewered shrimp for about 3 minutes per side.

5. Serve warm.

Fish Tacos

Fish tacos are healthier than beef tacos because fish is not high in saturated fat, and red meat is. Another reason is that fish tacos don't typically have cheese, and they taste best with healthy toppings of cabbage and fresh tomato salsa.

SERVES 4

8 corn tortillas

1 pound firm white fish such as halibut or snapper

½ cup cornmeal, seasoned with ½ teaspoon salt and ¼ teaspoon pepper

1 tablespoon olive oil

lime wedges

1 cup shredded purple cabbage

1 cup fresh tomato salsa

¼ cup diced avocados

¼ cup sour cream

1. Warm tortillas wrapped in paper towels in microwave. Discard paper towels and wrap in foil to keep them warm.

2. Cut the fish into strips, dredge in corn-meal mixture, and sear in olive oil for about 5 minutes. (If you like, you could grill the fish instead.)

3. Break the cooked fish into chunks; and put chunks in warm tortillas.

4. Squeeze a lime wedge on the fish, then top with cabbage, salsa, avocados, and sour cream.

Taco Tip

Sometimes soft tacos get a little too juicy and they fall apart while you are eating them. Try using two tortillas to help pre-vent this problem. It also makes a more filling taco.

tip

Boiled Lobster

Cooking lobsters is cheaper than if you were to order it at a restaurant, but it can be a bit of an experience! Try rubbing the forehead of the lobster by applying pressure with your thumb to hypnotize it before you place it in the boiling water.

SERVES 2

2 *live 1–2 pound lobsters*

8 *tablespoons salt*

5 *tablespoons butter, melted*

1. Fill an 8 quart or bigger stockpot or soup pot ¾ full with salted water. Make sure that you have enough water to completely cover lobsters (use two pots if necessary). Add 1 tablespoon of salt per quart of water.

2. Bring to a boil and pick up the lobster by the top of the body and put it head first into the boiling water until it is completely under water.

3. Put the lid on the pot and boil for 18 minutes. Do not remove from water until the shell turns bright red.

4. Remove from the pot and serve hot or plunge in ice water for chilled dishes. To serve hot, use a nutcracker to crack the shell and pull or push out the meat inside. Dip hot lobster meat in melted butter.

Eating Lobster

Stay away from the tomalley, which is the lobster's liver (it is green). You may also want to avoid eating the red roe, or unfertilized eggs, that you will find in a female lobster, although it is not harmful and many lobster enthusiasts enjoy eating it.

tip

Lobster Rolls

These are standard fare on the coast in New England, where they are served without pomp and circumstance from beachside lunch shacks. They are delicious sandwiches of lobster salad served on special hot-dog buns, usually split down the middle.

SERVES 4

4 hot-dog buns

2 tablespoons soft butter

1 cup cooked lobster meat chunks

¼ cup mayonnaise

¼ cup diced celery

Salt and pepper to taste

1. Butter the insides of the buns and toast them on a griddle or skillet.

2. Combine lobster meat, mayonnaise, celery, salt, and pepper, and mix well.

3. Spoon lobster salad onto toasted buns.

Lobster-to-Go

Purchase lobster from the grocery store fish counter. They will steam the lobster for you if you ask.

tip

Halibut with Papaya Salsa

This is a light fish dish that is simple to make. The fish is baked and the salsa is put together at the last minute. Serve this with roast fingerling potatoes and sautéed green beans for a lovely, easily prepared meal. Leftovers make good Fish Tacos.

SERVES 4

1 1½-pound piece of halibut

1 teaspoon olive oil

Salt and pepper

½ cup diced papaya

¼ cup diced red onion

¼ cup diced jalapeño pepper

¼ cup diced red bell pepper

2 tablespoons lime juice

2 tablespoons chopped fresh cilantro

1. Preheat oven to 350°F.

2. Brush halibut with oil, sprinkle with salt and pepper, and bake in the oven for about 15 minutes, or until fish flakes when you test it with a fork.

3. Combine papaya, onion, peppers, lime juice, and cilantro. Season with salt and pepper.

4. Spoon salsa onto baked fish before serving.

Salsa Suggestions

Salsa can be made with a variety of fruits, not just papaya. Try some of the following in fresh salsa: mangos, nectarines, peaches, plums, persimmons, apples, pears, guavas, and bananas. You can also use different acids, such as flavored vinegars, lemon juice, grapefruit juice, lime juice, or orange juice.

tip

Potato-Crusted Salmon

This is a quick and easy way to make an elegant dinner entrée.
Serve it with mashed potatoes and peas and carrots any night of the week.

SERVES 4

1 1½-pound side of salmon, skin-on

½ teaspoon honey

1 tablespoon Dijon mustard

½ cup dry bread crumbs

½ cup crushed potato chips

1 teaspoon dried dill

2 tablespoons butter, melted

1. Preheat oven to 350°F.

2. Place fish, skin side down, on an oiled baking dish.

3. Mix honey with mustard and spread it on the flesh side of the fish.

4. Combine bread crumbs, potato chips, and dill. Sprinkle the mustard-coated fish with all of this mixture.

5. Drizzle melted butter on top of the crumb mixture; then bake fish for 20 minutes. To serve, lift fish off the skin and place fish on individual plates.

One-Dish Meals
(Casseroles)

Basic Polenta

*Polenta is a classic Italian dish that is very versatile. You can serve warm
polenta with almost any vegetable or sauce, mix it with freshly-grated
Parmesan cheese, or simply serve it plain as a creamy and satisfying side dish.*

SERVES 4

4 cups water

1 cup coarse cornmeal

1 teaspoon salt

2 tablespoons butter

1. Put water and salt in a medium-sized saucepan and bring to a boil.

2. Turn heat down to medium-low. Gradually add cornmeal, stirring constantly, until it has thickened; about 15 minutes. Polenta should be thick without becoming stiff, and should have large bubbles rising and popping on the surface.

3. Stir in butter.

4. Serve immediately for soft polenta, or pour into a greased 9 × 13" baking dish and allow to cool. When cool it can be sliced and grilled, fried or baked.

Polenta Bake

When using precooked polenta that has been chilled and molded solid in a loaf pan, cut it in slices and lay them down on the bottom of the casserole dish instead of pouring hot creamy polenta (cooked cornmeal) into it. Proceed as directed for the remaining steps.

SERVES 6

1 cup uncooked coarse-ground cornmeal

3 cups water

1 teaspoon salt

1 egg

½ cup milk

2 ounces cream cheese

¼ cup grated Parmesan cheese

1 cup shredded mozzarella cheese

1 tablespoon butter

1 tablespoon olive oil

1 8-ounce can tomato sauce

3 cloves garlic, sliced

½ teaspoon dried oregano

2 fresh basil leaves, chopped

1. Preheat oven to 350°F.

2. Over medium heat, cook cornmeal in salted water and milk, stirring with a wooden spoon or whisk until cooked and creamy, about 10 minutes.

3. Add egg and beat in completely, followed by butter, cream cheese, Parmesan cheese, and half of the mozzarella.

4. Grease a 9 × 13" baking dish with olive oil; pour in polenta mixture.

5. Drizzle 1 tablespoon olive oil over polenta, and then pour tomato sauce over it. Sprinkle garlic, herbs, and remaining mozzarella over top. Bake 25 minutes.

Chicken with Rice

This is a basic meal made in one pot. A variety of ingredients can be added, such as sausage or seafood, which will make it resemble jambalaya or paella.

SERVES 6

3 boneless, skinless chicken breasts, cubed

½ cup olive oil

1 large onion, diced

1 cup diced green bell pepper

½ cup diced red bell pepper

½ cup diced yellow bell pepper

5 cloves garlic, minced

1 tablespoon turmeric

3 cups white long-grain rice, uncooked

4 cups chicken broth

¾ cup chopped green olives

2 bay leaves

Salt and pepper to taste

1. Brown chicken in oil in a large pot. Remove chicken and set aside.

2. Add onion, peppers, garlic, and turmeric to the pot, and sauté until onions are translucent.

3. Add rice and cook for 5 minutes, stirring occasionally. Add chicken broth, browned chicken, olives, and bay leaves. Stir to combine, bring mixture to a simmer over medium heat, and cover pot with a lid.

4. Simmer 20 minutes or until rice is cooked.

5. Remove bay leaves. Season with salt and pepper.

Arroz con Pollo

Arroz con Pollo is Spanish for "rice with chicken." It is a meal in itself, but when served with black beans and fried plantains it becomes a feast. The rice itself is colored vibrant yellow with annatto seeds, similar to the paella of Spain.

tip

Easy Jambalaya

This is a quicker version of the traditional Creole/Cajun spicy chicken and rice dish, which is made with tomatoes, andouille (pork sausage), and shrimp.

SERVES 6

1 recipe Chicken with Rice (see below)

½ cup chicken broth

1 smoked sausage, sliced

½ cup diced ham

½ cup canned diced tomatoes

1 cup cooked, peeled shrimp

1 teaspoon cayenne pepper sauce

Stir together all ingredients in the pot the chicken and rice were made in, and cook over medium-low until all ingredients are heated through.

Chicken with Rice

Brown 3 boneless, skinless chicken breasts (cubed) in oil. Remove chicken and set aside. Add 1 large diced onion, 1 cup of diced green bell pepper, ½ cup diced red bell pepper, 5 cloves of minced garlic, and 1 tablespoon of turmeric to the pot and sautee until onions are translucent. Add 3 cups of white long-grain rice and cook for 5 minutes. Add 4 cups of chicken broth, browned chicken, ¾ chopped green olives, and 2 bay leaves. Stir to combine and bring mixture to a simmer. Remove bay leaves add salt and pepper.

tip

Quick Paella

A quicker version of the traditional Spanish rice dish, which is made with saffron, peas, chicken, chorizo (spicy pork sausage), and shellfish. Dress up this recipe by adding cooked lobster claws and crab legs at the end.

SERVES 6

1 recipe Chicken with Rice (page 350)

1 cup frozen peas

1 smoked sausage, sliced

½ cup calamari, cut into 1" slices

½ cup diced canned clams

1 cup (about ½ pound) uncooked cocktail shrimp in the shell

1. Preheat oven to 375°F.

2. Combine everything except mussels and put in a 9 × 13" shallow baking dish. Cover with foil and bake 20 minutes.

3. Arrange mussels on top and return to the oven uncovered for 15 minutes.

Shepherd's Pie

*Shepherd's Pie is basically stew with a top crust of mashed
potatoes. Lamb is a traditional filling, but you can fill it with chili,
or you can make it with all vegetables, like a potpie.*

SERVES 4

1 small onion, diced

2 carrots, peeled and diced

1 celery stalk, sliced into ½" slices

2 tablespoons vegetable oil

1 pound ground beef

2 tablespoons all-purpose flour

1½ cups beef broth

Salt and pepper to taste

2 cups mashed potato

2 tablespoons butter, melted

Paprika

1. Preheat oven to 400°F.

2. Sauté onions, carrots, and celery in oil.
When the onions and celery are translucent,
add the beef and cook until browned.

3. Sprinkle meat mixture with flour; stir. Add
broth. Simmer until the mixture is thickened,
season with salt and pepper, and pour stew
into ungreased 9 × 13" casserole dish.

4. Spread mashed potatoes over the meat
mixture, drizzle with melted butter, and
sprinkle with paprika.

5. Bake for 20 minutes.

Potpie

This recipe is an open-top potpie with a vegetable filling. The filling can also be made from chicken, beef, or seafood in the same sauce, using chicken, fish, or beef broth to match the appropriate filling. It can be made vegetarian with vegetable broth.

SERVES 8

Pie dough

1 egg

2 tablespoons water

½ medium onion, diced

1 celery stalk, diced

1 leek, diced (white and light green parts only—discard dark green part)

2 carrots, peeled and diced

2 tablespoons butter

¼ cup all-purpose flour

Pasties

Pasties are little pocket pies made from meat and vegetable stew wrapped in pie pastry like a turnover. These portable potpies originally went down the shafts with Welsh coal miners to be enjoyed for their subterranean lunch. Immigrants spread the traditional miner's lunch to mining communities in Michigan, Kentucky, and West Virginia.

1. Preheat oven to 400°F. Roll out pie dough and cut into 2-inch circles with a round cookie cutter. You will need 4 circles for each serving.

2. For each potpie "cup" turn one ramekin upside down, oil it, and overlap four circles of pie dough around it, leaving an open hole in the bottom for juice to flow through when served. Attach dough circles to each other with egg wash (1 egg beaten with 2 tablespoons water). Bake pastry cups for about 15 minutes. Let cool and remove them from ramekins. Set aside.

3. Sauté onion, celery, leek, and carrot in butter until onions, celery, and leeks are translucent. Dust with flour; stir and cook a few minutes.

tip

Potpie

(continued)

3 cups chicken broth

1 large potato, peeled and cubed

1 cup cubed butternut squash

2 parsnips, diced

½ cup cut green beans

1 sprig fresh thyme or
¼ teaspoon dried

1 bay leaf

½ cup frozen peas

½ cup heavy cream

Salt and pepper to taste

¼ cup chopped fresh chives

4. Add chicken broth, then add potato, squash, parsnips, and green beans. Bring to a boil, add thyme and bay leaf, and simmer for 40 minutes, until the vegetables are cooked and the liquid is thickened.

5. Stir in peas and cream and remove from heat. Remove thyme sprig and bay leaf; season with salt and pepper. Add chives. To serve, place a pastry cup on a plate and spoon vegetables and sauce into it.

Tortilla Lasagna

This southwestern version of lasagna tastes like baked enchiladas but doesn't require the labor-intensive rolling.

SERVES 8

½ cup chopped onion

1 clove garlic, minced

1 teaspoon olive oil

1 pound ground turkey

¼ teaspoon cumin

3 cups enchilada sauce

12 corn tortillas

2 cups shredded Monterey jack cheese

1. Preheat oven to 400°F. Sauté onions and garlic in oil. Add turkey and cook until it is browned. Stir in cumin. Set aside.

2. Spoon a layer of enchilada sauce on the bottom of a 9 × 13" casserole dish. Layer tortillas, meat mixture, and cheese; then sauce, tortillas, meat, and cheese again. Top with a layer of tortillas, sauce, and cheese.

3. Bake 15–20 minutes.

Tamale Pie

This hot tamale pie is sure to be a hit with your family—
and it's so simple, you'll love to make it.

SERVES 8

1 cup coarse-ground cornmeal

3 cups water

1 teaspoon salt

1 pound ground beef

½ cup chopped onion

1 8 ounce can tomato sauce

1 tablespoon chili powder

1 cup corn frozen kernels

1 cup shredded Cheddar cheese

1. Boil 3 cups water in a medium saucepan. Add 1 teaspoon salt to boiling water, followed by the coarse cornmeal. Over medium heat, cook, stirring, until mixture thickens.

2. Preheat oven to 400°F. Brown meat in a skillet; add onion and cook until translucent, about 5 minutes. Add tomato sauce and chili powder and simmer for 10 minutes. Set aside.

3. Stir corn into cooked cornmeal. Layer half the cornmeal mixture on the bottom of an ungreased 9 × 13" casserole dish. Spoon meat filling on top of this layer. Spread remaining cornmeal on top of meat mixture.

4. Sprinkle cheese on top and bake for 20 minutes.

Quick Cassoulet

For this rustic French dish, put 2 cans of cannelini beans in 9 × 13" a casserole dish that has been rubbed with bacon fat or olive oil. Add 2 turkey legs, 1 sliced smoked sausage, ¼ cup diced onion, 1 tablespoon tomato paste, 1 clove garlic, and seasonings (thyme, salt, and pepper to taste). Sprinkle top with bread crumbs and bake for 40 minutes at 375°F.

tip

357

Tuna Noodle Casserole

This recipe is the real thing from scratch! It is just as easy as a packaged mix, and you get to control the seasonings and quality of ingredients.

SERVES 6

8 ounces egg noodles, cooked

1 cup sliced mushrooms

2 tablespoons butter

2 tablespoons all-purpose flour

2 cups milk

2 cans drained tuna

¾ cup frozen peas

Salt and pepper to taste

1 cup crushed potato chips

1. Preheat oven to 375°F and butter a 9 × 13" casserole dish. Lay cooked noodles in the dish.

2. Sauté mushrooms in butter, sprinkle with flour, and cook for a few minutes. Add milk, and cook until thickened. Stir in tuna and peas. Season with salt and pepper.

3. Pour mushroom sauce mixture over noodles and gently toss if necessary to distribute evenly.

4. Sprinkle potato chips over the top and bake for 20 minutes.

Recipe Options

This recipe uses crushed potato chips for a topping, but you can use bread crumbs instead for a more elegant presentation. Enrich the recipe with 1 cup shredded Cheddar cheese stirred in before baking.

tip

Stuffed Peppers

*This can be made with red, yellow, or orange bell peppers,
and the filling can be made with other meats, such as lamb or
turkey. Tofu can be substituted for a meatless version.*

SERVES 4

4 green peppers

1 pound ground beef

¼ pound ground pork

*½ cup white long-grain rice,
uncooked*

½ cup diced onion

1 16-ounce can tomato sauce

1. Preheat oven to 350°F.

2. Cut peppers in half through the stem and discard seeds, stem, and membrane. Lay pepper cups in an ungreased 9 × 13" casserole dish.

3. In a bowl mix together the meat, rice, onion, and ½ cup tomato sauce. Season mixture with a bit of salt and pepper.

4. Stuff each pepper half with a ball of meat mixture, mounding it on top.

5. Pour tomato sauce over tops of stuffed peppers, cover with foil, and bake 45 minutes to 1 hour.

Choux Farci

Choux farci is French for "stuffed cabbage." The same filling in stuffed peppers can be used to stuff blanched (quickly boiled, then immersed in cold water) cabbage leaves, which are rolled up after the filling is added. Bake cabbage rolls covered in tomato sauce for a taste of home-cooked comfort food.

tip

Chicken and Dumplings

In this dish, a roasted chicken adds depth of flavor and also makes this recipe easier than using a raw chicken, which would need to be boiled first.

SERVES 6

1 oven-roasted whole chicken

1 cup diced onion

1 cup sliced, peeled carrots

½ cup sliced celery

4 tablespoons butter

¼ cup all-purpose flour

4 cups chicken broth

Salt and pepper to taste

½ cup frozen peas

Biscuit dough

1. Remove chicken meat from the skin and bone, cut into bite-size pieces, and set aside.

2. In a large soup pot, sauté onion, carrot, and celery in butter until translucent. Sprinkle flour over vegetables and stir, cooking for a few minutes.

3. Add chicken broth and chicken meat and cook until thickened.

4. Season with salt and pepper, and add peas.

5. Drop 1-inch pieces of biscuit dough onto the stew, put a lid on the pot, and simmer 15 minutes.

Adding the Dumplings

The dumplings are steamed floating on top of the stew, but you can instead drop thinly rolled squares of dumpling dough into boiling water to cook them first and then add them to the finished stew.

tip

CHAPTER

12

Holiday Classics

Roast Turkey

Here is a recipe for the most important part of Thanksgiving. You may stuff the bird before roasting it, or bake the stuffing on the side. But don't limit yourself or your family to having turkey only one night a year!

SERVES 8

1 red onion, cut in big chunks

2–3 cups Stuffing (see below)

1 10-pound turkey (giblets removed)

4 tablespoons butter, softened

Salt

Pepper

1. Preheat oven to 325°F. Scatter onions on the bottom of a roasting pan.

2. Stuff turkey and place it on the onions. Massage butter on the skin of the turkey; season with salt and pepper.

3. Roast turkey, basting occasionally, for 3¾ hours, or until you can easily move the leg and the juices run clear.

Stuffing

Combine 2 cups corn bread cubes, 2 cups French-bread cubes, ¼ cup diced cranberries, ½ cup chopped pecans, 1 box Bell's seasoning and 1 cup chicken broth together in a bowl. Put this in a buttered baking dish (if not in a turkey), cover with aluminum foil and bake at 350°F for 25 minutes.

tip

Green Bean Casserole

This is a holiday tradition for many Americans.
Enjoy any night of the year!

SERVES 6

1 can cream of mushroom soup

½ cup milk

Salt and pepper to taste

1 small can sliced mushrooms

2 14-ounce cans green beans

2 cups French-fried onions

1. Preheat oven to 350°F. Butter a 9 × 13" casserole dish.

2. In a bowl, whisk together the canned soup and milk. Season with salt and pepper.

3. Stir in the mushrooms, green beans, and 1 cup of the French-fried onions.

4. Turn bean mixture into prepared casserole dish and cover the top of it with the remaining French-fried onions.

5. Bake for 45 minutes.

Indian Pudding

*Serve this cornmeal pudding warm
with vanilla ice cream for a real treat.*

SERVES 8

5 cups milk

½ cup cornmeal

1 teaspoon vanilla extract

½ cup unsulfured molasses

1 teaspoon salt

1 cup sugar

16 tablespoons unsalted butter, cubed

1 teaspoon ground dried ginger

1 teaspoon cinnamon

1 cup currants

1 cup corn kernels, fresh if possible

1 cup golden raisins

1 cup heavy cream

1. Preheat oven to 350°F. Butter a 9 × 9" baking dish and set aside.

2. Scald (heat to just to under a boil—when steam starts to rise, reduce to low) 1 cup of the milk in a saucepan, add cornmeal, and stir over medium heat until it thickens. Remove from heat.

3. Add all the remaining ingredients, except the cream and 1 cup milk, to the cooked cornmeal. Stir to combine. Pour the mixture into the prepared baking dish.

4. Pour the cream and 1 cup milk over the top of the mixture to prevent a skin from forming during baking.

5. Bake uncovered for ½ hour. Stir the cream and milk on the top into the pudding; bake for ½ hour more.

Scalloped Oysters

If you don't have access to fresh oysters in the shell, it is perfectly fine to use the kind that comes preshucked in a container from the grocery store. Oysters were part of the original Thanksgiving meal shared by the Pilgrims and Indians.

SERVES 4

½ cup butter, melted

1 cup soda cracker crumbs (crushed soda crackers)

½ cup dry bread crumbs

1 pint shucked oysters, drained, with juice reserved

¼ teaspoon salt

¼ teaspoon pepper

2 tablespoons heavy cream

2 teaspoons Worcestershire sauce

Few drops cayenne pepper sauce

1. Preheat oven to 425°F. Butter a 2-quart baking dish.

2. In a bowl toss together the melted butter, cracker crumbs, and bread crumbs. Spread half of this mixture on the bottom of the prepared baking dish.

3. Arrange the oysters on top of the crumb mixture. Sprinkle them with salt and pepper.

4. Mix the cream, Worcestershire sauce, cayenne pepper sauce, and 3 tablespoons oyster juice together. Pour this mixture over the oysters.

5. Sprinkle the remaining crumb mixture over the oysters. Bake for 25 minutes.

Oyster Stuffing

Enhance the Stuffing (page 362) for the holiday turkey by adding fresh or smoked oysters to it. Cut back a little on the chicken stock if using fresh oysters, and replace the cranberries with sliced green onions.

tip

Roast Beef—Prime Rib

This succulent roast is traditionally served with Yorkshire Pudding (page 367) and horseradish cream. Horseradish cream is made by mixing 1 cup of sour cream with ¼ cup of prepared grated horseradish.

SERVES 8

18-pound boneless beef rib roast

2 tablespoons chopped fresh rosemary

¼ cup kosher salt

2 tablespoons cracked black pepper

Have Leftover Prime Rib?

Leftovers from this classic holiday roast can be chilled and then thinly sliced for hot roast beef sandwiches.

1. Preheat oven to 450°F.

2. Rub the outside of the roast with the rosemary, salt, and pepper, leaving a crust.

3. Put the roast in a roasting pan and put it in the oven. Roast for 15 minutes.

4. Reduce the oven temperature to 325°F and continue to roast for 1½ hours. Check internal temperature with a meat thermometer; when it reaches 115°F, remove the roast from the oven. Let the roast stand for at least 15 minutes before carving to let the temperature rise and allow the juices to settle back into the meat,

5. Roast internal temperature will rise 10°F during the resting period after it is removed from the oven. Finished temperatures are 125°F for rare, 130°F for medium rare, and 135–145°F for medium.

tip

Yorkshire Pudding

This is a batter that basically bakes into a beef-flavored popover. It is the traditional partner to Roast Beef—Prime Rib (page 366). It can be baked in the pan the roast was cooked in, or in muffin tins for individual puddings.

SERVES 8

½ *cup beef fat (drippings from the beef roast)*

2 cups milk

4 eggs

1 teaspoon salt

2 cups all-purpose flour

1. Preheat oven to 400°F. Divide beef fat evenly among 8 muffin tin cups.

2. Combine remaining ingredients in a blender or bowl with a whisk. Pour the batter into the muffin tin cups that have been prepared with beef fat.

3. Bake 15 minutes. Reduce the oven temperature to 350°F; bake 15 minutes more.

Ham Loaf with Pineapple

This is a good way to use leftover holiday ham. Serve ham loaf with steamed asparagus with hollandaise sauce and scalloped potatoes.

SERVES 6

1¼ pounds ground ham

¾ pound ground pork

2 eggs

1 cup dry bread crumbs

½ cup buttermilk

¼ cup pineapple juice

1 pineapple ring

1. Preheat oven to 350°F.

2. Combine all ingredients except for the pineapple ring and form into a loaf.

3. Place the loaf in a loaf pan; place the pineapple ring on top.

4. Bake uncovered for 1 hour.

5. Cut into 1-inch-thick slices and serve warm.

Pecan-Crusted Roast Pork Loin

This meal is both festive and filling on a cold winter night.
Serve it with something chocolaty for dessert.

SERVES 4

1 garlic clove

1 teaspoon olive oil

1 teaspoon brown sugar

¼ teaspoon dried thyme

¼ teaspoon dried sage

¼ teaspoon freshly ground black pepper

½ pound boneless pork loin roast

¼ cup chopped or ground pecans

1. Crush the garlic with the side of a large knife. Remove the skin. Put the olive oil, garlic, brown sugar, and seasonings in a resealable plastic bag. Mix well. Add the roast and turn it in the bag to coat the meat. Marinate in the refrigerator for 6 to 12 hours.

2. Preheat oven to 400°.

3. Roll the pork loan in the chopped pecans and place it in a roasting pan. Make a tent of aluminum foil and arrange it over the pork loin, covering the nuts completely so that they won't burn. Roast for 10 minutes, then lower the heat to 350°. Continue to roast for an additional 8 to 15 minutes or until the meat thermometer reads 150 to 170°, depending on how well done you prefer it. Let sit for 10 minutes before serving.

4. Serve with garlic mashed potatoes and freshly steamed asparagus.

Create a Celery Roasting Rack.

If you want to bake a roast in a casserole alongside potatoes and carrots, elevate the roast on 2 or 3 stalks of celery. The celery will absorb any fat that drains from the meat so that it's not absorbed by the other vegetables. Discard the celery.

Caramelized Pearl Onions

*Although you can use already-peeled onions or even frozen
ones, you will get a far better taste from fresh pearl onions.
It's worth the 15 to 20 minutes it will take to peel them!*

SERVES 8

2 cups pearl onions

2 teaspoons brown sugar

¼ teaspoon salt

1 tablespoon butter

1 cup cold water

1. Peel the pearl onions.

2. In a heavy-bottomed skillet over medium heat, combine the onions, sugar, salt, butter, and water. Bring to a simmer. Cook gently until all the water is absorbed and the onions are coated in a light glaze, about 5 minutes. Turn heat to low. Cook slowly until the glaze browns and the onions appear golden brown, about 5 minutes more.

Preparing Pearl Onions

When using pearl onions, cook them first in boiling water for 3 minutes. Plunge them into cold water. Remove them from the water and cut off the ends before easily removing the stems.

tip

Holiday Goose with Cranberries

Garnish with fresh orange slices, baked sweet potatoes,
and parsley to create a festive-looking meal.

SERVES 4

1 wild goose, gutted and skinned

½ teaspoon table salt

½ teaspoon ground black pepper

1 (15-ounce) can whole-berry cranberry sauce

1 envelope dry onion soup mix

½ cup orange juice

1. Wash the goose cavity with cold water and sprinkle with salt and pepper. Place the goose in a slow cooker.

2. Combine the cranberry sauce, dry onion soup mix, and orange juice. Pour the mixture over the goose.

3. Cook, covered, on low setting for 8 to 10 hours, depending in the size of the goose.

A Goose Is Not a Goose Is Not a Goose

Geese can taste very different depending on the grains they have eaten during the summer. Look for geese that have nested near rice or wild rice fields. Domestic geese are much greasier than wild geese and should not be substituted in slow cooker recipes or any recipe that doesn't allow the grease to drip away.

tip

Herbed Beef Rib-Eye Roast with Potatoes

Serve with baked asparagus for a complete, festive meal.

SERVES 8

2 large sweet potatoes

2 medium Yukon gold potatoes

4 small red potatoes

2 teaspoons dried rosemary

4 garlic cloves

1 teaspoon dry mustard

1 teaspoon salt

1 teaspoon cracked black pepper

4-pound boneless beef rib-eye roast

2 tablespoons vegetable oil

Meat Safety

Store meat unopened for up to two days in the refrigerator. Freeze it if it will not be used within two days. Meat wrapped in butcher paper should be unwrapped and rewrapped in foil, freezer bags, or freezer paper. Frozen meat is best used within two months. Meat in transparent film can be frozen in the package for up to two weeks.

1. Preheat oven to 350°. Peel all the potatoes and cut them into pieces that are roughly 2 inches square.

2. Combine the rosemary, garlic, mustard, salt, and pepper, and divide in half. Rub or press half the mixture into the surface of the meat.

3. Place the meat on a rack in a shallow roasting pan and place a meat thermometer (if using) into the thickest part of the meat. Place the roast in the oven. The total roasting time will be 1½ to 2 hours for medium-rare (135°) or 2 to 3 hours for medium (150°).

4. Mix the remaining seasonings with the oil in a large bowl. Add the potatoes to the oil and herb mixture and toss well to coat.

5. About 1 hour before the meat will be done, place the potatoes in the roasting pan around the rack.

tip

Sauerkraut-Stuffed Roast Duck

Serve with garlic mashed potatoes.

SERVES 6

1 domestic duck

1 cup distilled white vinegar

¼ teaspoon salt

¼ teaspoon ground black pepper

2 Granny Smith apples

1 medium-sized yellow onion

4 cups sauerkraut

1 pound pork spareribs

1. Clean and wash the duck, then place it in a large kettle. Cover with water and add the vinegar. Soak for 3 hours. Remove the duck from the liquid, dry it off, and season with salt and pepper. Cover and place in the refrigerator overnight.

2. While the duck is being soaked, core and chop the apples. Peel and chop the onion into ½-inch chunks. Combine the apple, onion, sauerkraut, and spareribs in a slow cooker. Cook for 6 hours or until the meat from the ribs falls from the bones. Discard the bones and refrigerate the slow-cooker mixture.

3. The next day, stuff the spare-rib sauerkraut mixture into the duck. Place the stuffed duck into the slow cooker and cook on medium for 8 hours or until golden and tender.

High-Altitude Slow-Cooking

Since water boils at a higher temperature in high altitudes, you may want to cook most of your slow-cooker dishes on the high setting to ensure they're getting hot enough. You also can easily test the slow cooker by heating water in it and determining the temperature with a thermometer.

tip

Poached Salmon with Béarnaise Sauce

*Serve with fresh green beans and carrots and
a side of white rice for a light, festive meal.*

SERVES 4

½ cup water

¼ cup dry white wine

2 salmon steaks

¼ cup mayonnaise

2 tablespoons lemon juice

1 tablespoon Dijon mustard

1 teaspoon granulated sugar

1 teaspoon tarragon

½ teaspoon salt

1 teaspoon freshly ground black pepper

1. In a skillet, bring the water and wine to a gentle simmer. Add the salmon and cook without boiling for 8 to 10 minutes or until the fish flakes easily when tested with a fork. Cut the steaks in half and arrange on warmed plates.

2. In a small saucepan, whisk together the mayonnaise, lemon juice, mustard, sugar, and tarragon. Cook over medium-low heat, whisking, for about 3 minutes or until warmed through but not boiling. Season with salt and pepper and spoon the sauce over the salmon.

Freshly Ground Black Pepper

If possible, use freshly ground black peppercorns when pepper is called for in a recipe. These retain their flavor better than preground pepper and you'll need less of it to get the same flavor.

tip

Zucchini-Stuffed Chicken

A little twist on a stuffed turkey for Thanksgiving, this stuffed chicken can be served any night of the year. Adults and kids alike will gobble up this hearty dish.

SERVES 8

8 bone-in, skin-on chicken breasts

2 medium zucchini

1 small yellow onion

2 eggs

3 cups matzo farfel

2 tablespoons chicken bouillon powder

¼ teaspoon garlic powder

¼ teaspoon onion powder

½ teaspoon salt

½ teaspoon ground black pepper

Onion Varieties

Onions vary in sweetness. Vidalia tend to be the sweetest, followed by red, then yellow. White onions are the least sweet and are better in meat dishes than in soups.

tip

1. Preheat oven to 375°F. Grease a 9×13" baking pan.

2. Rinse the chicken breasts under cold, running water. Pat dry. Shred the zucchini using a vegetable grater. Peel and chop the onion. Beat the eggs and set aside.

3. Place the farfel in a bowl and cover with hot water for 5 minutes. Drain and squeeze out water.

4. In a medium-sized mixing bowl, combine the zucchini, farfel, eggs, chicken bouillon, onion, garlic powder, onion powder, salt, and pepper.

5. Place 2 to 3 tablespoons of the stuffing under the skin of each chicken breast and arrange them in the baking pan.

6. Bake for 40 to 50 minutes. Drain off excess fat and serve.

Braised Lamb with a Sour Orange Marinade

*If you are unable to find sour oranges, substitute
a combination of orange and lemon juice.*

16 SERVINGS

4 sour oranges

4 garlic cloves

1 large white onion

1 tablespoon dried oregano

2 bay leaves

1 cup dry white wine

6 pounds deboned leg of lamb

1 teaspoon salt

1 teaspoon ground black pepper

2 tablespoons vegetable oil

Cooking with Lamb

Lamb is underused in North America, yet it has a wonderful flavor. Substitute it for pork in your next slow-cooker recipe for an unexpected treat.

1. Juice the sour oranges. Peel and mince the garlic. Peel the onion and slice thinly. Combine the orange juice with the garlic, onion, oregano, bay leaves, and white wine in a large bowl.

2. Place the meat in the marinade. Make sure all the meat is covered. Cover the bowl and refrigerate for 2 to 4 hours.

3. Remove the meat from the marinade, reserving the marinade. Sprinkle the meat with the salt and pepper. In a large pot, heat the oil on medium-high. Place the meat in the pan and sear on all sides.

4. Decrease heat to low. Pour the reserved marinade over the meat in the pan and cover. Cook until the meat is fork-tender, about 3 hours. Add water to the pot if necessary to keep the meat from scorching.

tip

Fish in Red Sauce

This traditional dish is reminiscent of foods
shepherds would have eaten centuries ago.

SERVES 6

¼ cup minced fresh parsley

8 ounces pimientos

3 red tomatoes

2 carrots

2 celery ribs

2 garlic cloves

½ teaspoon salt

½ teaspoon ground black pepper

1 (28-ounce) can tomato purée

¼ cup water

3 tablespoons fresh lemon juice

6 (3-ounce) cod fillets

1 teaspoon white granulated sugar

1. Mince the parsley. Chop the pimientos into ¼-inch pieces. Chop the tomatoes into ¼-inch pieces. Peel and slice the carrots. Slice the celery. Peel and mince the garlic.

2. In a large saucepan, combine the parsley, pimiento, tomatoes, salt, pepper, and tomato purée. Bring to a boil. Add the carrots, celery, and garlic. Cook until the carrots can easily be pierced with a fork but are still firm.

3. Stir in the water and lemon juice. Place the fish into the pan without stirring. Baste the fish with the liquid. Sprinkle the sugar on top of fish but do not stir. Continue basting periodically.

4. When the fish is opaque and warmed through, remove from heat. Let cool and serve cold.

Venison Medallions with Cranberry Chutney

Venison should never be cooked past medium
or it will become very dry and tough.

SERVES 4

2 small shallots

2 cups mushrooms

1 cup fresh cranberries

1 teaspoon honey

1 tablespoon Dijon mustard

2 teaspoons butter, divided

1 teaspoon salt

1 teaspoon ground black pepper

8 (2½-ounce) venison medallions

1 cup dry red wine

¼ cup cider vinegar

½ cup chicken stock

1 tablespoon red currant jelly

Venison Definition

Venison isn't necessarily deer meat. It also is the term used for elk or caribou meat. These meats can vary widely in taste depending on what the animal has eaten. As a result, they are best served in stews or other dishes that blend many flavors.

tip

1. Peel and mince the shallots. Clean the mushrooms with a damp towel and quarter.

2. In a sauté pan, combine the cranberries, honey, mustard, and 1 teaspoon of the butter. Season with salt and pepper. Cook over low heat until the cranberries start to pop, about 4 minutes. Remove from heat and set aside.

3. Season the venison with salt and pepper. Melt the remaining butter in a sauté pan over high heat until very hot. Add the venison and sear for about 2 minutes or until golden brown. Turn over and sear for another 2 minutes. The meat should be medium-rare at this point. Transfer to a warm platter and keep warm.

4. Return the sauté pan to medium heat. Add the shallots and cook for 2 minutes. Stir in the mushrooms and cook until softened. Add the wine, vinegar, and stock, and scrape the pan with a wooden spoon to loosen browned bits. Raise the heat to high and cook for 10 minutes or until the liquid is reduced to ½ cup. Stir in the jelly and adjust seasoning to taste. Spoon the cranberry sauce on top of each venison medallion. Ladle the sauce on top and around the venison.

Shrimp Scampi

Serve with a dry white wine or champagne.

SERVES 6

16 jumbo shrimp

16 clams

3 garlic cloves

1 pound fettuccine

1 tablespoon olive oil

¼ cup butter

1 cup dry white wine

1 teaspoon dried oregano, crumbled

1 teaspoon dried basil, crumbled

1. Peel and devein the shrimp. Split each shrimp along the back from the tail to the head, but not all the way through. Scrub the clams well. Peel and mince the garlic.

2. Cook the fettuccine in boiling salted water until al dente. Drain the fettuccine, place in a warmed bowl, and toss with the olive oil.

3. Meanwhile, melt the butter in a large skillet over medium heat. Add the garlic and sauté until soft and translucent, about 10 minutes.

4. Add the shrimp, clams, wine, oregano, and basil. Cook until the shrimp are pink and the clams have opened, 5 to 10 minutes. Discard any clams that did not open.

5. Toss the shrimp and clams with the pasta and serve.

Preparing Fresh Shrimp

When using fresh shrimp, boil them for 3 minutes. Run under cold water. Remove all of the shell, although you can keep the tail on if you like. Take a small fork and run it along the back of the shrimp to remove the black vein.

tip

Filet Southwestern

Chipotle peppers canned in adobo sauce are available at most large grocery stores. Purée the entire contents of the can and store what you don't need for this dish in a covered bowl in the refrigerator. It adds flavor to any southwestern recipe.

SERVES 4

6 shallots

1 tablespoon cilantro

2 teaspoons chipotle peppers in adobo sauce

¼ cup butter, softened

1 tablespoon lime juice

4 (1-inch-thick) filets mignon

1 tablespoon vegetable oil

1. Peel and mince the shallots. Mince the cilantro. Purée the chipotle peppers in adobo sauce in a blender or food processor.

2. Adjust oven rack so the filets will be 4 inches from the heating element, and preheat broiler.

3. Beat the butter and lime juice with an electric mixer until light and fluffy. Mix in the shallots, cilantro, and peppers.

4. Remove the filets from the refrigerator about 15 minutes before you are ready to begin cooking them. Flatten them slightly by pressing with a plate. Oil 1 side of the filets lightly and place on the broiler pan, oiled-side down. Spread about 1 teaspoon of the butter mixture on each fillet. Broil for 4 minutes for rare or 6 minutes for medium.

5. Turn the filets. Top each with another teaspoon of the butter mixture and broil an additional 4 to 6 minutes. To serve, top each filet with a quarter of the remaining butter mixture.

Classic Waldorf Salad

Serve as a small salad before a beef or chicken dish,
or make it a bigger serving for an entire meal.

SERVES 6

2 *large red delicious apples*

2 *celery stalks*

½ *cup walnuts*

½ *cup mayonnaise*

1 *tablespoon granulated sugar*

1 *teaspoon lemon juice*

½ *teaspoon salt*

1. Dice the apples into ½-inch pieces. Finely slice the celery. Coarsely chop the walnuts.

2. Blend the mayonnaise with the sugar, lemon juice, and salt.

3. Combine the apples, celery, and nuts, and fold in the dressing mixture.

4. Chill for at least 1 hour before serving.

Freezing Cooked Rice

Cooked rice can be frozen up to six months. The next time you make some for a meal, make twice what you need and freeze the rest in an airtight container. It needs virtually no thawing when added to a casserole.

tip

Cheesy Golden Apple Omelet

This is the perfect way to re-create a delicious breakfast at night.

SERVES 2

1 golden delicious apple

2 tablespoons butter, divided

4 eggs

1 tablespoon water

¼ teaspoon salt

¼ teaspoon ground black pepper

2 tablespoons crumbled blue cheese

2 tablespoons grated Parmesan cheese

1. Pare, core, and slice the apple. Sauté in 1 tablespoon of the butter in a medium-sized pan on medium heat until barely tender. Set aside.

2. Combine the eggs, water, salt, and pepper until blended. Heat the remaining butter in a skillet. Add the egg mixture. Cook slowly, lifting the edges to allow the uncooked portion to flow under.

3. When the eggs are cooked, arrange the apple slices on half of the omelet. Sprinkle with cheeses. Fold in half.

Roast Duckling with Orange Glaze

*Fresh steamed asparagus tips give a pleasing
complement in both taste and color to this meal.*

SERVES 2

2 cups prepared poultry stuffing

1 duckling, fresh or thawed

½ cup granulated sugar

½ teaspoon salt

1 teaspoon cornstarch

1 (6-ounce) can frozen orange
juice concentrate, thawed.

1. Prepare the stuffing according to the package directions and stuff into the duckling cavity. Place the duckling, breast-side up, in a slow cooker. Cover and cook on low setting for 6 hours.

2. One hour before serving, combine the sugar, salt, and cornstarch in a medium-sized saucepan. Add the thawed orange juice concentrate. Stir over moderate heat until slightly thickened. Brush the entire surface of the duckling with the glaze. Repeat every 15 minutes for the remaining 1 hour.

Put It All in the Fridge

Food can be stored in the crockery container of your slow cooker for up to four days in the refrigerator. However, never freeze food in the container, because the crockery may crack.

tip

Beef and Horseradish Salad

This salad is a meal in itself, enjoy!

SERVES 4

1 cup fresh green beans

1½ cups fresh baby carrots

¾-pound beef sirloin steak, 1-inch thick

4 cups torn Boston or Bib lettuce

1 (16-ounce) can julienne-cut beets

For the dressing:

1½ ounces softened cream cheese

2 tablespoons prepared horseradish sauce

3–4 tablespoons milk

1. Wash the green beans. Remove the ends and strings and cut in half lengthwise. Cook the beans, covered, in boiling water in a medium-sized saucepan for 5 minutes.

2. Add the carrots and cook for 10 to 15 more minutes or until the vegetables are tender. Drain. Cover and chill the vegetables for 4 to 24 hours.

3. Remove broiler pan from the oven. Preheat broiler.

4. Place the steak on unheated rack of broiler pan. Broil 3 inches from the heat for 13 to 15 minutes for medium, turning once.

5. In the meantime, combine the cream cheese, horseradish sauce, and milk in a small container with a cover. Cover and shake until well mixed.

6. Arrange the torn lettuce on plates. Top with steak. Drizzle with dressing.

Bar Harbor Fish Chowder

Although the recipe calls for discarding the salt pork, many people like to add it to the soup at the end to create an interesting array of flavors.

SERVES 6

¼ *pound salt pork*

4 *cups cubed small red potatoes*

3 *medium-sized onions*

2 *teaspoons salt, divided*

3 *pounds flounder, haddock, or cod*

2 *cups milk*

1 *tablespoon butter*

¼ *teaspoon freshly ground black pepper*

1. Dice the salt pork into ½-inch pieces. Cut the red potatoes into ½-inch pieces. Peel and thinly slice the onions. Scald the milk by heating it in a saucepan on medium heat until a thin film appears on top.

2. Fry the salt pork in a large skillet. Set aside, leaving the drippings in the pan. Add the potatoes, onion, and ½ teaspoon of the salt. Cover with hot water and cook over medium heat, covered, for 15 minutes or until the potatoes are just tender.

3. Meanwhile, cut the fish into large chunks and place in another saucepan. Add boiling water to cover and the remaining 1½ teaspoons salt. Cook slowly, covered, until the fish is fork-tender, about 15 minutes. Remove from heat. Strain and reserve liquid.

4. Remove any bones from the fish. Add the fish and strained liquid to the potato-onion mixture. Pour in the milk and heat through, about 5 minutes. Mix in the butter and pepper. Serve at once.

Selecting Fish

When purchasing fresh fish, check for clear and bright eyes, firm skin that bounces back when touched, and a fresh, clean smell. Try not to keep fresh fish more than a day in your refrigerator before cooking.

tip

Easy Chicken Cordon Bleu

Serve with fresh peas and carrots for a well-balanced meal.

SERVES 2

2 whole chicken breasts

4 small ham slices

4 small Swiss cheese slices

¼ cup all-purpose flour

¼ cup grated Swiss cheese

½ teaspoon fresh or ¼ teaspoon dried sage

¼ teaspoon ground black pepper

1 (10¾-ounce) can condensed cream of chicken soup

1. Remove the skin and bones from the chicken breasts. Cut each breast in half and pound with a kitchen mallet until about ¼ inch thick.

2. Place a ham slice, then a Swiss cheese slice on each piece of chicken. Roll up and secure with toothpicks.

3. Combine the flour, cheese, sage, and black pepper in a small bowl. Dip the chicken rolls into the mixture. Place in the bottom of a slow cooker. Pour the condensed soup over the chicken rolls. Cook, covered, on low heat for 4 to 6 hours.

Grate Your Own Cheese

As a time and money saver, buy blocks of cheese and grate them yourself. To keep the cheese from sticking together, add a little cornstarch and toss the cheese until mixed through.

tip

Quail Baked in White Wine

If you don't have wine handy for your recipe, substitute 1 tablespoon of red or cider vinegar mixed with 1 cup of water.

SERVES 2

2 quail or game hens (fresh or frozen)

2 garlic cloves

1 small yellow onion

1 tablespoon shortening

2 whole cloves

1 teaspoon black peppercorns

1 bay leaf

1 teaspoon fresh-chopped chives

1 cup dry white wine

½ teaspoon salt

⅛ teaspoon ground black pepper

⅛ teaspoon cayenne pepper

1 cup heavy cream

1. Thaw the quail, if necessary, and clean by running under cold water. Peel and chop the garlic and onions into ¼-inch pieces.

2. Melt the shortening in a medium-sized frying pan on medium heat. Add the garlic, onions, cloves, peppercorns, and bay leaf. Cook for several minutes. Add the quail and brown on all sides.

3. Place the quail and the mixture from the frying pan into a slow cooker. Chop the chives into ¼-inch pieces. Add the chives, wine, salt, pepper, and cayenne pepper to the slow cooker. Cook, covered, on low setting for about 6 hours.

4. Remove the quail and set aside. Remove the bay leaf and discard. Strain the liquid, then add the cream to the liquid. Stir well for 5 minutes. Pour over the quail to serve.

Game Hens

Rock Cornish game hens weigh only 1 to 1½ pounds and are all white meat. They are a separate breed of poultry, unlike capons, which are small male chickens that have been neutered.

tip

Pasta and Smoked Trout with Lemon Pesto

Serve with fresh fruit and freshly steamed broccoli for a healthy, festive meal.

SERVES 4

2 garlic cloves

2 tightly packed cups fresh basil leaves

⅛ cup toasted pine nuts

2 teaspoons fresh-squeezed lemon juice

2 teaspoons water

5 teaspoons extra-virgin olive oil, divided

4 tablespoons grated Parmesan cheese, divided

4 ounces uncooked linguini

2 ounces boneless smoked trout

1 teaspoon freshly ground black pepper

1. Place the pasta in 1 quart boiling water and 1 teaspoon olive oil. Boil until the pasta is soft but firm. Drain and set aside.

2. Peel the garlic. In a food processor, pulse the garlic until finely chopped. Add the basil, pine nuts, lemon juice, and water; process until puréed. Add the remaining 4 teaspoons of the olive oil and 3 tablespoons of the Parmesan cheese; pulse until the pesto is smooth. Set aside.

3. Flake the smoked trout and add to the pesto mixture. Add the pasta and toss. Divide onto 4 plates and sprinkle each serving with Parmesan cheese.

Smoked Fish

Smoking is not just a way to add flavor to meat. Native Americans would smoke fish over their fires in the fall as a way to preserve it through the winter. Unlike other preservation methods, a well-smoked fish will remain flaky and tender for months.

tip

Baked Red Snapper Almandine

Serve with rice pilaf and fresh fruit for a festive yet light meal.

SERVES 4

1 pound red snapper fillets

1 teaspoon sea salt

½ teaspoon freshly ground white pepper

4 teaspoons all-purpose flour

1 teaspoon olive oil

2 tablespoons raw almonds

1 teaspoon unsalted butter

1 tablespoon lemon juice

1. Preheat oven to 375°. Rinse the fish fillets and pat dry between layers of paper towels. Season with salt and pepper. Sprinkle the front and back of the fillets with the flour.

2. In an ovenproof, nonstick skillet on medium-high heat, sauté the fillets in the olive oil until they are nicely browned on both sides.

3. Finely grind the almonds and combine with the butter in a microwave-safe dish. Microwave on high for 30 seconds, or until the butter is melted. Stir.

4. Pour the almond-butter mixture and the lemon juice over the fillets.

5. Bake for 3 to 5 minutes, or until the almonds are nicely browned.

Fusilli with Chicken and Coriander Pesto

Serve with a green salad and fresh fruit for a traditional Italian dinner.

SERVES 4

2 *whole chicken breasts, halved*

1 *pound fusilli pasta*

4 *garlic cloves*

4 *serrano chile peppers*

½ *cup slivered blanched almonds*

3 *ounces cilantro*

2 *tablespoons olive oil*

1 *cup low-fat mayonnaise*

1. Preheat oven to 375°. Cook the pasta in boiling water until al dente.

2. Place the chicken breasts in a baking pan. Bake until cooked through and tender, 15 to 20 minutes. Remove from the oven and let cool. Remove and discard the skin and bones and shred the meat. Place the meat in a medium-sized bowl, cover, and chill.

3. Meanwhile, peel the garlic and cut into ¼-inch pieces. Remove the stems and seeds from the chili peppers. In a food processor or blender, combine the garlic, chilies, almonds, and cilantro; process until finely chopped. With the motor running, add the oil in a thin, steady stream, processing until the pesto is the consistency of a thick paste.

4. Place the pesto in a bowl. Whisk in the mayonnaise.

5. In a large bowl, combine the chilled pasta, shredded chicken, and the pesto; stir to mix well. Cover and chill for 1 hour before serving.

Index